The POWER of CONTEXT

The
POWER
of
CONTEXT

How to Manage Our Bias and Improve
Our Understanding of Others

DANIEL R. STALDER

Prometheus Books

59 John Glenn Drive
Amherst, New York 14228

Published 2018 by Prometheus Books

Cover image © Shutterstock
Cover design by Nicole Sommer-Lecht
Cover design © Prometheus Books

Inquiries should be addressed to
Prometheus Books
59 John Glenn Drive
Amherst, New York 14228
VOICE: 716–691–0133 • FAX: 716–691–0137
WWW.PROMETHEUSBOOKS.COM

22 21 20 19 18   5 4 3 2 1

Library of Congress Cataloging-in-Publication Data Pending

Printed in the United States of America

CONTENTS

SOCIAL JUDGMENT AND ERROR

Do not judge, and you will never be mistaken.
                    —Jean-Jacques Rousseau, philosopher

To err is human.
                                —Alexander Pope, poet

This has been a great era for the study of error.
                    —David Brooks, *New York Times* op-ed author

People who do crazy things are not necessarily crazy.
                    —Elliot Aronson, author of *The Social Animal*

It is easy to assume that other people have enduring patterns of beliefs and desires that caused them to act as they did and difficult to consider the surprisingly strong role played by their temporary circumstances. When we observe others, we always do what is easy and only sometimes do what is difficult, and whatever form or shape future explanations may take, this small fact is surely one of the reasons why we so often misjudge each other.
                    —Daniel Gilbert, Brett Pelham, and Douglas Krull,
                    authors of "The Psychology of Good Ideas"

In our lives with other people, we judge each other. We make social judgments. "Judging" might be considered a dirty word, but sometimes we have to do it.

If someone likes you and asks you out on a date to have coffee or to see a movie, and if you're available, then you have to decide what you think of this person. You have to judge this person. You have to say yes or no or a diplomatic version of no or convey some opinion at some point. You're not a bad person for judging. A social judgment need not be negative or certain. Maybe give this person a try—go on one date and see what happens. It's not a marriage proposal. But if someone does propose marriage to you, then you do really have to decide what you think. Certainty in judgment may be more desirable for a marriage proposal compared to a first date.

If you decide to exercise a right to vote, then you have to make a judgment about those who are running for office. You can watch the news and speeches and read articles about the candidates to try to make an informed decision, or you can go with your gut. Most of us think we're making an informed decision when we're actually doing the gut thing.[1] Jury members have to judge defendants. Interviewers have to judge job applicants. Teachers have to judge students. On *Project Runway*, celebrities have to judge designers. And so on.

Of course, these judgments do not have to cover every facet of the people being judged. Jury members need not judge whether the defendant would be a fun date but rather whether the defendant had motive to commit a crime. A teacher need not judge how extroverted a student is but rather how much the student has learned in a course. Often we can't help ourselves and we judge outside the required domain. Teachers have a variety of opinions about students (and vice versa).

Whatever the judgment domain, one message of this book is that we do judge each other. Sometimes we have to. The rest of the times, we just do. I am not writing this book to tell you to stop judging. Judging is part of being human, although some of us judge more often than others, and some judgments are more consequential than others.

One area of social psychology that falls under social judgment is attribution theory. An attribution is an explanation for someone's behavior or outcome and is part of many social judgments. Attributions are about *why* a behavior or outcome has occurred. This book is especially about attribution theory and the mistakes we make when we make attributions. Misunderstanding *why* a person acts or ends up a particular way makes it very difficult to accurately judge that person based on that action or outcome.

WHY GEORGE ZIMMERMAN SHOT TRAYVON MARTIN

Some social judgments are made with careful consideration and based on a lot of information. Most social judgments are made without much thought, with very little information, and very quickly—sometimes at "blink speed," in Malcolm Gladwell's terms. Under these conditions, errors are likely to occur. But most of all, most social judgments are made with undue confidence and certainty.[2]

In the high-profile story of George Zimmerman, and many race-related tragedies since then, absolute certainty abounded from all sides even within hours after the incident. In 2012, George Zimmerman, a white or Hispanic man, shot and killed Trayvon Martin, a black seventeen-year-old. Zimmerman belonged to the neighborhood watch. Martin recently started living in the neighborhood and was walking home. Why did George Zimmerman shoot Trayvon Martin? Was it self-defense? Did George Zimmerman racially profile Trayvon Martin? There was a man screaming on the 911 audiotape. Was it George Zimmerman or Trayvon Martin?

The judgments made by the jury were very consequential. George Zimmerman was acquitted on all charges. Judgments were also made by friends and family of both men, bloggers, reporters, cable news anchors and their guests, and many people on Facebook and Twitter. If you recall, did the outcome of the trial make you angry at the jury or the American justice system? Did the not-guilty verdict cause a sense of relief? Your emotional response probably depended on your judgments of Zimmerman and Martin and your attribution for the fatal shooting.

What most caught my attention about non-jury judgments was how absolutely certain so many people quickly became about why the shooting occurred. There were no eyewitnesses, and interpretations of the audiotape of the screams differed among experts and others who took the stand. Zimmerman's family said the screams sounded like Zimmerman. Martin's family said the screams sounded like Martin. But "obviously," for some people, Zimmerman was racially prejudiced in his lethal actions against Martin, and there was "no doubt" in some minds that Martin violently attacked Zimmerman. To think anything different would "obviously" be naïve, or racist, or harmful to society.

Of course, people have the right to form their own views, and I am sorry if my current openness to either side is upsetting to any reader still strongly entrenched on one side. My point is how could there be such pure, absolute certainty in seemingly reasonable people on both sides? There was certainty even before the trial, and even in some social scientists, whose training, in my view, should discourage jumping to conclusions.

The NBC-edited 911 tape can take some responsibility for pretrial certainty. Right before the shooting, Zimmerman called 911 and seemed to cite Martin's race as the reason for Zimmerman's suspicions about Martin. Zimmerman reportedly said, "This guy looks like he's up to no good. He looks black." But the full version of the tape revealed that Zimmerman only mentioned Martin's race when the 911 operator asked for it. The pieced-together audiotape left out the in-between question. Talk about quoting out of context![3] I will discuss this case further in chapter 2. I will discuss the possible causes of absolute certainty. And, regarding people who became certain about George Zimmerman's racism entirely because of the 911 tape, I will discuss why some of them might have held on to their certainty even after hearing the full version of the tape.

Of course, I don't know what happened that night in terms of motives and who was screaming on the audiotape. Another message of this book is that we may never know for sure why certain things happen. In the case of George Zimmerman, one side might indeed be right and the other wrong, or there could be an in-between reality in which both Zimmerman and Martin made bad decisions. I am not trying to excuse the behavior of either individual, but we may never know which side was more right. In fact, we will never know for certain the whys for most behaviors of individuals we don't know personally, and even sometimes for those we *do* know.

This concept of inevitable not-knowing is unsettling to a lot of people, so I mention it here in the introduction for you to start getting used to the idea. Being more comfortable with not knowing and with uncertainty is a little-known strategy to reduce biases.

EVERYDAY EXAMPLES OF BIAS

There are countless other examples of how we judge each other and how we make attributions. When others stumble, we might explain it by calling them clumsy. When others speak rudely to us, we call them mean. When someone tailgates us at high speed, we might call the tailgater an idiot, a jerk, or worse. When someone arrives late to our meeting or classroom, we might infer low interest, laziness, or just bad manners. When others physically attack us, we invariably infer evil. When faced with poverty in society, we often blame the impoverished. The likely reasons for this victim-blaming phenomenon might surprise you and will be discussed.

We make such judgments all the time. Not all of us make the same judgments, but through curiosity or evolution or other possible causes to be discussed, humans try to draw coherent conclusions about what they observe in each other. But another part of being human is often to get these conclusions wrong. Our social judgments are at great risk of a variety of biases. This risk is partly because of how quickly and overconfidently we usually make these judgments.

The pattern in my examples so far is explaining others' behaviors by focusing on others' personal characteristics or intentions with little, if any, consideration for the context (including the circumstance that something was left off a spliced 911 tape!). This pattern or tendency is extraordinarily common and is part of what's called the "fundamental attribution error" or FAE. Despite its name, conclusions resulting from this tendency are not always in error. For example, some high-speed tailgaters are indeed idiots and jerks. However, even when we have evidence to the contrary, we still tend to focus on others' personal characteristics or intentions when trying to explain their behavior. Most of us cannot seem to help ourselves. This automatic bias carries many consequences. There is much to discuss regarding the fundamental attribution error.[4]

What happens, though, when we try to explain the same behaviors in ourselves? If we stumble, is it because we are clumsy? Maybe we got pushed. If we speak rudely to an individual, is it because we are mean? Maybe the individual asked for it, or maybe we had a bad day. When we tailgate others, are we idiots? Maybe we are driving as carefully as we can to get somewhere very important on time. Maybe we even regret that we have to tailgate. When we arrive late, are we showing bad manners? Maybe something kept us from leaving home on time. Maybe the slow drivers in front of us causing us to tailgate caused us to be late!

In explaining our own behaviors, especially negative ones, we tend to do the opposite of the fundamental attribution error. We focus on context and specific circumstances. This difference in how we judge ourselves versus others for identical behavior goes by many names: double standards, speaking out of both sides of your mouth, the pot calling the kettle black, and just plain hypocrisy. In social psychology, it is called the "actor-observer bias."

There may indeed be circumstances to explain our own questionable behavior, but even when there aren't, we tend to invent circumstances or exaggerate irrelevant circumstances to relevant status. Many cases of the actor-observer bias arise out of ego protection and the plain fact that, of course, we give ourselves the benefit of the doubt. Such ego protection in moderation is a fundamental part of human functioning—it turns out to be mentally healthy. However, there are additional reasons for the actor-observer bias that have nothing to do with ego and mental health. They include simply having more knowledge about our own situations versus others'.

In many other ways, most of us are biased in how we perceive ourselves, others, and the world. We tend to take credit for our successes but blame other people or factors for our failures. We underestimate the likelihood that bad things will happen to us and overestimate the likelihood of good things. We overestimate how much others agree with us. We rate the skills we're good at as more important in life than the skills we're not so good at. We feel we have more control over our lives than we actually do. We think the world is a more just place than it actually is. We pay attention to the evidence that supports our views, ignore or distort the evidence that contradicts our views, and dislike those who provide the latter. We think that mainstream political news is biased in favor of the other party. We judge others based on stereotypes, based on whether or not they belong to the same group we do (racial, political, you name it), and based on what is most available or recent in our memories.[5]

Most of these mistakes or biases are difficult to see in ourselves but easy to see in others. And in our biased judgments, as already mentioned, we tend to be remarkably and unjustifiably confident. The list of biases and misperceptions goes on and on.

Biases and misperceptions are also the makings of many popular nonfiction books in recent years, such as *Blindspot, Blind Spots, Blunder, Don't Believe Everything You Think, The Invisible Gorilla, Mindware, Mindwise, Predictably Irrational, You Are Not So Smart,* and *Why We Make Mistakes.* The number of these books reflects how many biases are out there, how much readers care to know about these biases, and perhaps, for some readers, how much readers want to avoid these biases.

However, as conveyed by philosopher Jean-Jacques Rousseau, the only way to avoid mistakes in judgment is never to judge. Everybody makes mistakes. Live and learn. Nobody's perfect. There's no shortage of adages. Such views do not mean that we should stop judging each other, nor do they excuse our misjudgments or mistakes. Such views do not mean that we are all equally biased, nor that an individual cannot improve. We can improve.

After reading this book, hopefully your risk of bias will reduce from whatever level it currently resides at. On the other hand, some of you are too accurate or too biased in a negative way, and you need more positive illusions to function. I will discuss the fundamental role of positive illusions in mental health. Fortunately, in terms of mental health, most of us do not have the problem of being overly accurate.[6]

AN ANTI-BROAD-BRUSH APPROACH

So everybody makes mistakes at some point, in social judgments or otherwise. We do not all commit the same mistakes, and most of us do not own up to our mistakes very quickly or comfortably. But everybody makes mistakes. This is probably the only time in this book that I use the word "everybody." I try to avoid such all-inclusive language because another mistake most of us make in social judgment is to overgeneralize. It's part of stereotyping. Popular press authors in social science are especially guilty of this broad-brush approach.

Even psychologist Nicholas Epley—who wrote one of the best bias books in recent years, titled *Mindwise*—regularly overgeneralized. In the book, Epley often used all-inclusive language in which he was sure that "you" would react to A in a particular way, that "nobody" would ever do B, or that "everyone" is affected by or wants C. He referred to research about groups such as women and the poor but did not acknowledge individual differences within these diverse groups.[7]

A more striking example of a broad brush is in Christopher Chabris and Daniel Simons's *The Invisible Gorilla*. The authors made several excellent points, such as how co-occurrence does not imply causation and how science cannot retrospectively explain a single occurrence of something. But Chabris and Simons often overgeneralized. They often wrote "we all" or how something "affects us all" when it's not actually 100 percent of us. At times, they also referred to an effect as occurring in "people" in general or occurring "often" when they concurrently reported that it occurred less than half the time.

Chabris and Simons even overgeneralized the very result the book was named after. *The Invisible Gorilla* refers to a finding in which a study's participants didn't recall seeing someone in a gorilla suit walking through a group of people because participants had to focus on what those people were doing. It was as if the gorilla were invisible. This failure to recall the gorilla is a case of "inattentional blindness" and was found by the authors themselves in their 1999 study. They reported in their book that "roughly half" of the participants didn't see the gorilla. Although that means that roughly half *did* see the gorilla, the authors referred to the effect of missing the gorilla as "striking" and wrote that "we are completely unaware of those aspects of our world that fall outside of that current focus of attention."[8]

So when I first read *The Invisible Gorilla*, instances of such strong language and naming the book after the effect surprised me because the effect only pertained to half the sample. On the other hand, even half is still pretty amazing. It was a gorilla, after all!

My bigger surprise came when I read the actual 1999 study. It turned out that in the conditions that mirrored real-life viewing, the gorilla was invisible to *clearly less than half* of all participants. Approximately 57 percent of participants in these conditions reported *seeing* the gorilla. Perhaps the true percentage was even higher than 57 percent, because some of the participants who noticed the gorilla may have been excluded from the final report. About 7 percent of the original participants were excluded because they misrecorded or lost track of their count of the number of basketball passes they were asked to observe. Such miscounting could indicate not following directions or not focusing attention where they were supposed to (the apparent basis for excluding these participants), but it could also indicate a distraction because the participants noticed the gorilla.[9]

Many bloggers and other popular press authors who reviewed *The Invisible Gorilla* or referred to the result just went with the general line of "about half." But many writers generalized the finding of missing the gorilla even further. They referred to people in general not seeing the gorilla, even "most people." Even academic articles glossed over this issue in simply stating that observers "frequently" didn't see the gorilla, that observers "tend[ed] not to notice," or that "a substantial portion of the observers did not report seeing it."[10] But more than half of the participants did in fact see the gorilla. Not as invisible as it sounds.

One piece of advice I offer is to be on the lookout for such overinclusive language in not only popular nonfiction but also academic articles. Ask yourself what the author precisely means by "frequently," "most people," or even "everyone." If exact percentages are not provided, then consider the possibility that the actual frequency or amount might be less than it sounds. Of course, it helps if you can get hold of the original study to examine the results yourself.

An even stronger and more consistent example of the broad brush occurs in comparing men and women. As John Gray is known for claiming in his best-selling book, men are from Mars and women are from Venus. In other words, men and women are fundamentally different from each other. Right? No. Not really. Aside from sex-based anatomy, individual differences within either gender group greatly exceed the average differences between groups. Within each gender group, there are many people from different planets that are farther away from each other than Mars and Venus. A renowned expert on gender differences, Janet Hyde, has strongly argued that "gender similarities are far more common than gender differences." And some well-known average gender differences, such as in math ability, turn out to be minuscule or nonexistent.[11] A cleverly titled book on this topic is *Delusions of Gender* by Cordelia Fine.

Yet many authors who talk about gender differences take a black-and-white approach. Saying that men are one way and women are the other is a classic example of overgeneralization and a false dichotomy. Authors similarly need to be careful in comparing groups based on race, religion, sexual orientation, political orientation, and so on. No large-group comparisons are as black-and-white as they might first appear.

As a social scientist, I guard fiercely against overgeneralizing, not only in my language but also in my thinking (not that I'm always successful). There are so many individual differences within every group and in every social area of human life, and I cannot read the mind of anyone I observe—I am not telepathic. As an instructor who has taught thousands of students, I may still have a student next term who does not fit any previous student's profile, whose reasons for common behaviors are unique, and who is impossible to predict. Even if I had your older sibling in my classroom last year, that doesn't mean I know *you* when you arrive in my classroom. On some level, most instructors probably know this about individual differences among students, but we still might overgeneralize without realizing it.

Even if I were a clinical therapist with thousands of hours of experience helping people one on one, during which time I'd noticed patterns that went beyond research-based knowledge, that would not mean those patterns would apply to my next client (although they might). That would not mean that I could read your mind, decode your nonverbals in my office, and know what was really going on in your life. Psychiatrist Jim Phelps, author of *Why Am I Still Depressed?*, wrote, "Although many people think psychiatrists can 'read people's minds,' we cannot."[12]

Even if social science studies show the same thing about people over and over, the result is still on average and based only on samples of participants. There are almost always exceptions. Social science research does not allow us to perfectly understand or predict a particular individual. Social science research does *improve* our probability of understanding and predicting people in general. Social science research does identify processes and causes that underlie social phenomena, and this knowledge has led to successful interventions in education and mental health and business. But even "successful interventions" don't work on *everyone*.

The Myth of the Stable Personality

This problem of overgeneralization includes cases in which people think they can predict your behavior in a new situation after having interacted with you in only one or two narrow situations (such as at work, in the classroom, or in your therapist's office). According to well-known social psychologists Lee Ross and Richard Nisbett, people falsely believe they can predict your behavior from one situation to another because they assume there is a stable and easy-to-see personality that caused your behavior in the first place. People see stable dispositions behind your initial behavior, as opposed to particular circumstances.

Stable personalities, if they exist, are, of course, stable, so it would make sense to generalize them to new situations. But that initial assumption of a stable and visible personality impervious to situational specifics has long been known to be in error. In fact, that assumption amounts to the fundamental attribution error. Ross and Nisbett summarized decades of research in referring to a "fundamental unpredictability" of an individual from one situation to another.

Ross and Nisbett wrote,

> Neither the professional nor the layperson can do that well when obliged to predict behavior in one particular new situation on the basis of actions in one particular prior situation. Despite such evidence, however, most people staunchly believe that individual differences or traits can be used to predict how people will behave in new situations. Such "dispositionism" is widespread in our culture.[13]

Such cases of overgeneralization particularly occur when the previous situations contain social roles that might influence your behavior. Social roles include that of employee, boss, patient, doctor, student, teacher, parent, police officer, neighbor, man, woman, and so on. These roles and the norms for how to behave in these roles might make you behave in ways that don't match your behavior in other situations and that don't even fit your usual character, however stable it might be. To underestimate the power of social roles is a well-known case of the fundamental attribution error.[14] I devote an entire chapter to social roles (see chapter 5).

In general, just because you are hard-nosed or aggressive in one situation does not mean you will be unsympathetic or unkind in another. Just because you are soft-spoken or polite in one situation does not mean you will be unable to handle yourself in a confrontation in another situation. The 1999 movie *Blast from the Past* offered a good example of this in its over-the-top well-mannered protagonist Adam, played by Brendan Fraser. Adam seemed incredibly polite and naïve, having been raised in a fallout shelter by well-mannered 1960s parents. So Adam's new 1990s friends feared for Adam's safety around bullies. But Adam called out bullies for their bad manners and easily fended off their physical attacks, having been trained to box by his father.

Think of coworkers whom you get to know outside work. Think of acquaintances from the health club, yoga class, or pickup basketball whom you barely recognize outside the gym in street clothes. Think of the many murderers or mass shooters whose neighbors expressed shock that such a quiet, "kept to himself" person was capable of such behavior.

It's not just that a particular situation can constrain or prevent the expression of a certain behavior, making it impossible for you to know that someone is capable of that type of behavior in another situation. It's also that the specifics of a new situation might elicit or intensify a surprising behavior from the person you thought you knew. Soft-spoken or subdued students can scream their heads off at the right music concert. Polite coworkers don't usually run or jump in the hallway or committee meeting, but some of them can outrun and out-rebound you on the basketball court and purposely smash a tennis ball at your head in a tiebreaker.

My own drive and ability in some sports surprise many players and observers based on their interaction with one version of me off the court and away from the gym. Not that I am a stellar athlete or a brute. I've been told that I am too polite to pose a real on-court threat. I've also been called "disarming." After losing to me (which occasionally happens), one opponent actually said, "I'm sorry, but you didn't seem like you could play that well," and "I didn't think you were that strong." Thanks, I guess.

Similarly, I know a very kind professor who played on a big-city roller derby team a few years before we met. She called herself Irrational Velvet—very cool. There's also a professor who competes as an American Ninja Warrior—while dressed in a stereotypical sweater vest and necktie.[15]

My last example for now is a young man in my wife's yoga club who was very sweet and polite—and who was a Marine and trained to kill during wartime. War is an extreme situation, but that is part of my point. Extreme situations, and even some non-extreme ones, make our trait theories about people kind of meaningless. If it sounds like I am just describing a problem with stereotypes, that is indeed part of what I'm doing. Why can't yogis join the military? Why can't soldiers be sweet and practice yoga? Why can't professors knock people on their butts in skates? Of course they can.

But if you only know an individual from a classroom where she softly lectures, then it might surprise you to know she excels in a high-contact sport. If you only know an individual from a yoga club, then it might surprise you to know he is a Marine. Maybe on average, military men don't practice yoga, but some of them do. According to *Yoga across America*, yoga can greatly benefit service members and veterans. Their website shows dozens of yogi-soldiers on yoga mats.[16] On the other hand, you might not be surprised at all by an individual's multiple and seemingly contradictory roles, perhaps because you're aware of your own.

Authors Don't Know You

All the above is to say that I do not presume to know you, the reader. Even if I know that on average, people are surprised by certain things or respond to certain stimuli in certain ways, that does not mean that *you* have responded that way, nor that you will in the future. I am not pointing my finger at you. I am not judging you. How can I? I don't know you at all. *You* can decide how much of the research discussed in this book might pertain to you.

And I won't test you the way some popular press science authors do— setting you up to make a likely mistake and then saying, "See, I have something new to tell you about yourself." In particular, I won't tell you that you're unconsciously racist based on your performance on an implicit association test (IAT). The IAT is available these days at any number of online venues, from academic to pop psych to the Public Broadcasting Service to Oprah. com. But despite many of these sites' claims, including that all or most of us are secretly racist, the IAT has methodological and theoretical limitations connected to the fundamental attribution error. The IAT cannot definitively reveal hidden bias (to be discussed further in chapter 2).[17]

In any case, there are reasons so many popular press authors write with a broad brush, besides thinking they know what "everybody" is like. Broad-brush language often sounds better. It's simpler. It sounds authoritative and worth reading. It avoids the appearance of quibbling, evading, hemming, or hawing. Publishers or editors ask their authors for it. It's more efficient. How cumbersome it would be if every few sentences the author had to remind you that the results are on average, that some readers may operate differently, or that the author was not 100 percent certain of something. Adverbs and phrases such as "on average," "most of us," "typically," "usually," "probably," "possibly," "relatively," "in general," "may," "might," "seem," "tend to," "appear to," and "not necessarily" can make a statement about people so much more accurate, but, too often used, they can cloud the message and undermine the authority of the author. (I apologize to publishers and authors if I am giving away any secrets in selling popular nonfiction.)

GENERAL DISCLAIMER

Please consider this section my general disclaimer that even if I sound like I am broad-brushing it, what I am saying very likely does *not* apply to *everyone*. Even if I sound confident about people in general, there are almost always exceptions. I do believe it is more accurate in almost every instance to use qualifiers such as "almost," "very likely," "usually," and "on average." This accuracy in using qualifiers lies in that unsettling reality I've tried to convey about understanding an individual—that there is an "inevitable not-knowing" why a particular individual acts a particular way, or, in the words of Ross and Nisbett, a "fundamental unpredictability" of the individual. But that reality doesn't mean that I have to remind you of the uncertainty every few sentences. That reality doesn't mean that I have to sound wishy-washy or indecisive to convey a message.

So, for the most part, I try to write simply and efficiently and to highlight the bottom lines when they are evident to me. But when I do use explicit qualifiers, it's not indecisiveness—it's a truth about the complexity of people.

I set aside an entire chapter to delve into this complexity in more detail, where I will share research on individual differences (see chapter 9). My individual-differences chapter is one of many reasons that this book is unique among books about bias. Beyond the overarching truths that we are all different from each other and that tendencies to commit bias do not apply to everyone equally, I will discuss some of what social science knows about what type of person is more susceptible to certain biases.

Unlike most social psychology books that stress the role of social and situational forces to explain behavior, such as *The Lucifer Effect*, Elliot Aronson's *The Social Animal*, and *Situations Matter*, the message of this book is that the role of the individual is also important. Behaviors are usually caused by a combination of situational and personal factors. I will draw from my own research as well as that of many other social and personality psychologists. The power of context has limits.

A REQUEST OF YOU

I hope you will take my anti-broad-brush approach to heart. You are unique. You are not necessarily like most people. Just because you behave one way in one situation doesn't mean you will behave the same way in another situation. Perhaps it is easy to realize these things about yourself when others make incorrect presumptions about you based on stereotypes, based on how *most* people are, or based on how you are in one situation.

But sometimes you *are* like most people. Sometimes the way you are in one situation *does* fairly inform observers of how you will be in another situation. Perhaps you even like that idea, that you are consistent and stable in the way you live your life (especially when the way you live is praiseworthy). Indeed, some of us are more stable than others. And sometimes stereotypes apply to you. Sometimes the average result from social science research does pertain to *you*. I suggested earlier that you can decide how much of the research discussed in this book might apply to you. But I hope you are open to the *possibility* that most of it does.

One of the first steps to reduce biases is developing openness to the possibility that you have them. Yes, biases only occur on average, and not everyone shows every bias. But beware the above-average effect—the tendency to think you're above average in good ways and that you're not among the biased majority. The majority of us think we're not among the majority when it comes to negative attributes. We tend to think that a particular bias is something other readers have to worry about, not us. Most of us even think we're above average when it comes to avoiding the above-average effect![18]

Maybe you are the exception, or maybe not. Try to be open to the possibility that you are average. Sorry. It had to be said. If the majority of us can be open in this way, even if some of us are not prone to a particular bias, then on average, biases will reduce overall.

Psychologist Jamil Zaki once posted an article at his *Scientific American* blog, *The Moral Universe*, about how psychological research is "not about you" because it's based on averages. I posted a comment saying whoa, maybe, but it *might* be about you, so let's keep an open mind. In fact, if the research sample is normally distributed, there's an especially decent chance the research *is* about you. Zaki seemed to agree in his reply to me, although he cautioned science writers not to overstate what a particular study means for a particular reader. Indeed.[19]

LISTENING TO READERS

So social science research may or may not pertain to a particular reader. Every reader is unique. Partly for that reason, I've tried to listen to many different readers in writing this book. To learn their views, I read hundreds of reviews from everyday readers on Amazon.com and elsewhere for books on topics similar to mine. I've also paid attention to word of mouth. Of course, it depends on the particular book, but I have found several common complaints and points of praise within this social science genre. Unfortunately but predictably, the perspectives sometimes contradict each other, even among reviews of the same book.

Most readers really like anecdotes, real-life stories from the news, and personal stories from the author's life, while some find these stories or devices to be painfully boring or even irrelevant. Most readers feel overwhelmed or bored by research details, while some wish more of those details were provided. But most readers do want science authors to back up their statements with research, although some argue that frequently citing research reveals a book with nothing new to say. Most readers readily defer to the expertise of a professor-author and don't feel talked down to, while others find the same author to be arrogant, self-congratulatory, or condescending (some authors do come off that way, of course). Last, many readers lament that a 250-page book could have been written in half the space or less (even one page!). Very few wish that books were longer. A common sentiment is that authors add material to reach the page mark set by a publisher without caring that they are making the same point over and over again from chapter to chapter.

I have definite ideas for what would be most interesting, effective, and appropriate to illustrate my points and convey my message, but I have also carefully listened to readers. I could go with the views of the majority and not worry about the complaints from the few, but I try to incorporate all perspectives. I know that I will not please everyone in every chapter, but I hope that my approach can make the overall book more interesting and rigorous for more readers.

Even if I had read every single online review for every book in this genre, I do realize that this sampling has a selection bias because it excludes readers who do not submit their thoughts to be read online. Nonetheless, this information from everyday readers seems too valuable to pass up. In sum, I do the following.

1. I Regularly Describe Real-Life Stories and Personal Experiences

Sharing vivid stories and experiences is an effective way to show how concepts and research relate to everyday life. But I try not to overdo it. Indeed, anecdotes or case studies, especially colorful ones, are notorious for giving false impressions that large-sample research studies correct. And many popular press authors seem to indulge in cherry-picking real-life stories that support their viewpoint while leaving unmentioned countless stories that do not. Although I strongly encourage readers to trust large-sample research over single stories, I will mention some of the counter-stories when I'm aware of them to combat cherry-picking. I also sometimes use scenes from movies and television shows to illustrate a point. I defer to research-based conclusions when they are available.

2. I Include Some Research Details

I am a researcher, so most of my past writing has included details from research. But I understand that this approach can go too far in popular nonfiction, which is not about producing standard classroom textbooks. So when I report research results, I will sometimes include *some* research details, but never a lot. When further details might be relevant or interesting, I will include them in the endnotes for interested readers.

3. I Go Beyond a Reporting of Research Results

I am in the habit of backing up my statements with research, and I believe that offering brief summaries of dense research areas for lay readers is useful. But I also agree with some readers that I need to go beyond a reporting of research results. I need to draw new connections and to convey new insights based not only on research but also on theory, logic, current events, and my personal experiences. I do all of the above. Based on rigorous assessment of past research, I also provide new conclusions in research areas that readers, popular press authors, and even scientists think they understand but don't. For example, I will correct the long-standing belief that victims are less likely to receive help the more bystanders there are. A large group of bystanders is a powerful situational force, but not as powerful as popular press social science leads us to believe. In the usual telling of the famous 1964 story from New York City, Kitty Genovese was murdered while numerous bystanders did nothing to help, but in fact she was not abandoned by bystanders that night.

4. I Try Not to Sound Condescending

I apologize if I ever sound condescending or arrogant. I really don't mean to. Of course, I do need to sound a little like I know *something* (publisher's orders). And, of course, it's hard to see our own arrogance and relatively easy to think we see it in others. As a check on myself in this regard, I have sought feedback from colleagues and everyday readers. I know that some readers know as much as I do or more (even about the particular content of this book).

Keep in mind that a question is sometimes just a question and not arrogant opposition to a position. I've noticed that questions, proposed middle grounds, and even playing devil's advocate are sometimes perceived by one extreme side of a debate as arrogant attacks from the other extreme side of the debate. Revolutionary researchers including Paul Ekman, Anthony Greenwald, and Derald Wing Sue have had to deal with many questions over the years or just suggestions for possible alternative interpretations of their results, and these researchers sometimes responded as if the suggestions were full-blown or even deceitful attacks (perhaps an occupational hazard for revolutionary scientists!).

One of the messages of this book is that just because someone has questions about your position or doesn't fully agree with you right away, they don't necessarily hold negative intentions toward you (although they might) and aren't necessarily being purposely deceitful or willfully ignorant (although they might be). To automatically assume these characteristics based on someone's failure to fully agree with you can represent the fundamental attribution error. Asking questions is sometimes just asking questions, to gather more information in response to a new, confusing, or complex situation. A cigar is sometimes just a cigar. Or maybe you didn't state your position as clearly as you could have. Questions from listeners can clarify that ambiguity.

Some of you might know all this but still get upset at the questioner because of *how* the questioner questions. "I'm OK answering questions," you might think, "but not when the questioner uses that tone of voice." (If you know what tone I mean.) Fair enough. But try to be open to the possibility that your perception of a negative or accusatory tone can be an extension of the fundamental attribution error. Inferring negative characteristics or intentions would feel more validated if you also inferred a negative tone of voice.

Of course, if even asking questions about your viewpoint is annoying or offensive to you, that is your call. Be offended. You don't have to answer questions. If you cannot understand how a decent person would not fully agree with you, be confused. Stand up for your viewpoint.

I will pose many questions and take some middle grounds on controversial issues in this book. When doing so, I might upset both extreme sides of an issue. Please know that is not my intention. And please know that I don't usually have space to cover every important article on both sides of an issue, but I do my best to provide a balanced picture of complex debates.

5. I Try Not to Make the Same Points over and over Again

As for the length of books in this genre, I am very sensitive to the issue of unnecessary chapters. The readers who have complained about this phenomenon in other books have better things to do with their time than to read a book's second half that provides very little, if any, new information. Of course, an author may claim new information even if some readers don't see it. I have carefully evaluated each chapter, especially those that come later in the book, and asked myself what new information, new perspective, or new application is provided. This question is part of what has driven chapter revisions. I have even removed some chapters from initial outlines and drafts for this book. At the same time, I do stress some major themes throughout the book.

PREVIEW

In this book, I will focus on the classic and wide-reaching bias called the fundamental attribution error, in which we underestimate the power of context. This bias is fundamental to human perception and interpersonal relations but has surprisingly received very little attention in popular press books on bias.

Among a few exceptions, social psychologist Sam Sommers's book *Situations Matter* did cover the fundamental attribution error. But Sommers's focus appeared much broader. His recurring theme was that we underestimate the importance of the situation for both others and ourselves, with which I don't fully agree. For example, in the actor-observer bias, we *overestimate* the importance of our own situations. Sommers highlighted the power of multiple classic situations (as done in most social psychology textbooks), but he only mentioned the fundamental attribution error by name once, in a footnote.

I will share new information regarding the common reporting for some of those classic studies about the power of context. And I will discuss the fundamental attribution error more directly and in specific. I will describe its inner workings and some of its history. I will provide a wider array of examples of how we misjudge this way that are not typically covered in textbooks. I will discuss how the fundamental attribution error is part of why we can be misled by quote mining and by politicians, why the very study of microaggressions and implicit bias is flawed, why we misread each other in nonverbal decoding (including lie detection and gaydar), why we overestimate our ability to predict each other's behaviors in new contexts, why we blame victims for their own suffering and why we parent shame, and why we are so quick to anger while driving or at work or in many other interpersonal contexts.

I hope that reading this book can literally bring more peace into the lives of those who wish they were less quick to get angry or defensive. I will share some stories from students and others about the stress-reducing effects this book's message can have. Reducing the fundamental attribution error can reduce anger, stress, misguided retaliation, and interpersonal conflict.

In particular, I will discuss how the fundamental attribution error and victim blaming can occur during psychotherapy. I will highlight a potential flaw in cognitive-behavioral therapy that may reflect the fundamental attribution error. I will cite examples of how social psychologists and authors of popular press science books are also not immune to this error (nor am I). I will discuss how the fundamental attribution error expands beyond the error itself and is part of many other biases and processes in social perception, including prejudices and conspiracy theories.

In his 2005 book *Blink*, Malcolm Gladwell championed blink-speed judgments that amounted to the fundamental attribution error. I will offer many counterpoints to his position. But even Gladwell acknowledged years later that the fundamental attribution error speaks "to the very broadest questions of human perception"[20] and that a blink-speed judgment is "probably more often terrible than it is good."[21] (Better late than never!)

So yes, situations matter in why people act the way they do, and it usually takes a little extra time to see the situation. But in bringing readers' and students' attention to the power of the situation, many authors and educators go too far. They overly focus on the context and underestimate the power of the individual. The power of context has limits. Thus, I have a chapter titled *The Individual Matters Too* (see chapter 9). Most behaviors are caused by a combination of situational and personal factors, not just one or the other.

Even in the famous Stanford Prison Experiment, usually cited as showing only the power of the situation (behind abusive behaviors in prison settings), I will highlight the likely but little-known role also played by the guards' personalities.[22] Even in the classic bystander effect—the more bystanders, the less help to a victim—again usually cited as showing only the power of the situation, I discovered a computational mistake in the cornerstone meta-analysis. Based on my publication of its correction and new analyses, I will highlight how individual bystanders matter more in large-crowd emergencies than we thought. Even the famous Kitty Genovese received more help from bystanders than described in the classic story. As a general rule, it turns out to be untrue that victims are less likely to receive help the more bystanders there are.[23]

To lose sight of the individual and the individual's personal dispositions risks a less common bias in which we overattribute to the situation, a common criticism of political liberals when they try to explain society's problems. My individual-matters chapter will also share research on who is more susceptible to certain biases and why.

Last, I will take on the challenging task of explaining that, although biases have negative consequences, biases can also be good for us. Certain biases, misperceptions, and illusions in moderation are part of good mental health.[24] For example, *feeling* in control of negative life events may be more important than actually *being* in control of them. Certain biases and illusions are good for us in other ways as well, from the physical healing properties of the placebo effect to the general day-to-day efficiency in making quick (if biased) decisions. So if you can see any of these biases in yourself, I advise not to beat yourself up about it. Managing our bias doesn't automatically mean eliminating all biases. Some biases can be a good thing.

But ultimately, I will argue that the cons of being biased outweigh the pros. And I will suggest multiple ways to reduce bias, especially the fundamental attribution error. I will go beyond the simple route suggested by most popular press authors, which is to learn about bias. It turns out that just reading or learning about bias is limited in how helpful it can be.

I will also address how to reduce the biases committed by those who are close to us. Reducing our own biases is hard enough. How do we diplomatically tackle the task of correcting family, friends, significant others, spouses, and even coworkers? Maybe we're better off not trying. I will make some research-based suggestions and highlight the challenges. Be ever aware that your perception of bias in others might be biased.

In terms of your own potential biases and mental health, my moral dilemma in writing this book is that I don't want your mental health to suffer from you becoming more accurate. Certain positive illusions are fundamental to good mental health. People who do not hold these positive illusions are more likely to experience moderate depression, termed "depressive realism."[25] When I teach social psychology, I let my students know that I am walking a line between improving students' accuracy and preventing their depression. I want my students to become more accurate but not get depressed in the process. As attributed to President James Garfield and sometimes Mark Twain, "The truth will set you free, but first it will make you miserable."[26]

So in the epilogue, I will suggest ways to offset the mental health risks of truth, of accurate perception, in the goal of setting you free. In other words, our well-being tends to be irrational, supported by positive illusions and simplistic misperceptions, but I hope by reading this book and its epilogue, you can have a better chance at what I call "rational well-being." Rational well-being is having good mental health without committing the irrational biases to which so many mentally healthy individuals are prone. I believe we can be happy and rational.

CHAPTER 1

SPEECHES AND TRAFFIC JAMS: FAE BASICS

The persisting pattern which permeates everyday life of interpreting individual behavior in the light of personal factors (traits) rather than in the light of situational factors must be considered one of the fundamental sources of misunderstanding personality in our time. It is both the cause and the symptom of the crisis of our society.
—Gustav Ichheiser, social psychologist

Circumstances cause us to act the way we do. We should always bear this in mind before judging the actions of others. I realized this from the start during World War II.
—Thor Heyerdahl, adventurer

Have you ever noticed that anybody driving slower than you is an idiot, and anyone going faster than you is a maniac?
—George Carlin, stand-up comic

Traffic jams are no fun. You're wasting time and gas, breathing exhaust, probably bored, and now running late. On the highway it can be worse because you're trapped until the next exit. When you do reach an exit, you don't know if you should get off or stay the course in hope traffic will clear. And most of us get a bit irritable in heavy crowds, whether at a shopping mall or bumper to bumper in traffic.

So when you see an impatient jerk pull onto the shoulder and start passing everyone because he obviously doesn't think traffic laws pertain to him, you might get really mad. Who does he think he is? Right? What arrogance.

If you yell and honk your horn, maybe Mr. I'm-Better-Than-Everyone-Else will get the idea and get back in line with everyone else. And if you see this guy coming from behind and get angry enough, you might even edge out onto the shoulder to block him.

An everyday commuter, Peter Rowe, found himself in this scenario during a jam on the New Jersey Turnpike. In a letter to the editor in the *New York Times*, Rowe described how "there is nothing more infuriating than watching these shoulder drivers whiz by." Rowe decided to pull out and block a shoulder driver to make the shoulder driver drive as slowly as everyone else. Rowe wrote, "What a sense of power," and described how a nearby truck driver applauded him for righting this wrong. The editor titled the letter "Let Those Shoulder Drivers Stew in Their Own Juice." Yeah![1]

This screw-the-shoulder-driver sentiment appears universal. In a Russian video clip titled "Car Drives on the Shoulder to Avoid Traffic Jam, Gets Proper Payback" and posted at a blog called *22 Words,* a shoulder driver doesn't notice the end of the shoulder and so drives onto the guard-rail. The clip shows the motorist's car stuck on the guardrail with its tires hovering off the ground. The clip also shows Russian commuters strongly deriding the driver. My Russian-speaking friends were a little disturbed when I asked for translation help.

The blogger who posted the video wrote, "It feels good to see this car get owned. So, so good." Other commenters wrote, "That made my day," and "What an idiot."[2]

Of course, not everyone reacts this way to a stranded motorist or shoulder driver, but if either taking action or feeling moral indignation sounds like you, then you might be committing the fundamental attribution error or FAE. Shoulder drivers are breaking the law, and they might be arrogant. But maybe there's a situational factor in play, maybe even an emergency. What if some shoulder drivers have good reasons for their actions?

Once, during a family trip, my dad was the shoulder driver passing everyone and getting honked at. We were nearly out of gas on a Tennessee interstate in stop-and-go, bumper-to-bumper traffic. My brothers, sister, and I were kids, and we were a bit scared.

With the gas needle on empty, my dad decided to drive on the shoulder to the next exit ramp. Cars honked, and towering semi-trucks pulled out to block us. My dad swerved. My mom screamed. My sister recalls feeling very small. My dad decided it was better to risk being stranded than getting in a collision and pulled back into traffic. We made it to a gas station in time.

It's usually impossible for a bystander to be sure why a driver does something extreme. Being unwilling to consider even the possibility of an emergency amounts to the FAE, no matter how pinheaded that other driver appears. Even assigning a 10 percent probability to some unknown emergency is better than zero if your goal is to avoid this bias.

In the case of my family, even if running out of gas does not rise to the level of an emergency in terms of state law or social norms, my dad was worried about stranding his wife and four young kids in the middle of nowhere, before the age of cell phones. Yes, maybe my parents should have filled the tank sooner, but that is a separate issue. My dad drove on the shoulder for a more complex reason than being arrogant or a jerk. (By the way, my dad's nature is quite the opposite.)

Partly because of this experience, I find it hard to get angry at the shoulder drivers who occasionally pass me during traffic jams. Maybe the shoulder driver is a total jerk, or maybe something else is going on.

A FUNDAMENTAL MISTAKE

The FAE is a very common tendency in explaining an individual's behavior or outcome, especially in Western cultures.[3] The FAE has two co-occurring parts. First, we quickly overestimate the causal role of dispositional factors, such as the individual's traits, attitudes, feelings, preferences, motives, abilities, or inadequacies. Arrogant jerk. These explanations are called internal or dispositional attributions. Second, we overlook or underestimate the possible contribution of situational factors or specific circumstances. Running out of gas. Explanations involving such circumstances are called external or situational attributions. In social psychology parlance, an attribution is an explanation.

Put simply, in the FAE, we jump the attributional gun. We don't stop to explore the possibilities. We quickly narrow in on one or two traits and then feel satisfied. Ironically, as in the shoulder-driving examples, this satisfaction sometimes arises from, helps to maintain, or even causes interpersonal anger (see chapter 7).

Because of this connection to anger and to perceptions of being slighted or mistreated, the FAE may be involved in many if not most forms of human interpersonal conflict—from blocking shoulder drivers to confrontations at work to world wars. If a person or group or country behaves in a way that has negative consequences for us or makes us feel mistreated, then the person or persons engaging in that behavior must have negative personal characteristics or intentions, or so most of us believe. As spoken by Austrian social psychologist Gustav Ichheiser, this cognitive habit may be "both the cause and the symptom of the crisis of our society."[4] The FAE also applies to our explanations of neutral and positive behaviors, but negative behaviors or those that are unexpected or salient are more likely to make us want to provide an explanation.

Of course, sometimes the person or persons who behave negatively do indeed have negative personal characteristics or intentions—end of story. But what is clear from decades of research is that it's not nearly as often as most people think. It's usually not that simple.

Keep in mind that explaining is not excusing. Even if there are a multitude of situational factors to help explain an action, whether or not to excuse the actor is not my call as a social psychologist. As I tell my students, social science helps people to accurately *explain* others' behaviors, but the individual who feels mistreated gets to decide whether to *excuse*.

WHO HAD THE IDEA FIRST?

The idea that people overlook situational factors has probably occurred to many individuals over the centuries, and not only well-known philosophers or social scientists. In particular, most of us who have been criticized or punished over a negative outcome that was not our fault can see that those who sit in judgment are missing something in our situation. Shoulder drivers with legitimate emergencies might feel a sense of injustice when getting honked at and blocked. Whether or not they extrapolate from that experience and see a more general phenomenon in human perception is a harder question, and most of us have not conducted our own research.

Kurt Lewin, who is considered a pioneer of social psychology, criticized psychology at large for overly focusing on individuals' dispositions to explain behaviors and outcomes. Lewin observed that by 1931, psychologists were starting to get it, that psychology was beginning a transition to greater consideration of the environment and the specific context in which behaviors occur.[5] But what about the dispositional bias from everyday people? I credit the first articulation of the everyday FAE to Gustav Ichheiser.

Gustav Ichheiser

Ichheiser came to the United States in 1940 after losing his family in Poland in World War II.[6] The war and his experience of it seem to have influenced much of Ichheiser's writings. Psychologists Daniel Gilbert (author of *Stumbling on Happiness*) and Patrick Malone suggested in a brief history of the FAE that many intellectuals, including Ichheiser, thought World War II and the "Nazi phenomenon . . . demonstrated that social situations can be fantastically powerful determinants of action" and that people can be "prisoners of their times" more than "captains of their destinies." Gilbert and Malone referred in large part to the conforming and obedient nature of soldiers.[7]

Ichheiser also observed that the power of context went unnoticed by everyday people in everyday times who overlooked powerful social forces in trying to understand each other. Ichheiser argued that this common oversight contributed to a crisis in our society, specifically to social injustices and to misperceptions and mistreatment of the underprivileged who were victims of such forces.[8]

Surprisingly, Ichheiser is not well known in social psychology, even though many of his ideas foreshadowed and influenced classic contemporary work. His ideas predated and related to aspects of both attribution theory and cognitive dissonance theory, probably the two most prominent, long-lived theoretical frameworks in social psychology. A host of factors contributed to Ichheiser's lack of renown, but what caught my attention was that critics seemed to misjudge Ichheiser in a form of the FAE.

In a biography of Ichheiser, Floyd Rudmin and colleagues commented that important contributions, including Ichheiser's, can go unrecognized because of historical circumstances.[9] But in addition to having many of his ideas go unrecognized, Ichheiser was strongly criticized by those who overlooked such circumstances. In particular, critics jumped on Ichheiser's 1970 volume that reprinted much of his earlier work from the 1920s through 1940s. Because the 1970 volume did not cite the contemporary works that conveyed similar ideas, critics accused Ichheiser of poor scholarship and of falsely claiming others' ideas as his own. But Ichheiser's ideas preceded those contemporary works. Rudmin argued that those contemporary authors should have been citing Ichheiser.

Ichheiser's 1970 volume did cite Ichheiser's earlier publications. I'm not certain why that was not enough for critics. Perhaps it was because the earlier publications were in German and difficult to obtain. Perhaps it was because Ichheiser had not followed up with empirical studies, scholarly presentations, or more prominent publications. Rudmin argued that such follow-up was hampered by a number of circumstances, starting with the loss of Ichheiser's notes and books when he fled from his home during World War II. In addition, during much of his time in the United States, Ichheiser lived in poverty or at a psychiatric hospital. Lacking an academic affiliation made data collection, presenting, and publishing extremely difficult.

Ichheiser had explored, importantly, how we misinterpret everyday behaviors of individuals by overattending to personal characteristics and overlooking situational factors. This concept is the FAE. However, unlike most social psychologists, Ichheiser went out of his way to avoid the FAE in explaining why people commit it. Whereas contemporary social psychologists typically attribute the FAE to the individual's imperfect cognitive processes or self-protecting personal motives, Ichheiser described the FAE as conditioned by society.

It is not that contemporary social psychologists disagree that society or culture plays a role in committing the FAE and other biases. It is accepted that the FAE is somewhat stronger in Western than Eastern cultures. Rather, social psychologists usually place culture in the background or describe it more as a moderator than as a central cause. Ichheiser put culture at the forefront. He went as far as saying that people who commit the FAE are not ignorant but rather stuck in a culture that promotes individualistic ideals. We are raised to believe that we are not victims of circumstance or that we have more control over our lives' successes and failures than we actually do.

Yes, culture is an omnipresent situational factor that should be part of any careful thinking about why people behave and think the way they do. To not consider relevant cultural factors is to commit the FAE. I commend Ichheiser for trying to avoid the FAE in explaining the FAE.

In my own assessment, however, Ichheiser went too far in how much he blamed the social system for mistaken judgments. Ichheiser argued that people were not ignorant. Culture was to blame. Well, maybe it is a combination. Even if culture is the culprit—even if all of us in a culture or social group commit the same bias—that does not mean we are not ignorant. A long time ago, we were conditioned to believe that the earth was at the center of the universe and to punish those who said differently. But as data came to light to the contrary, we realized (eventually!) how ignorant we had been. Nietzsche referred to such collective misjudgment as "inherited stupidity."[10]

After Ichheiser

In 1958, Fritz Heider, another Austrian social psychologist, presented the idea that perceivers only see the behavior and the actor, not the field or context in which they exist, and thus inevitably underestimate the causal role of the situation. The famous slogan attributed to Heider is that "behavior engulfs the field."[11] Although Ichheiser referred to this bias as "one of the fundamental sources of misunderstanding,"[12] the actual naming of the "fundamental attribution error" is credited to another social psychologist, Lee Ross. Ross coined this term in a well-known 1977 work titled "The Intuitive Psychologist and His Shortcomings."[13] One reason besides the FAE label that Ross is so much better known today for discussing the FAE compared to Ichheiser is because by 1977, numerous research studies had further verified the existence of the FAE. These studies established a research record that Ichheiser could not provide but Ross could. Social psychology is very much a research-based discipline.

WHAT'S IN A WORD?

The first research study on the FAE is credited to Edward Jones and Victor Harris in 1967. In this study, the participants read debate speeches with particular viewpoints about Fidel Castro, but participants were told in one condition that the speechwriters were forced to take those viewpoints (through assignment from a debate team advisor). Nonetheless, in this condition, the average participant attributed the speeches to the personal attitudes or beliefs of the speechwriters. If John writes that the people of Cuba are better off under Fidel Castro, then it must be because John believes that the people of Cuba are better off under Fidel Castro. Duh. It does seem like a sensible inference except for the information that the speechwriter was forced by the situation to take that viewpoint.[14]

The Absence of Logic

Daniel Gilbert and Patrick Malone, in their well-cited 1995 article on the causes and consequences of the FAE, emphasized the absence of logic in committing the FAE. They wrote that committing this bias is a violation of attribution theory's "fundamental rule" and "logical canon."[15] However, Gilbert and Malone failed to cite any formal principles of logic being violated. One of them is the principle that A implies B does not mean B implies A. To think that B implies A, based only on the fact that A implies B, is sometimes called the "converse error."[16]

An example of this principle is that all ants are insects, but not all insects are ants. In other words, being an ant (A) implies being an insect (B), but being an insect (B) does not necessarily imply being an ant (A). There are so many other insects out there besides ants.

More relevant to understanding attributional processes, consider the following. Let A stand for taking a drug—say, atorvastatin—and B for lowered blood cholesterol. For most people, taking the drug lowers cholesterol. A implies B (not that there are no side effects). However, even if we assume a 100 percent success rate for atorvastatin, does B imply A? Does lowered blood cholesterol imply that that individual had ingested atorvastatin? No. Not necessarily. There are plenty of people whose blood cholesterol lowers without taking the cholesterol-reducing drug. Taking the drug is not the only way to reduce cholesterol. People could change their diet, increase their exercise, or curb their drinking and smoking. Changes in cholesterol level can also be random fluctuations.

So just because you observe someone whose blood cholesterol has lowered doesn't mean it's the drug that did it, although it could be. Many examples in physical science tend to be this straightforward.

Moving back to (messier) social science and the FAE, let A stand for attitude and B for behavior (a happy coincidence in terms of first letters). For most of us, a strongly held attitude leads us to express some form of that attitude when we're asked how we feel or leads us to behave in a way that supports or is consistent with that attitude, like the viewpoint we take in a debate speech. A implies B. However, even if we assume that outcome occurs 100 percent of the time, does B imply A? Does the existence of a behavior reflect a consistent attitude? No. Not necessarily. Other factors can lead to the same behavior (B), instead of our personal attitude (A), including directions from an authority figure (like Jones and Harris's debate team advisor), peer pressure, political pressure, financial or career incentives, or otherwise wanting to please a particular audience (even if that audience comprises only one close other asking how you feel). Other nonattitudinal causes are also possible, including stress, provocation, or our culture.

In terms of peer pressure, real life and social science are replete with examples of conformity in which teens and young adults say and do things that do not reflect their personal views. Conformity pressure is a situational factor that is often overlooked when inferring an individual's personal view.

In social psychology, Solomon Asch was one of the first to demonstrate how strong conformity pressures can be in making you say something you don't really believe. In Asch's classic study, participants were asked to judge the lengths of geometric lines after several confederates (actors pretending to be other participants) gave an incorrect answer. The majority of participants went along with the group and gave the wrong answer at least once among multiple trials. Just observing the participant's behavior (and not the confederates'), it might have seemed like the participant was inattentive or stupid, didn't care about the task, or had a problem with vision. But there was a situational factor in play—conformity pressure, or social norms. Most of us have probably gone along to get along at some point in our lives, maybe even saying something that was the complete opposite of how we thought or felt.

Career incentives are another common situational factor that can influence behavior. How many of us do things to get or keep a job? How many politicians might vote a particular way to please their constituents or their political party? In the entertainment industry, movie reviewers might write positive reviews to become more recognized and not just because of positive regard for a movie. A staple of Hollywood moviemaking is advertising and the quoting of movie critics in print and television ads. According to some movie critics, there is thus pressure for even famous reviewers to write glowing reviews to stay in the limelight.[17]

I knew a faculty member who, during an interview, agreed to carry out certain duties, then declined to carry out those duties, and when reminded about the earlier agreement, explained simply that of course you're going to agree to things during the interview to get the job. (Of course, there are also many stories of faculty members who verbally agree to something and mean it.) Beyond conformity and career pressures, there are countless other examples of saying something for reasons other than meaning it.

So if all we have in front of us is B, a speech or essay or movie review that supports a particular viewpoint, it does not logically follow that the speaker or writer holds that viewpoint, especially if there is evidence of nonattitudinal causes. I suspect that committing the FAE in most cases arises from this logical fallacy, from transposing a fair belief that A implies

B to the unjustified conclusion of A in the presence of B. Internal factors can lead to expressions of behavior, but expressions of behavior need not reflect what might seem like obvious internal factors.

Discomfort with Uncertainty

This truth about explaining behaviors—that behaviors and even statements of how one feels need not reflect consistent feelings or attitudes—is very unsettling to a lot of people. Upon this realization, some of my social psychology students look disheartened, especially when we apply it to topics like prejudice. Others can discriminate against us based on our race or sex or sexual orientation without holding a prejudiced attitude. It's true. Even if others shout out a derogatory slur at us based on our group membership, they still might not hold a prejudiced attitude against us.

In the 2012 movie *The Perks of Being a Wallflower*, Brad disparagingly called Patrick a "faggot," but both Brad and Patrick were gay and had been romantically involved. Brad was sitting with his male friends from the football team at the time and used the slur to fit into that group. Classic peer pressure. Researchers have documented the direct and immediate role of male social norms in countless contexts, particularly in the use of homophobic epithets.[18]

Discrimination or mistreatment of someone based on their group membership is not excusable. It's horrible behavior. But discrimination or mistreatment is precisely a behavior, and it may or may not reflect prejudiced personal feelings about a group of people. Institutional racism is another clear example of how this pattern is possible (again, not to excuse institutional racism).

In apparent response to discomfort with the idea that behaviors need not reflect consistent feelings, some of my students ask, "Then how can we ever know anything for sure about anyone's real feelings?" Right. You've got it. We can't. At least, not nearly as often as we think. Most people need to feel like they know stuff about other people with certainty. But justification for 100 percent certainty is rare, if it exists at all, in inferences about what other people are feeling or thinking. The message is that we cannot read each other's minds.

Gilbert and Malone wrote,

> The problem, of course, is that a person's inner self is hidden from view. Character, motive, belief, desire, and intention play leading roles in people's construal of others, and yet none of these constructs can actually be observed. As such, people are forced into the difficult business of inferring these intangibles from that which is, in fact, observable: other people's words and deeds. When one infers the invisible from the visible, one risks making a mistake.[19]

Even if we *could* read minds, and even if people believe what they're saying about themselves, their motives, and their reasons, what they say still might be false. It's not as simple as lying versus honesty. According to Malcolm Gladwell (author of *Blink*) and Timothy Wilson (author of *Strangers to Ourselves*), sometimes we don't know our own selves. Sometimes we don't know our own motives and reasons.[20] There are self-serving biases and neurological processes that operate below our conscious radar. And our memories are far from perfect. So even with telepathy, the most we could learn is what someone *thinks* their reasons are, which may or may not be the actual cause of their actions.

In the television show *Star Trek: The Next Generation* (the one that came after the first *Star Trek* with Kirk and Spock), Captain Picard often asks his partially telepathic counselor, Deanna Troi, whether a potential alien enemy is telling the truth. Sometimes all the counselor can say for sure is that the alien believes it.

But it's not just uncomfortable or unsettling to realize the uncertainty of this difficult business of inferring the invisible from the visible, of explaining behavior and inferring feelings. The *logic* of this business is tricky. Even prominent social science educators have difficulty with the idea that A implies B does not mean B implies A.

Applying the Logic to Word Choices

David Myers wrote several editions of a popular undergraduate textbook on social psychology in which he followed the logic when discussing Jones and Harris's study. Myers conveyed that just because someone makes pro-Castro statements doesn't mean he actually holds a pro-Castro attitude. In general, Myers's text is thorough, illustrative, and well written (all reasons why I've used it for years in my courses). But in another chapter, Myers strongly argued that the labels people use in everyday language and that social psychologists use in their reports necessarily reflect personal attitudes or value judgments. (Many other social science writers have made a similar case, such as Eric Shiraev and David Levy, authors of a cross-cultural psychology textbook, and Derald Wing Sue, a well-known author on microaggressions.)

Myers wrote, "Whether we label a quiet child as 'bashful' or 'cautious,' as 'holding back' or as 'an observer,' conveys a judgment. . . . Whether we call public assistance 'welfare' or 'aid to the needy' reflects our political views." Whoa. Talk about mind reading. Yes, A implies B, as Myers conveyed when he explained how it is "inevitable that prior beliefs and values will influence what social psychologists [and others] think and write." I'm not certain it is inevitable, but yes, personal attitudes and values (A) can influence what we write (B). But even if it were inevitable, does that mean that B implies A, that what we write reflects our personal attitudes? No. Not necessarily. To assume that it does is not only illogical but constitutes the FAE. There are other possible causes behind what we write or say.[21]

If I'm talking with colleagues at my university about those who receive public assistance, and I say "aid to the needy" instead of "welfare," is it because I have liberal values? Maybe. (I'm actually not certain what values Myers thinks these different phrases might reflect, but I'm going with liberal when one talks about "aid to the needy.") Going back to my previous paragraph in discussing Jones and Harris's study, I wrote, "Other factors can lead to the same behavior (B), instead of our personal attitude (A), including directions from an authority figure . . ., peer pressure, political pressure, financial or career incentives, or otherwise wanting to please a particular audience." Do any of these possible causes ring true in why I might say "aid to the needy" instead of "welfare?"

If the colleagues to whom I'm speaking are all self-professed liberals, then I might use the liberal phrase even if I do not hold liberal values so as to please my audience or because of peer pressure. If others know the political leanings of my group without knowing mine and infer my political leanings based on my use of a phrase, then that inference counts as the FAE. I'm not calling myself a spineless conformer in this hypothetical. But conformity to the norms of our social group can play a role in our language choices without our even realizing it.[22]

What if I write "aid to the needy" instead of "welfare" in an article submission? If the magazine is known to have liberal leanings, then I might use the liberal phrase to help get my article published. Or maybe I originally wrote "welfare," and the editor strongly suggested that I change it to "aid to the needy." Publish or perish. I'm changing it. If others know the political leanings of my publication outlet without knowing mine and infer my political leanings based on my use of a phrase, then that inference counts as the FAE. Even if we cannot think of an alternative cause (other than the personal values of the author), that does not mean an alternative cause does not exist. That A implies B is technically insufficient evidence to infer A from B.

Politics aside, editors routinely play a role in exact wording in a final draft. But how often do we think about that role when making dispositional inferences from particular word choices? Authors can fight for their original wording, but sometimes authors have to pick their battles and compromise when putting together a final product. Other times, editors can change wording without the author's input.

At the *New York Times*, the author of an op-ed titled "Defeating My Anxiety" offended at least one reader because of the word "defeating," but apparently that word was put there by the editor and not the author.

According to the comment section, the reader thought the author held a "really harmful" perspective, and author J. L. Cowles had to explain that he had submitted a different title.[23] Some newspaper and magazine policies reserve the right to make such changes. But how often do we think about that possibility when getting upset at an author for word choices?

What about authors or speakers who grew up using a different language? My wife grew up with British English and, shortly after coming to the United States, got an unintended burst of laughter as a teaching assistant when she asked a math class for a rubber, intending an eraser, not a condom. Most of the students probably understood my wife's request (eventually). Anyone who didn't understand and who decided my wife was overly informal or socially inept was overlooking a cultural context (and the math classroom context).

What about academicians trained in earlier decades with different terminology or before attention to diversity issues changed the terms we typically use? "Retarded" did not always have the negative or offensive connotation that it does today. In fact, the Global Down Syndrome Foundation urges its readers to show "the utmost respect" to the "MANY [*sic*] older advocates who fought for human and civil rights for our children back in the 1960s and 1970s who still say 'mentally retarded' even when talking about their own family member."[24]

What about individuals who object to political correctness on principle? I've seen bumper stickers that read, "Politically incorrect and proud of it," and "Your political correctness offends me." Individuals who espouse these views might use the politically incorrect term in response to a society that is very concerned about political correctness. Many supporters of Donald Trump in the 2016 United States presidential election praised Trump for using politically incorrect language, and maybe Trump used such language to oblige them.

What about bloggers or shock jocks who want to provoke a reaction to generate debate or to increase viewership? Such communicators might purposely use an offensive phrase without personally holding the corresponding values. I'm not saying that we should not take offense (that is for each listener to decide), but a full analysis of why people write or talk the way they do requires consideration of the context and cannot assume the values people display are the values they hold.

Being Realistic

By this point (if not much sooner), some of you might be thinking I'm going overboard. You might want to say, come on, be realistic. Maybe it makes sense when reading edited publications or listening to shock jocks, but you might feel that we cannot function in daily life by applying principles of logic to daily interactions. We have to make some assumptions about how others feel based on what we see or hear, even if we cannot be 100 percent certain.

To such ideas, I say yes, absolutely. Often we need to risk the FAE and make our best guesses about how others feel based on how they behave and what they say so we can get along or navigate our social worlds. We don't have unlimited time for a full analysis to discern the absolute truth, even if discerning the absolute truth were possible. And maybe our best guesses are often correct, depending on the situation.

But then let's truly realize that our inferences are, in fact, best guesses at risk of the FAE. We don't need absolute certainty to function in most of our daily social interactions. In fact, "best" in "best guess" is comparative and doesn't technically even mean "good." Still, people far too often feel absolute certainty. They think they can see a controversial story for "what it really is" and will unfriend you on Facebook if you do not agree. "I've seen it with my own eyes" and "I heard it with my own ears" are not, unfortunately, as ironclad as they sound. In interpersonal perception, there is rarely a simple "it" to be so easily seen or heard. And a little less certainty allows us to be more open to corrections if further information comes along.

And for most of us, even if it's uncomfortable or cumbersome to pause mentally during a conversation, there is room for improvement in the initial assumptions that we make based on how others act or what they say. With just a little extra effort, external training, or forethought, we can try to postpone our conclusions about each other. Indeed, some of us can be incredibly and immediately set off by a single word choice and might appreciate a way not to be. For Marty McFly in the *Back to the Future* movies (and perhaps for many young men), that word was "chicken," and the triggered response got Marty into trouble. Maybe Marty's defensive response was classically conditioned from a childhood experience with a bully, but it doesn't matter—them's fightin' words. Don't disrespect me. The *New Yorker* published an article actually titled "Fighting Words" that described the power of the trigger word "whatever."[25]

Do you have a word that sets you off and leads you to make inferences of negative intentions? Do you have a coworker or friend who has a word that sets him or her off? Have you ever accidentally set someone off? Accidents happen, and you didn't mean to offend anyone. Even psychoanalysts acknowledge the possibility that "sometimes a cigar is just a cigar." Or maybe you're from a different part of the country and use that trigger word a little differently. And maybe you didn't know that this individual had a trigger word.

But try explaining that you didn't mean anything. Once the anger or tears come, despite your pleas that you did not harbor negative intentions, the offended often cannot help but commit or maintain the FAE against you and infer negative intentions, at least in the moment. Not that I blame them. Not that their feelings aren't real. Not that you don't regret having used that word. I will discuss later why so many people stick with the FAE after taking offense.

For example, the offended sometimes think to themselves or say out loud, why else would you say it if you didn't mean it? This question is usually meant rhetorically and as solid justification for upset feelings and for internal attributions against you. But there are possible answers to this question. It may not be realistic to always look for these answers. But not considering the possible answers or that they could even exist is part of the FAE.

Beyond Jones and Harris

In Jones and Harris's classic study that used speeches about Fidel Castro to test for the FAE, participants might have asked themselves why the speech givers would say something so particular if they didn't mean it. The real answer, underconsidered by the participant, was because the debate coach made them do it. This study has come to be known as the attitude-attribution paradigm, or essay paradigm, in which participants have to decide how much to attribute an essay or speech to the personal attitude of the writer. Although it's a classic and well-cited study, one study is not enough to draw the firm and broad conclusions that I am making.

Jones and Harris's study was followed by a vast number of other studies in which participants read essays or speeches or viewed videotaped talks on a variety of topics, including whether marijuana should be legal, whether abortion should be legal, whether federal money should be spent on AIDS research, whether university final exams should be comprehensive for graduating seniors, and whether a consumer should purchase a particular product. In one condition in all of these studies, participants learned that the writer or speaker was forced to take the particular viewpoint. Thousands of participants (the majority) still tended to attribute what they read or heard to the personal attitudes of the writer or speaker.

In further studies, researchers tested the limits of Jones and Harris's form of the FAE. For example, researchers wondered if they first required participants to take an assigned viewpoint—thereby experiencing the same condition as the writer—then maybe the participants would not commit the FAE. Turns out no—the participants still committed the FAE. The FAE occurred even when participants were warned ahead of time about the risk of the FAE, when participants learned that speech-writers did not come up with their own arguments (but rather were handed arguments to use by the experimenter), and when participants were aware that they themselves were the ones who placed the situational constraint on the writers.[26]

So this form of the FAE has ample research support, and I've described a few real-life scenarios in which it can occur. In the next chapter, I will focus even more on real-life instances of this form of the FAE. I will also discuss how the FAE can be applied to many other biases and misperceptions of others.

CHAPTER 2

POLITICS AND HEARSAY: FAE APPLIED

We're not going to let our campaign be dictated by fact-checkers.

> —Neil Newhouse, pollster for Mitt Romney

The biggest liar in the world is They Say.

> —Douglas Malloch, poet

Even people who study situations for a living still revert to bad habits in the mindless midst of the daily grind . . . it becomes all too easy to revert to looking past the context that's right in front of your eyes.

> —Sam Sommers, author of *Situations Matter*

The words in the debate speeches in research like that by Jones and Harris do not necessarily reflect writers' personal views. But as highlighted in chapter 1, very little seems to convince research participants of that possibility.

What about the words in real-life speeches from high-profile political candidates and even presidents? FAE experts Daniel Gilbert and Patrick Malone suggested that the FAE can be applied to voters who hear actual political speeches.[1] Indeed, there are many examples of politicians, both liberal and conservative, whose words are trusted even when the politicians say things they themselves may not believe. I start at the top.

Before the implementation of the Affordable Care Act, President Obama told Americans in multiple speeches that they could keep their health-care plans under his new health-care law if they wanted to. Did he really believe that? Putting partisanship aside (if that's possible), there is a tendency in the perceiver to attribute such a strong and repeated statement to the personal belief of the speaker—that's part of the FAE—perhaps especially if the speaker is the president of the United States (and someone you voted for).

It turned out that a small percentage of individuals could not keep their health-care plans, and President Obama seemed to know that could happen. Writers in the often-liberal *New York Times* did not uniformly support President Obama on this point, but when a particular *New York Times* editorial summed up the situation by saying the president simply "misspoke," there was quite a backlash.[2] I am speculating that the backlash was so strong not only because of divisiveness in American politics but also because of the FAE.

Because of the FAE, many of us initially trusted that what we heard from the president stemmed from personal conviction (and truth), despite the presence of strong political pressures on the president. When the truth came out, many felt betrayed. Although I cannot know for sure, pressures to pass the health-care law—and perhaps just the high number of uninsured Americans—apparently led to repeated, strong, but untrue statements (not that such pressures or the millions of uninsured Americans would necessarily excuse lying).

When we consider political ads, it becomes even more clear that there are reasons not to attribute what we hear to the personal beliefs of the speaker. Elections are on the line and are a major situational factor to explain (but not necessarily excuse) election behaviors. In 2012, as Mitt Romney's pollster Neil Newhouse famously announced after one of their ads failed multiple fact checks, "We're not going to let our campaign be dictated by fact-checkers."[3] Newhouse probably did not mean that the campaign wanted to ignore facts. He probably meant that just because

fact-checkers call something wrong doesn't mean it is. I can only speculate on what Newhouse meant, but he was driven to make this statement
in response to a flood of criticism of the ad from both liberal and conservative sources. The Romney campaign let the ad stand, which was commonly interpreted as ignoring facts.

Whatever you thought of the 2012 United States presidential candidates in terms of fact-checking, the 2016 election was worse. Among
many commentaries on this topic, White House correspondent Linda
Feldmann wrote that "fact-checkers are having a field day" in a piece
titled "How 2016 Became the Fact-Check Election." At this mid-summer
point, she cited PolitiFact in reporting that only about 10 percent of
Donald Trump's statements had been found to be either true or mostly
true, compared to about 50 percent of Hillary Clinton's.[4]

The popular wisdom among campaign managers is that even when
speeches and ads miserably fail a nonpartisan fact check, voters seem
unaffected—that is, seem just as likely to believe what they hear as when
the fact check is successful. Journalists speculate about why. They suggest
that some voters have become so disillusioned about politics that they are
simply not surprised by the red flags and therefore don't pay full attention
to failed fact checks. Journalists also point out that the many partisan
fact-checkers whose fact-checking needs fact-checking make it difficult
for voters to distinguish between biased and impartial fact-checkers.[5]

Of course, most voters who already support one candidate will probably embrace fact checks that support their candidate and discount those
that do not, thus maintaining their original view of their candidate. In
2016, the fact-checkers themselves highlighted this partisan bias but also
noted that the news cycle was so fast that it was hard to "get people to
stand still long enough to hear" the fact checks.[6]

What is noticeably missing from this discussion of why voters may
not care more than they do about fact-checking is the FAE. On a subconscious or automatic level, most of us cannot shake an initial assumption
that if somebody repeatedly says something persuasive, then it must in

55

some way reflect some actual personal belief or conviction on the part of the speaker. That is the essence of the FAE. We have an implicit resistance to disconnecting the speaker's statements from the speaker's actual feelings. And inferring personal conviction behind words makes the words sound more trustworthy or truthful.

Some voters manage to infer personal conviction behind words even while doubting the truth value of the words. In the 2016 election, many Trump supporters said they didn't really believe Trump's campaign promise that he would build a wall between the United States and Mexico. They explained that though they didn't believe Trump's claim, "it's just such a strong vision" or "I think he's making a stand" or "I think he's just trying to set his tone that we have to separate the countries."[7] Such explanations might have been realistic at the time. Or maybe the FAE drove an attempt to find *something* consistent between Trump's words and intentions. Why would he keep saying it unless he meant it on some level?

The tendency for people to believe what others tell them has its own label—the truth bias. Lie-detection researchers suggest that this bias stems from a desire to get along or from social norms.[8] But an obvious additional factor is the FAE. Straight from Jones and Harris's attitude-attribution paradigm, we can't help but connect someone's words to their personal beliefs. There is no need to get along with anyone in this paradigm because those who wrote the speeches or essays are not in the room and are not expected to show up.

It may not be rocket science to say that politicians don't always speak from the heart. But the FAE is an overlooked factor in why so many people still trust what their politicians say to them and why failed fact checks don't have a bigger impact on voters' views. So in this environment of political ads and speeches that routinely ignore or bend facts, committing the FAE has clear consequences. It can contribute to believing false information.

POLITICAL INCORRECTNESS AND MICROAGGRESSIONS

Aside from the truth value of what politicians say, many voters care about *how* politicians say things or what words they use. There are politically incorrect and correct ways to talk or to refer to groups of people. Professors and students have also come under greater scrutiny for their language as efforts to promote diversity have increased on college campuses. As discussed in chapter 1, David Myers and many other social scientists argue that the word or label you choose necessarily reveals your personal views or values. Your choice of label for a group of people would reveal how you really feel about that group of people, even if you're not conscious of it.

So be careful. Is it "welfare" or "aid to the needy," "disabled" or someone "with a disability," "homosexual" or "gay"? If you go with the politically incorrect label (even if you're unaware that it's politically incorrect), then according to many prejudice researchers, you would be guilty of a microaggression. Microaggressions are verbal or nonverbal slights or snubs against members of a particular group. Microaggressions can be intentional or unintentional by definition but are almost always discussed as being committed by well-intentioned majority-group members who hold an unconscious bias against members of a minority group.[9]

Even positive adjectives can be deemed microaggressive when applied to certain groups. For example, microaggression researchers argue that a white individual referring to a black individual as "articulate" reflects a subtle bias or negative view against black individuals in general. The hidden message supposedly conveyed is that "it is unusual for someone of your race to be intelligent." Even Joe Biden was not exempt from being criticized when he used the wrong adjectives such as "articulate" to compliment Barack Obama in 2007.[10]

But as I've tried to emphasize (see chapter 1), it is a logical fallacy and the FAE to automatically assume that a person's particular word choices in themselves necessarily reveal that person's personal values or views, even unconscious views. This fallacy introduces a fundamental problem in the study of microaggressions. And it would be a sad irony for a bias-free compliment to a member of a minority group to be automatically interpreted as a hidden insult. I'm not saying we shouldn't try to "correct" the speaker for language that offends some people. I'm not saying we shouldn't share a concern with the speaker about the choice of words, especially in case there *is* a hidden bias behind it. Obama and others made Biden aware of the issue, and Biden expressed regret in a public statement.[11]

What I *am* saying is that we cannot read the mind of the speaker. Let's try to address the language but not assume we always know where it comes from. Maybe the speaker holds a biased racial view, or maybe not. Unfortunately, microaggression researchers and presenters often speak in absolutes and don't allow for both those possibilities. The wrong label reveals a biased view. The wrong question reveals a biased view. Period.

Wrong-Question Microaggressions

A common example of a wrong-question microaggression is to ask an Asian American "where are you from?" The hidden message is supposedly, "You are not American."[12] John McWhorter, a linguistics professor and author of *Losing the Race*, once described a wrong-question example in which a black journalist attended a writers' program and was asked by a literary critic, "So why are *you* here?" McWhorter asserted that "it was obvious" what the critic meant.[13]

I was not at this event to hear the question as it was spoken, but in my view, to think a hidden racist meaning is obvious is too common among those who fight against microaggressions. Advocates for minority groups have enough evidence to raise concerns about microaggressions but not enough to claim 100 percent certainty in any particular case. The evidence in the microaggression literature is limited in that it is self-report, sometimes hearsay, correlational, often based on small focus-group interviews, and always based on averages. The microaggression literature has strengths but also severe limitations that have led some well-known social scientists to call for a moratorium on microaggression training.[14]

I know that when someone offends or condescends to you and you think the intent is obvious, it's probably very hard to consider my message, that what seems obvious may not be true when it comes to reading minds. Go ahead and share your interpretation with the speaker if you're able, but my advice is try not to assume your initial interpretation is obvious.

Even McWhorter had such reservations about the microaggression concept. He thought that some claims of microaggression go too far, like when a white person is called microaggressive for claiming to be color-blind. According to Derald Wing Sue and colleagues, as well as a growing number of university diversity handbooks, the hidden message is that the white person who claims to be colorblind is "denying a person of color's racial/ethnic experiences."[15] McWhorter reasoned that "it's considered racist for whites to treat any trait as 'black'" and so "we can't turn around and say they're racists to look at black people as just people."[16]

The Scientific (Lack of) Logic

In the case of colorblindness as a microaggression, McWhorter essentially levied a charge of nonfalsifiability against the microaggression concept by highlighting that microaggression authors claim there's a microaggression no matter what a white person does—whether the white person carries out a particular act or its opposite. This is a "Damned if you do, damned if you don't" scenario. The microaggression accusation becomes nonfalsifiable because it cannot be shown to be false regardless of how an individual behaves, which is a no-no in the scientific method. McWhorter was not the first academic to make this point of nonfalsifiability. Kenneth Thomas and coauthors commented that "one is damned regardless of whether he or she makes distinctions between people of different races or treats them all the same."[17]

I believe this point of nonfalsifiability is a fair logical argument from McWhorter and others against the validity of the microaggression concept, not that white people are limited to the dichotomous choice between colorblindness and calling a trait black. But researchers are not limited to formal scientific logic to identify a general problem with inferring a microaggression. As detailed in chapter 1, there are known situational factors that can contribute to language choices in place of or in addition to personal feelings or views (again, not to excuse those whose language choices upset certain groups of people). In particular, politicians sometimes choose their words based on focus groups or the audience at the moment. Many teens mindlessly mimic their peers. Older people and even longtime advocates for civil rights grew up in a different time and might not be up on current politically correct language. Sometimes certain words spoken by some people do reflect an unconscious racial bias, but to automatically assume this underestimates the role of these potential situational factors and constitutes the FAE.

Well-known microaggression researcher Derald Wing Sue regularly acknowledges the existence of potential situational factors behind alleged microaggressions. For example, in discussing inferences of a microaggression, Sue and colleagues asserted that "there will *always* [sic] be an alternative explanation."[18] But amazingly, such acknowledgments have not softened Sue's resolute claims of unconscious racism behind particular words or questions. Rather, Sue points out only that these potential situational factors make it even more frustrating for people of color who have just been microaggressed against, because people of color in good conscience cannot be certain that someone just mistreated them. Wow. That "in good conscience" thing sounds like an attempt by people of color to avoid the FAE, which is good to hear, but Sue and colleagues seem to discount any need to avoid the FAE. Sue and colleagues regard the uncertainty by people of color as simply part of the painful and draining experience of unquestionable microaggressions.

I regret this very real experience of many people of color. I'm not trying to invalidate their emotional reactions, as done by some academics who oppose Sue's viewpoint. For example, Kenneth Thomas wrote that "it seems ridiculous, if not a bit pathological, to experience emotional distress" over certain word choices—which Sue justifiably called victim blaming.[19] But this experiential reality for people of color doesn't change the physics of social situations. There are other causes for saying things that hurt besides unconscious racism.

I dearly hope I am not upsetting or losing any readers at this juncture in my book. I hold a middle-ground position when it comes to micro-aggressions. I truly praise Sue and other microaggression researchers for raising awareness of this real issue, but I suggest greater caution in thinking we can read the minds of everyone who uses certain words or asks certain questions.

QUOTING OUT OF CONTEXT: CONTEXTOMY

Listening to the words or labels used by politicians or professors who talk for themselves is one thing. If they use politically incorrect language, it's risky to think we can read their minds, but at least we know for a fact that it is they who said it. Then there is hearsay.

When presented with hearsay, which is what someone says someone else said, it is even more risky to make confident dispositional attributions about the someone else. Even direct quoting is technically hearsay and secondhand information, which carries a host of risks, including that quotes can be taken out of context.

Quoting out of context goes by a variety of names, including quote mining, proof texting, and contextomy. Contextomy refers to the surgical excision of context. The general process refers to quoting in which one removes or fails to mention nearby words or phrases or entire sentences, thus removing the original context. One can exclude these portions for brevity or to purposely mislead, but what's left can imply a very different meaning from that intended, even the exact opposite. The removed context can explain or be the actual cause for the choice of the visible words, but without knowing the context had been removed, listeners are likely to commit the FAE. Listeners would overlook that context and the plain fact that the quoter left out a bunch of words.

Journalist Carl Bialik referred to the selective quoting from a movie review as the "blurb racket." Bialik went as far as to categorize the common types of contextomy used to sell a movie. For example, there's the misplaced adverb. By removing the in-between words, an advertising blurb can make an adverb modify the wrong word. Bialik noted a case in which the critic wrote, "hysterically overproduced and surprisingly entertaining," but the ad wrote, "hysterically . . . entertaining." So I guess I could write "incredibly stupid and never enjoyable" and be quoted to say, "incredibly . . . enjoyable." Then there's the old actor-movie switcheroo. Critics sometimes praise an actor but pan the movie, and advertisers simply leave out the actor's name and quote the words of praise as if the words refer to the entire movie.[20]

The Case of George Zimmerman

A more serious case of contextomy and a clear case of the FAE occurred in 2012 in reporting on the story of George Zimmerman. Zimmerman is a white or Hispanic man who shot and killed Trayvon Martin, a black seventeen-year-old. The Florida case became a national media story. Why did George Zimmerman shoot Trayvon Martin? Was it self-defense? Did George Zimmerman racially profile Trayvon Martin?

About a month after the event, NBC played a segment of a 911 tape from that night. The content of this segment enraged many listeners. Zimmerman belonged to a neighborhood watch group and had called 911 upon observing Martin walking through the community. On the tape segment, Zimmerman said, "This guy looks like he's up to no good. He looks black."

Wow. A racist caught on tape. Open and shut. Right? A lot of minds

POLITICS AND HEARSAY: FAE APPLIED

probably got made up right then. Why would Zimmerman say "he looks black" right after saying "no good" if Zimmerman were not a racist? There's no other explanation.

Oh, wait a minute. The 911 operator had in fact asked Zimmerman about Martin's race. The operator had asked this question in between the two quoted statements from Zimmerman, but the question had been excluded from NBC's version of the recording. Here is a fuller version of the exchange:

> Zimmerman: "This guy looks like he's up to no good, or he's on drugs or something. It's raining and he's just walking around, looking about."
> 911 operator: "OK, and this guy—is he white, black or Hispanic?"
> Zimmerman: "He looks black."[21]

A direct multiple-choice question by the 911 operator was the context that was removed. Being asked such a question is a strong situational factor. Responding to such a question with one of the provided choices reflects that the question was asked and not much more. Sure, Zimmerman could still be racist, but attributing these particular words of his to a racist attitude fits the definition of the FAE. How many people's views of Zimmerman became dispositionally fixed beyond repair after hearing that highly edited tape?

Even though listeners who inferred racism were committing the FAE by definition, it is, of course, not their fault that NBC edited this tape. It's understandable that a listener would not assume such an important chunk of the recording got skipped. On the other hand, with so many documented cases these days of quotes presented out of context, listeners are well advised to reserve judgment until the news media, other sources, or even the individual being quoted has a fair chance to verify or address the evidence. (I'm sure some listeners did just that.)

Reserving judgment does not mean never judging. Just give it a little more time. Maybe even wait for the trial. It may be an unsatisfying or uncomfortable way to listen to breaking news, but it can help to avoid the FAE.

Even Comedians Get It

Cable news and many other outlets jumped on this NBC mistake, from Sean Hannity of Fox News to Jon Stewart of *The Daily Show*. Stewart ran a skit called "The Splice Channel," and after highlighting the NBC mistake, Stewart showed another example. He played a highly edited clip of *Jeopardy!* in which all we could hear was the contestants' questions (which of course is how that show works): "What is a solarium?" "What is a cul de sac?" Stewart made fun of how these supposedly smart people didn't know these terms. He asked, "Don't you guys go to college?" In apparent response, the next contestant said, "What's the University of Texas?" Stewart emphasized that editing out Alex Trebek's answers, in the context of that game show, made the contestants sound like "morons." Stewart then drew the obvious parallel that the edited NBC tape made Zimmerman sound like a racist. Stewart spelled it out: the edited tape assigned a motive to Zimmerman that he may or may not have had, and we didn't have any idea why Zimmerman did what he did. NBC's response to the controversy was that a "bad mistake" had been made, but Stewart didn't let them off the hook. He pretended to understand and said how they "must have just hit the Remove Context button by accident." He then showed a picture of a big red Remove Context button on the side of a fancy-looking editing machine.[22]

A Remove Context button pressed without realizing it is an apt metaphor for the FAE. We unknowingly press that button all the time in observing others, or we fail to look for a Show Context button. But the FAE is not an accident. The FAE is an automatic response for most of us, whether a cognitive byproduct or driven by motive, and without context, we are at great risk to make dispositional attributions that are in error.

Making these attributions when someone else withheld relevant context doesn't make us bad people. We obviously don't always have control over the release of information. But the conclusions we draw can still be wrong.

If a math student arrives at a wrong answer because the teacher provided the wrong formula, the answer is still wrong. And it's still the FAE when someone withholds situational information from us. Such instances might be uncontrollable on our end, but reserving judgment can still reduce such instances of the FAE. When there's no time available to reserve judgment or to gather more information, then all we can do is make the best attribution we can, knowing that we might be missing necessary context. But in most cases when a news story first breaks, there would seem to be time available.

In the end, NBC probably did realize how serious it was to withhold contextual information. Several NBC employees lost their jobs over the matter.

Belief Perseverance

What makes such real-life stories worse is that once someone is misquoted or quoted out of context, retractions or corrections don't usually undo the effects, even if printed on page 1. This general phenomenon of holding on to a belief even after its original evidence is discounted is called belief perseverance. We may hold on to the belief out of simple ego protection. Or we may hold on to it because our brains created enough justifications for the belief that went beyond the original evidence.[23]

There were, of course, political effects of the edited 911 tape. Liberals and liberal-leaning outlets in particular conveyed great concern about racial profiling, fueled in part by the tape. After Zimmerman was acquitted, liberals conveyed great concern about general racial inequities and racial injustice. Protesters held rallies for weeks. I am not discounting the existence of racial inequities or racial profiling, and I'm not criticizing the rallies. And maybe Zimmerman should have been found guilty. But I wonder whether the left's outrage might have been less if it were not for the FAE and belief-perseverance aftermath resulting from the edited 911 tape.

More Politics

Perhaps the epitome of quoting out of context is to quote someone quoting someone else without mentioning the quoting-someone-else part. The Romney campaign did just this in a 2011 television ad. That ad showed President Obama saying, "If we keep talking about the economy, we're going to lose." The quote was accurate. Obama did say those words. However, Obama was quoting someone from the 2008 McCain campaign. The full statement from Obama was, "Senator McCain's campaign actually said, and I quote, 'If we keep talking about the economy, we're going to lose.'" Putting Obama's statement back into its context completely changes Obama's meaning. Oops. The "and I quote" part sort of got left out. Someone must have accidentally hit the Remove Context button.[24]

Many liberals didn't think the out-of-context quote was an accident. Nor do many conservatives think ads are accidents when they quote conservative candidates out of context. Romney's statement, "I like being able to fire people who provide services to me . . . if someone doesn't give me the good service I need," found its way to liberal outlets as, "I like being able to fire people." Someone must have accidentally hit the Remove Context button again.[25]

So moveth the political ad wars. CNN political correspondent Jim Acosta said of the 2012 presidential election, "Welcome to the 'out of context' campaign."[26]

Perhaps political examples most clearly fit the definition of contextomy. However, many scientists, philosophers, and historians have studied contextomy in other arenas. Several authors have even crossed over from their discipline to social psychology to cite FAE research in explaining the effects of contextomy. For example, Matthew McGlone, a cognitive psychologist, argued that the FAE makes it hard to undo the false impressions caused by quoting out of context. McGlone's chief example showed how opponents of affirmative action selectively quoted from Dr. Martin Luther King Jr.'s "I Have a Dream" speech to make King sound like he would have been against affirmative action.[27] Even the originator of evolutionary theory, Charles Darwin himself, has been selectively quoted to sound like he was against evolutionary theory.[28]

It can feel so validating for those against affirmative action that a mega civil rights leader said things against affirmative action. It can feel so comforting for those against evolutionary theory that the original evolutionary theorist himself said things against the theory. If even these icons did not believe their own movements, then why should the rest of us? But these iconic examples against their own causes are FAE-based illusions. Maybe King and Darwin secretly had mixed feelings about the positions they publicly espoused, but out-of-context quoting is not valid support for such a possibility.

FUNDAMENTAL BUT UNDERRECOGNIZED

The FAE is fundamental not only because it is so common and robust and automatic but also because it is so broadly applicable. The list of everyday FAE examples is unending. Beyond the driving, political, historical, and classroom contexts discussed in some detail thus far, researchers have demonstrated or applied the FAE in conspiracy theories, courtrooms, hiring, international relations, marriage, prejudice, prison, psychotherapy, religion, texting, and tweeting and in the public's response to national issues including poverty, unemployment, racial disparities, gun violence, and terrorism.

In addition to these real-life instances of the FAE, the FAE can be applied to many other social-psychological biases and related perceptual phenomena. Daniel Gilbert and colleagues wrote that the FAE is "fundamental to many of social psychology's most important phenomena,"[29] but even Gilbert underrecognized this reach of the FAE by omitting numerous examples. A fuller list of FAE-related phenomena includes stereotyping, prejudice, the actor-observer bias, the anchoring-and-adjustment heuristic, anthropomorphism, the bias blind spot, conspiracy theories, defensive attributions, essentialism, false-consensus beliefs, hedonic relevance, the group-serving bias, the halo effect, the hostile attribution bias, the hostile media bias, illusion of control, illusion of freedom, immanent justice reasoning, the inherence heuristic, the interview illusion, the invisibility cloak illusion, just-world beliefs, the outgroup homogeneity bias, parent shaming, pluralistic ignorance, the romance of leadership, scapegoating, the self-fulfilling prophecy, the social-roles effect, spontaneous trait inference, temporal extension, the truth bias, the ultimate attribution error, and victim blaming.

I will cover a subset of these biases and additional real-life instances of the FAE by the end of this book. But one of my points is that the FAE is one bias, one way of thinking, that reaches so many facets of life and connects to so many other types of distorted judgments.

In sum, the FAE is probably the most studied, most discussed, and most central or wide-reaching bias in the history of social psychology. So it is ironic that so many social psychologists readily commit the FAE or at least put themselves at great risk of it. It is ironic that so many popular press books about bias don't even mention the FAE, and those that do mention it usually underrecognize the breadth of its application. I briefly discuss a few examples of such social psychologists and popular press writing to expose this very common difficulty in avoiding the FAE and to expose this gap in what authors tell us about the FAE and its role in our daily lives.

Social Psychologists Who Commit the FAE

Sam Sommers, social psychologist and author of *Situations Matter*, related a story in which he angrily honked at a man for not proceeding quickly enough through a rotary (or roundabout). Sommers thought the man was a lousy driver and an imbecile. But Sommers later noticed there was a funeral procession blocking anyone from entering the rotary. Oops. A perfect example of the FAE. Sommers regretted his error, and I appreciated his willingness to discuss it in his book.[30]

Other social psychologists seem unaware of their apparent bias. The author of *Mindset*, Carol Dweck, often explained anecdotal behaviors or outcomes as necessarily reflecting a particular mind-set with no consideration for immediate circumstances. For example, she described that if you suddenly feel tired or hungry and want to quit a difficult activity, "don't fool yourself. It's the fixed mindset." Dweck also typically explained the negative outcomes experienced by individuals with fixed mind-sets as due to a lack of trying. For example, in explaining how such individuals react to heartbreaks, she wrote, "Some people *let* [italics added] these experiences scar them and prevent them from forming satisfying relationships in the future." Such interpretations of failure technically fall under victim blaming, another form of the FAE—not that I think Dweck's intentions were anything but good.[31]

More generally, as already discussed, many social science authors have argued that word choices necessarily reflect personal values, a logical no-no despite the number of academics who believe it. Emily Pronin, known for her work on our difficulty in seeing our own biases, demonstrated another version of this logical fallacy in stating that certain nonverbal behaviors necessarily reflect racial feelings. In referring to the potentially prejudiced nonverbal behavior of white participants interacting with black participants, Pronin wrote that such behavior "notably, flowed from implicit attitudes" and "revealed their implicit attitudes."[32]

Derald Wing Sue not only believes that certain word choices reveal implicit bias (which may sometimes be true) but also once falsely concluded that an author disagreed with Sue's position because the author was white. It turned out that the author, Rafael Harris Jr., was not white. During a debate in a series of articles written by Sue, Harris, and others, Sue and coauthors referred to Harris and two others opposed to Sue's views as "well-intentioned Whites" who "are working to impose their racial realities on POC [people of color]." Sue and coauthors added that "it seems truly arrogant for any White person to define and impose their racial reality on marginalized groups." Oops.[33]

In an often-told story from Sue that began the debate, a white flight attendant mistreated Sue and a colleague (two people of color) because of the flight attendant's racial bias. Harris raised the possibility of situational causes for the flight attendant's behaviors as opposed to racial bias.[34] Ironically, after Harris suggested that Sue might be committing what amounted to the FAE (by inferring racial bias in the flight attendant), Sue seemed to commit the FAE (by inferring that Harris made his arguments because Harris was white or held a white-privileged perspective). In subsequent articles, Harris pointed out Sue's error in assuming Harris was white, and Sue apologized.[35]

In addition to Pronin, Sue, and many other social scientists who have made automatic dispositional attributions by inferring implicit attitudes, there are those who constructed and use the Implicit Association Test (IAT) and regularly make similar attributions. The IAT measures the test taker's reaction time in associating positive or negative words with certain groups of people, such as blacks and whites. The idea is that if one is biased against blacks, then one will take longer to associate positive words with blacks than with whites. Similar to the academic debate on microaggressions, there is an ongoing debate about what we can reasonably infer from an IAT score. Advocates for the IAT are sure there is implicit bias behind poor scores, but others have raised the possibility of situational or cultural factors to explain response times.[36]

Mahzarin Banaji and Anthony Greenwald, authors of *Blindspot: Hidden Biases of Good People*, might have committed the FAE in their assessment of George Zimmerman. Before the Zimmerman trial even started, Banaji and Greenwald called Zimmerman a "neighborhood vigilante" who "mistakenly assumed that Martin was dangerous when in fact he was unarmed."[37] I don't want to overinterpret the word "vigilante," in the spirit of my earlier section on trying not to think we can read minds from a single word choice. Vigilante has a negative connotation, but Banaji and Greenwald might have meant to convey that Zimmerman was a member of a neighborhood watch group with no judgment attached about illegal or aggressive intentions.

Still, Banaji and Greenwald explained Zimmerman's actions by citing his thoughts or assumptions. But how do we know what Zimmerman assumed? Someone on a neighborhood watch might follow or stare at an individual without assumptions about whether that individual is armed. The *New York Times* article cited by Banaji and Greenwald as support for their statements made reference to Zimmerman's voiced concerns about recent break-ins in the neighborhood. Those recent break-ins constitute a situational factor for Zimmerman's initial actions, even if those actions were illegal and even though those actions turned lethal. The article made no mention of a claim from Zimmerman that Martin was armed.

In terms of Zimmerman's claims of self-defense, it is of course relevant that Martin was unarmed, and I am in no way excusing Zimmerman's actions that night. But Banaji and Greenwald went into Zimmerman's mind and inferred internal assumptions to explain Zimmerman's behavior when situational factors from the external environment presented a sufficient explanation.

On a broader scale, some social psychologists explain evil behavior with almost entirely dispositional causes. One example is Roy Baumeister in his book *Evil: Inside Human Violence and Cruelty*. Baumeister identified four dispositional "roots of evil," including greed and ego.[38] The epitome of this FAE message in explaining evil behavior is conveyed by the title of another book, *Evil Genes*, by engineering professor Barbara Oakley. Social psychologist Philip Zimbardo, on the other hand, argued for the centrality of situational causes of evil in his book *The Lucifer Effect: Understanding How Good People Turn Evil*.

In fact, it's usually not one or the other, dispositions or situations. There is research support for both. Evil can be caused by both dispositions and situations and by their interaction. I think that Baumeister and Zimbardo probably understood that complexity, and please know that I am in no way excusing evil behaviors. But some of those citing Baumeister's four dispositional root causes of evil, including social psychologist Jonathan Haidt, have written in more black-and-white terms. Haidt referred to the four dispositions as the "four main causes" of "violence and cruelty."[39] I think the message that gets conveyed is that evil is caused by dispositions, an example of the FAE.

And of course I have racked up my own FAE infractions over the years (perhaps even somewhere in the pages of this book). Put me in the anonymity of my own car, and when I am driven off the road by a fellow driver, my initial reaction can sometimes be described as FAE-ish. I am sometimes aware of it, and I immediately take back my curse on the house of the other driver.

I'm trying to say that even a whole lot of social psychology education is not enough to eliminate the FAE. I wouldn't go as far as saying that social psychologists commit the most biases, as in the adage that doctors make the worst patients, but social psychologists are not immune to the errors that they try to help their students avoid. As noted by Sam Sommers, author of *Situations Matter*, "Even people who study situations for a living still revert to bad habits."[40]

Despite the limitations of social psychology education in reducing bias, education is the primary advice given by popular press authors for how to reduce bias. I will offer several additional suggestions in this book for how to reduce the FAE (see chapter 10).

Books about Bias That Don't Cover the FAE

Beyond the irony that social psychologists commit the FAE is the irony that most popular press books on bias give the FAE very little, if any, direct attention. Richard Nisbett only briefly described the FAE in an opening chapter of *Mindware*. Nicholas Epley similarly spent less than a chapter on the FAE in *Mindwise*. As discussed in my introduction, Sam Sommers's *Situations Matter* covered the FAE idea but only mentioned the FAE by name once in a footnote.

Jonathan Haidt very briefly covered some FAE territory in *The Happiness Hypothesis* but framed it as a different bias, the self-serving bias.[41] It's an interesting take but so far not shared by FAE researchers. In *How We Know What Isn't So: The Fallibility of Human Reason in Everyday Life* by Thomas Gilovich, the FAE would definitely count as an everyday-life fallibility. But the FAE didn't make the cut.

Most books about bias, such as *Blindspot, Blind Spots, Blunder, Don't Believe Everything You Think, The Invisible Gorilla, Predictably Irrational,* and *Why We Make Mistakes*, cover many biases but not the FAE. Of course, authors can write about whatever biases they choose, and these listed books have other strengths. But a main goal of my book is to address this enormous FAE gap. Readers of popular press social science have been learning about other biases and misperceptions but very little about the FAE. Because of how fundamental the FAE is, I think the FAE should be a starting point in trying to understand flawed social judgment.

So Relevant That It Goes without Saying?

Even when directly asked, notable social psychologists do not seem to think of the FAE as the big deal that it is, perhaps because it has been so absorbed into the foundation and background of social psychology. Is the FAE so obviously relevant to daily life that it goes without saying for social psychologists?

Steven Pinker (author of *How the Mind Works* and *The Blank Slate*) once asked, "What scientific concept would improve everybody's cognitive toolkit?" and Edge.org published the responses from "164 thinkers." Although numerous social psychologists were among those thinkers, not one of them nominated the FAE. In discussing this exchange, columnist David Brooks took the initiative and nominated the FAE as his first suggestion. Brooks wrote, "If I were presumptuous enough to nominate a few entries, I'd suggest the Fundamental Attribution Error: Don't try to explain by character traits behavior that is better explained by context."[42]

This FAE nomination from a nonpsychologist, who has been a prolific writer in public discourse, reflects how everyday and impactful the FAE is. Brooks notwithstanding, I want to introduce the FAE in contemporary public discourse on social errors and interpersonal understanding. Let's really keep our eyes out for it. The FAE is incredibly relevant and common almost everywhere we look in human interaction.

TESTING FOR THE FAE: AN ACKNOWLEDGMENT

The attitude-attribution paradigm used by Jones and Harris and so many others is probably the most common method to test for the FAE. However, particularly for those readers who know something of social psychology's history, let me acknowledge that the attitude-attribution paradigm has not been without critics.

In particular, some have questioned whether an error in this largely laboratory setting would translate into an actual mistake in everyday interactions with people. This issue is one of external validity. In the attitude-attribution paradigm, in the condition with a speechwriter forced to take a viewpoint, participants are given a (usually persuasive) speech to read that logic dictates they should ignore. But then why were they given the speech in the first place? According to David Funder, a distinguished researcher in personality and social psychology, this paradigm violates an unspoken rule in everyday communication: "that the speaker tell the listener what he or she thinks the listener needs to know" and "not give information . . . that he or she believes has no relevance to the situation at hand."[43]

As I alluded to earlier, politicians or their campaigns don't necessarily follow this rule. So the attitude-attribution paradigm may generalize at least as far as politics. But even everyday people with whom we have everyday conversations often don't follow conversational rules. In particular, according to Bella DePaulo and colleagues, authors of *Lying in Everyday Life*, lying is an "everyday social interaction process."[44]

In sum, I think there is clear value in using the attitude-attribution paradigm. But in any case, there are additional FAE paradigms, including one that Funder himself finds quite applicable to real life and "unusually realistic."[45] This realistic paradigm is often called the quiz-game or questioner-contestant paradigm, and sometimes called the social-roles paradigm. This paradigm tests the degree to which participants overlook the effects of social roles in explaining others' behaviors. Chapter 5 delves into social roles. First, I discuss how the FAE affects our nonverbal decoding.[46]

CHAPTER 3

NONVERBAL DECODING: AN ILLUSION OF INSIGHT

It's not the case that our internal computer always shines through, instantly decoding the 'truth' of a situation. It can be thrown off, distracted, and disabled. Our instinctive reactions often have to compete with all kinds of other interests and emotions and sentiments.
— Malcolm Gladwell, author of *Blink*

There's an illusion of insight that comes from looking at a person's body. . . . Body language speaks to us, but only in whispers.
— Nicholas Epley, author of *Mindwise*

I want to stand up for all the slightly effeminate dorks that are actually heterosexual. Just 'cause the gaydar is going off, doesn't mean your instruments aren't faulty.
— Jon Cryer, actor who played Duckie in *Pretty In Pink*

In January 2014, in the small town of Sheboygan Falls, Wisconsin, a local newspaper ran a feel-good story about three brothers. They were born and raised in a big city but moved to Sheboygan Falls with their parents. The boys "were looking for a change" from a "big school system." Of their new town and school, the boys said, "The people here have been so accepting of us," and "the classes are much better."[1] All three joined the Sheboygan Falls High School (SFHS) basketball team. Jeff Pederson, the editor for the *Sheboygan Falls News*, described the story as "a positive article about high school student-athletes adjusting to a new school and contributing to an SFHS sports program."[2] The newspaper took a few photos of the brothers and chose one to run with the story.

Then the trouble began.

Figure 3.1. (Photo courtesy of the *Sheboygan Falls News*.)

The hand gestures of two of the three brothers in the article's photo resembled hand signals used by big-city gangs (see figure 3.1). Community members voiced their concerns to the school district. The associate principal and local police investigated. They held a meeting with Jordan Jackson, the boy on the far left, and with Jordan's parents.

According to the police report, Jordan said he was using the hand sign for a successful three-point basketball shot and was not involved in any gangs. Indeed, many college and professional players use the same sign as Jordan after hitting a three. In the center, Juwaun Jackson was apparently just having fun. Jordan explained that Juwaun wasn't even making a sign but was just "pointing up in the air as if he was saying 'what's up.'" The boys' mother also said the boys were not involved in any gangs. The police did not pursue any charges nor recommend any disciplinary action to the school. The police report concluded that "there was no evidence indicating that the boys meant to display gang signs."[3]

But for the school district, the words of explanation from the students who made the gestures seemed less important than the photographed gestures themselves. Actions speak louder than words, and a picture is worth a thousand words, right? The school district suspended the two students from the next game.

The days following the suspension were very stressful for the teens. Their parents asked for a hearing to appeal the decision. Four days after the decision to suspend, the school district held a closed appeal hearing, after which the suspensions were lifted in time for the boys to play in the game that night. The Sheboygan Falls mayor agreed with the decision to overturn the suspension. Despite the appeal decision, the ACLU began an investigation of the high school's disciplinary policies.[4]

Nonverbal decoding refers to drawing inferences about people based on nonverbal behaviors. Nonverbal behaviors include facial expressions, tone of voice, body language, and gestures. Is this overreaction to photographed hand gestures a rare occurrence? Turns out no, unfortunately. Most people are less accurate in nonverbal decoding than they think and are more confident than is justified. Nicholas Epley, author of *Mindwise*, called nonverbal decoding an "illusion of insight."[5] What I add to this analysis is the role played by the FAE.

INFERRING INTENTIONS

The FAE is about overlooking context while inferring personal characteristics or intentions. At least regarding their inferences about Jordan, some community members and the school administration appeared to commit the FAE by overlooking or underestimating the role of the basketball context: It's a basketball photo for a story about basketball, and we're in our basketball jerseys, so hey, I'm going to use a basketball hand gesture.

The administration also seemed to overlook the more immediate context that also played a role. According to the newspaper editor, the photographer had taken a previous photo "with the boys standing still with no gestures or signs." Boring. "For the second photo, he [the photographer] suggested that the boys do a 'fun pose,' as is a common practice for newspaper photographers to spice up the generic nature of posed photographs where the subjects are in a prone state."[6] The police report also noted a direction from the photographer to be "goofy."[7]

So the teens came up with something to comply with the photographer's request. Jordan went with the three-point sign. Juwaun used a more generic positioning of his hands as if to say "what's up." The photographer succeeded in "spicing up" the photo.

Just as George Zimmerman said "he looks black" of Trayvon Martin in direct response to a question from the 911 operator (discussed in chapter 2), the Jackson brothers moved their hands and fingers in response to a direction from the photographer to be more "fun" or "goofy." In both cases, there was an authority figure who gave a direction that was neither visible nor audible. Both directions led to the behavior of the judged individual, and both directions appeared overlooked in the initial negative judgment.

I don't mean to equate George Zimmerman's actions with the teens' less serious behavior. But in both cases, negative dispositional judgments were made against individuals who were only responding in fair or polite ways to their immediate situations. (Obviously, whether all of Zimmerman's actions were "fair" was at issue in the trial.)

LESSONS IN (NOT) MIND READING

Assuming we believe Jordan Jackson's words, as the police who questioned him did, then one lesson from this event is not to think we can read minds based on nonverbal behavior, even when that behavior matches a gesture associated with a gang. At a minimum, we should probably not feel certain enough to enact a punishment, at least when those who behaved nonverbally also verbally communicated a different and plausible story.

Maybe this advice seems obvious to many readers. But some nonverbal behaviors or gestures might seem so obvious in their meanings in the moment. In these cases, we might be automatically affected even if our rational selves know better outside the moment. Malcolm Gladwell, in *Blink*, described a variety of examples of interpreting nonverbal behaviors very quickly and without knowing why. It's intuition or instinct. In general, Gladwell contended that such interpretations and instinctive decision-making tend to be accurate, even more accurate sometimes than conscious slower decisions.

Gladwell, along with other popular press and some academic authors, even referred to the supposedly accurate process of nonverbal decoding as "mind reading," a colorful phrase, but one that taps the psychic ability of telepathy. Annie Murphy Paul wrote for *Psychology Today* that "we're all street-corner psychics" and that "every day . . . we're reading each other's minds."[8] But according to *The Feeling Good Handbook* by David Burns and according to other cognitive-behavioral therapists, "mind reading" is one of the top ten cognitive distortions or "forms of twisted thinking."[9] After implying that people have the ability to read minds, Paul later cited psychologist William Ickes on how poor we actually are at mind reading or nonverbal decoding. According to Ickes, our accuracy rates vary between 20 and 35 percent, depending on how well we know the person whose mind we are trying to read.

Yet Gladwell wrote that "we can all mind-read effortlessly and automatically."[10] More than any other author, Gladwell popularized this belief. So I devote some time here to Gladwell's argument to offer some counterpoints. I want to try to slow down blink-speed decoding.

First, let me discuss Gladwell's claim about accurate nonverbal decoding of teachers. Gladwell cited research by Nalini Ambady and Robert Rosenthal that showed how students' judgments of a "teacher's effectiveness" based on thirty or fewer seconds of viewing the teacher were "very similar" to end-of-semester ratings. Gladwell contended that such results demonstrated the "power of our adaptive unconscious." However, such results can also demonstrate the fallibility of end-of-semester ratings. More important, I found several problems with Gladwell's reporting of the actual results. For example, the actual snap judgments regarded a variety of traits and not "effectiveness" per se.[11]

A centerpiece in Gladwell's reporting comprised interviews with experts on nonverbal decoding such as Paul Ekman. Ekman is known for his foundational work on connecting certain facial expressions to certain emotions. Good choice to interview. *Lie to Me*, a television show about a nonverbal-decoding expert who helped the FBI, was based in part on Ekman. *Lie to Me* ads even cited connections to research and sold the show as being based on real science.

Needless to say, *Blink* and *Lie to Me* stirred up a bit of controversy. Cognitive and social scientists have raised questions about *Blink*'s main assertions about accuracy. Civil rights organizations and numerous researchers have strongly questioned whether *Lie to Me*–style deception-detection techniques, currently used by some airport security personnel, are supported by science. The scientific consensus largely says no.

One group of researchers, led by Timothy Levine, even wondered whether watching *Lie to Me* and learning about the principles of decoding might make viewers *worse* at deception detection. In their study, Levine and colleagues randomly assigned college students to watch the series premiere of *Lie to Me*, the series premiere of a different crime drama (*Numb3rs*), or no show. The *Lie to Me* watchers turned out to perform the worst of all three groups in detecting deception. The researchers suggested that *Lie to Me* viewers became indiscriminately skeptical of others' truthfulness, which decreased the ability to recognize honesty.[12]

Even before *Blink* and *Lie to Me*, some researchers in nonverbal communication had begun a heated debate with Ekman. Unlike the days when Ekman first standardized and published his facial-decoding system, it is no longer a foregone conclusion that certain faces necessarily reflect certain emotions. And detecting deception is generally regarded by researchers as about as accurate as a coin toss, even after training. The current state of these facial-decoding debates will be summarized in the next chapter.

My unique contribution to the general debate for now is to highlight that the FAE detracts from the accuracy of nonverbal decoding. Numerous researchers have stressed that the context and other specific social or situational factors can influence nonverbal behavior. Therefore, the FAE—that is, overlooking the context and situational factors—can impair our nonverbal decoding. It's not just Gladwell and Ekman and airport security personnel who may underestimate these situational factors. It's also everyday people when they think they "know" what someone is really like or what someone means to say based on nonverbal behavior.

Sharon Weinberger, writing for *Nature*, raised the issue that airport security personnel might underestimate the very situation of flying when trying to use nonverbal cues to uncover deception or the intent to cause harm (for which Weinberger coined the term *malintent*). Weinberger wrote that flying and related worries about terrorism or missing flights can "heighten the emotions that would be monitored . . . but may have nothing to do with deception, let alone malintent."[13]

New York Times science writer John Tierney also raised several red flags about thinking we can nonverbally decode at the airport. He wrote that "the T.S.A. seems to have fallen for a classic form of self-deception: the belief that you can read liars' minds by watching their bodies." Tierney cited psychologist and deception-detection researcher Maria Hartwig, who said that "the common-sense notion that liars betray themselves through body language appears to be little more than a cultural fiction."[14]

Decoding Failures

Gladwell did highlight some counterexamples to the quick-and-accurate mind-reading position reflected in the title of his book. In particular, Gladwell devoted an entire chapter to a 1999 case in New York in which inaccurate nonverbal decoding led to the fatal shooting of an innocent man by police officers.

Amadou Diallo, an unarmed twenty-two-year-old black immigrant from Guinea, was shot and killed by four plainclothes white police officers. The first mistake was in misreading Diallo as suspicious as he stood on a stoop outside an apartment building in the Bronx near midnight. An overlooked situational factor that explained why Diallo was standing there was that it was where he lived. Wow. According to *New York Times* reporting, the officer who first decoded Diallo's body language as suspicious "acknowledged that he never considered that Mr. Diallo might have had a legitimate reason for being where he was, or that he might have lived in the building."[15]

As such nonverbal-decoding mistakes accumulated, Diallo, who was apparently terrified, was misread as dangerous. Diallo fled from these plainclothes officers, possibly fearing that they would rob him, due to a recent robbery of someone Diallo knew under similar circumstances.[16] In the ultimate mistake, an officer thought Diallo was going for a gun, when actually it was a wallet. Going for a wallet makes sense if you think you are being robbed. All officers "acknowledged that they never considered the situation from Mr. Diallo's point of view."[17]

It's one thing for a police officer to think you're going for a gun during a chase when you're just going for your wallet. That's sad enough. It's another thing for a police officer to think you're going for a gun when you're going for your wallet *after* the officer asked you to present your driver's license. This scenario appeared to occur in July 2016, when Philando Castile was shot and killed by a police officer during a traffic stop in Falcon Heights, Minnesota. As noted in chapter 1, people commit the FAE even when they themselves placed the situational constraint on the observed individual. Castile apparently went for his wallet because he was requested to do so by an authority figure, who then apparently underestimated the role of that request.[18]

Despite the massive nonverbal-decoding failure in the shooting death of Diallo in the Bronx in 1999, Gladwell took several opportunities in the same chapter to restate how accurate our blink-speed decisions normally are. For example, Gladwell wrote, "Ordinarily, we have no difficulty at all distinguishing, in a blink, between someone who is suspicious and someone who is not ... and, most easily of all, between someone terrified and someone dangerous; anyone who walks down a city street late at night makes those kinds of instantaneous calculations constantly." Then Gladwell added, "Yet, for some reason, that most basic human ability deserted those officers that night."

This description of a "basic human ability" reminded me of a scene from the 1999 movie *She's All That*, in which the teen heroine's father sat in front of the television in his bathrobe watching the trivia game show *Jeopardy!* He was "constantly" and confidently answering the game-show questions out loud, one after another. But every answer was incorrect, sometimes hilariously so.

Yes, most of us probably instantaneously interpret nonverbal behavior often, if not constantly, but why does regularity of an action elevate its status to an ability? And how can we be sure of our instantaneous calculations from our late-night city walks? We'd have to interrogate each person we see during that walk to try to verify our decoding—and even then not be sure.

To explain the existence of quick-but-inaccurate nonverbal decoding, Gladwell wrote that our instinctive decision-making can often be "thrown off" by competing "interests and emotions and sentiments." In other words, instinctive decoding is not the problem and is not inherently flawed, but it can be thrown off by other processes that *are* biased. This distinction might sound semantic; after all, if a decision-making process can be easily thrown off track, then that process is indeed flawed.

But even if we accept this distinction, inaccurate decoding due to the FAE may still not be about getting "thrown off." The FAE may be one of those natural, intuitive, or automatic decision-making processes to which Gladwell generally referred, except without the inherent accuracy. According to some social psychologists, the FAE is even more automatic in explaining nonverbal behavior compared to explaining verbal behavior.[19] Even if these automatic processes are a product of human evolution, which many intuition proponents claim, the resulting decisions need not be uniformly accurate. The theory of evolution easily allows for evolved aspects of humanity to have lost their usefulness in current-day humans. For other examples of presumably evolved decision-making processes that routinely lead to mistakes, see the classic work on heuristics by Tversky and Kahneman.[20]

Motives That Drive the FAE

In truth, social psychologists are not sure whether the cause of the FAE is predominantly cognitive or motivational. In other words, the FAE might not be a natural cognitive process per se, but rather, it could be driven by the individual's motives or sentiments, which would be consistent with Gladwell's reasoning about a cognitive process (blink-speed decoding) getting thrown off by other sentiments (the FAE). The FAE may be driven by a need to feel in control of our surroundings or by a desire to be able to predict and understand more than we actually can.[21] For example, in a classic case of the FAE, explaining an individual's unemployment or poverty by calling the individual lazy can reduce uncertainty and increase feelings of control over negative life events, as in, "I'm not lazy, so thank goodness I won't ever be poor." Social psychologist Melvin Lerner has called victim blaming a "fundamental delusion."[22]

In general, connecting an observed outcome or action to the nearest visible and moving stimulus—namely, the actor engaged in the action—is the quickest way to come to closure and to satisfy a need for control.

The situational factors are often motionless—in the background or in the past—and more spread out, if even visible. A prolonged absence of closure is uncomfortable for many people, so committing the FAE by going straight to the actor can be comforting by providing fast closure. Hypothetically, the brain of an individual who does not bear such discomfort over the absence of closure would better incorporate the situational factors. Indeed, my own research has shown that such individuals are less prone to the FAE. I will discuss this individual-difference research further in chapter 9.[23]

So in the basketball hand-gesture story, maybe interpretation of the hand gestures was thrown off by a basic need for closure or control. Rather than wonder what the heck these Jackson boys are doing with their hands, our brains might try to come up with something quick and concrete and connected to the gesture maker, even if wrong.

This need for control can also cause the creation and spreading of conspiracy theories. Conspiracy theories by definition fit the FAE concept. Conspiracy theories are essentially exaggerations of an enemy's power and negative traits or intentions for the purpose of explaining random or situationally caused negative events. Indeed, studies have shown that threatening someone's feeling of control causes not only the endorsement of conspiracy theories but also all sorts of other biases and misperceptions in which we see patterns or connections that do not actually exist.[24]

Perhaps the officers who shot Diallo had felt an elevated need for control over negative events in the crime-ridden neighborhood. These four officers were part of a special unit assigned to the high-crime area to prevent assaults, murders, and robberies.[25] Being entrusted and paid to protect people from out-of-control negative events would understandably increase the protectors' need for control over those events.

A More Obvious Sentiment: Racism

A sentiment more obvious than a need for control that might have thrown off the mind reading in both the Sheboygan Falls and Bronx stories was racism—that is, at its core, the instantaneous negative emotional reaction to members of a racial group other than your own. In the case of Amadou Diallo in the Bronx, Gladwell acknowledged that some saw racism in the shooting of Diallo. And following the acquittal of the four officers, many protest rallies decried racism. On January 6, 2004, the city gave $3 million in a settlement to Diallo's parents, who accused the officers of racial profiling, though no wrongdoing was admitted.[26] A reason why civil rights organizations have been questioning the deception-detection techniques used at airports is a concern over the biasing effect of racial profiling.

Gladwell also cited research by Keith Payne, who believed that "when we make a split-second decision, we are really vulnerable to being guided by our stereotypes and prejudices."[27] Reading Payne's original study reveals that the Diallo shooting was in fact the inspiration for Payne's research. Payne showed that flashing a black (as opposed to a white) face on a computer screen and giving participants only a half second to respond led to higher rates of misperceiving a hand tool as a gun. All participants were non-black college students.[28]

Even when given more time to decide, white participants still tend to make prejudiced judgments based on racial cues or skin color. In fact, Birt Duncan described this tendency as committing the FAE against black people. Duncan referred to his classic study in which he videotaped staged interactions between two people who were in a disagreement. White college students watched the interaction under the impression that it was actually occurring live in a nearby room. Near the end of the interaction, one actor shoved the other in an "ambiguous" way, in one of four conditions: a black person shoved a white person, black shoved black, white shoved black, or white shoved white. Participants rated the ambiguous shove as more violent, more person caused, and less situation caused when the shover or "harm-doer" was black—whether the "victim" of the shove was white or black—compared to conditions in which the harm-doer was white.

Using the words of Fritz Heider, who is often quoted to describe the FAE as behavior engulfing the field, Duncan wrote the following:

It would appear that the black man is imbued (stereotyped, categorized, etc.) with such salient personality properties (e.g., given to violence) that these traits tend to engulf the field rather than be confined to their proper position, the interpretation of which requires additional data about the situation.[29]

Although Gladwell raised the issue of racism and cited Payne's research, Gladwell amazingly downplayed the possibility of racism for why the white officers misread Diallo in the Bronx shooting. Racism actually fits quite well into Gladwell's general thesis, but Gladwell did not feel that the racism theory was "particularly satisfying" because "there was no evidence that the four officers in the Diallo case were bad people, or racists, or out to get Diallo."

Of course, I cannot know whether the four officers harbored racist feelings or not. But I was struck by a sense of irony that the author who championed humans' natural ability to read minds within seconds, and to discern an individual's true feelings just by looking at that individual, was concerned about the existence of external hard evidence in simply speculating about the feelings of the four officers. Surely there was video footage of these officers available. Why not get a nonverbal-decoding expert to watch the videos? Researchers such as John Dovidio have claimed that there is nonverbal race bias, a set of nonverbal cues that supposedly reflect racist feelings.[30] Or why not simply decode the actions of the officers? Mistaking a wallet for a gun sounds a lot like mistaking a hand tool for a gun, doesn't it?

To be sure, I agree that we need harder evidence than nonverbal decoding to levy a charge of racism or racial profiling. But why did these officers get special treatment from Gladwell? Why did Gladwell separate these officers from the everyday people throughout his book whose minds, in Gladwell's terms, can be effortlessly and automatically read by even the untrained among us?

The answer possibly lies in the US justice system. Innocent until proven guilty. Hearsay is inadmissible. Polygraph results are inadmissible. Gladwell was perhaps giving the courtroom decision special treatment and not the officers per se. As a society, we have established a higher threshold of certainty in our justice system. We need hard evidence and cannot trust the don't-even-know-why-we-feel-it impressions that we form of each other, especially because racism and stereotyping can influence such impressions and prevent consideration of situational factors.

What I want to suggest is that the valid reasons we don't allow court cases to be decided by nonverbal decoding or lie-detection machines should apply to everyday interactions. Obviously, the consequences of a court case are usually more serious than those of an everyday interaction. Best-guessing the secret feelings of your date or coworker doesn't usually rise to the level of what can happen in a court of law. But everyday consequences are not trivial. Dating can lead to marriage and having children. Conflicts in the workplace can lower productivity and cause stress and poor health.

Yet many of us feel a courtroom level of certainty when we nonverbally decode outside the courtroom. "It's obvious" is uttered or felt too often. But another apparent cause of such confidence are the many popular press books and pop-culture articles and websites that encourage such feelings of certainty. These outlets provide steps or tips to read others' body language or to know what your boyfriend or boss is really thinking.

And the main message of Gladwell's book also encourages such certainty when we form instantaneous impressions of our dates, coworkers, or teachers. Many reviews of Gladwell's book from everyday readers, including the "most helpful" reviews at Amazon.com, reflect newfound and strong certainty. Some readers wrote comments like the following:

> Malcolm Gladwell skillfully presents several case studies that inspire me to recognize my own intuitive talent. . . . As a result of this book, I feel more confident and freer to express myself spontaneously! Tuning in to my first impressions is fun and actually gives me a greater sense of well-being and living in the moment, wow![31]

Indeed, there are mental health benefits to judging people this way (see chapter 10). Gladwell encouragingly wrote,

> We can all mind-read effortlessly and automatically. . . . We make these kinds of complicated, lightning-fast calculations very well. We make them every day, and we make them without thinking. . . . Our powers of thin-slicing and snap judgments are extraordinary.[32]

Happy news indeed. Our social world is an easily and quickly understood place. Whew.

So when even Malcolm Gladwell, the author of *Blink* and champion of human mind reading, admitted in the same book that "mind-reading failures happen to all of us," are "surprisingly common," and "lie at the root of countless arguments, disagreements, misunderstandings, and hurt feelings,"[33] it seems so very wise to listen.

The new message I want to emphasize here is not that Gladwell acknowledged some mind-reading failures (although that might sound new to some readers). My new message is not that nonverbal decoding is much less accurate than most of us think (as argued by contemporary nonverbal-communication researchers). My new message is that one of the reasons nonverbal decoding is not more accurate is the FAE. Most of us cannot help but connect nonverbal displays to the traits or intentions of the displayer. That is how the FAE works, whether the FAE is a cognitive heuristic or driven by a desire for control. The context and ever-present social and situational factors can influence nonverbal displays, and so to overlook these factors, to commit the FAE, can cause mistaken interpretations.

REVISITING SHEBOYGAN FALLS

If any readers were wondering when I was going to further discuss racism for the Sheboygan Falls story, here it is. The Jackson brothers are black. As of 2010, Sheboygan Falls was over 96 percent white.[34] Maybe some of the concerned community members and school officials were influenced by the race of these boys to interpret their hand gestures as gang related or otherwise negative. This racial issue is probably why the ACLU got involved.

Recall that Gustav Ichheiser wrote that the FAE is a "symptom of the crisis of our society." Racism is, of course, still a problem in America, even a crisis. And racism can reveal itself in the FAE when people infer negative traits or intentions because of race while ignoring relevant situational factors. Birt Duncan showed that white participants committed the FAE against black students because of racism. The white officers in the Diallo case admitted to committing the FAE against a black man, perhaps because of racism. And some of the community members in Sheboygan Falls appeared to commit the FAE against the Jackson boys, again perhaps because of racism.

It is of course impossible to read the minds of the concerned community members, whoever they are. But that issue of the *Sheboygan Falls News* ran a baseball team photo on the very next page with about a dozen white boys using a variety of hand gestures, all of which matched gang signs (based on a quick check of police-run websites) (see figure 3.2). Some of the signs also matched sport signs such as the extended forefinger for being "number one." To my knowledge, the police and school district did not hear any concerns about that photo and did not question those boys. Or if the police heard any concerns, they apparently did not act on them.

Figure 3.2. (Photo courtesy of the *Sheboygan Falls News*.)

None of the hand signs from the baseball team exactly matched those used by the Jackson brothers. So it is technically possible that some community members recognized a gang sign in the Jackson photo and not the baseball photo. Or maybe the most vocal community members didn't get to the baseball photo in the newspaper before voicing their concerns. I hope I don't sound naïve, but as obvious as it seems that racism was involved, this story is still just a case study and based on hearsay—we don't know exactly what the community members told the school officials. That said, the aforementioned studies by Payne and Duncan are just two of countless reports that demonstrate that racism is still around in America. And the Sheboygan Falls case apparently raised enough concerns to trigger the ACLU investigation.

SOMETIMES WE GET IT RIGHT

So the inference of gang signs in Sheboygan Falls seemed very mistaken and was maybe due to racism. An almost identical case occurred a month later in Olive Branch, Mississippi. Two black teens were suspended for their hand gestures in a photo but then allowed to return.[35] In 2011 and 2013, hearing-impaired individuals using sign language were stabbed after being mistaken for using gang signs.[36] The list goes on.

But as is always the problem with case studies, an author can handpick vivid examples that fit a viewpoint. I don't want to seem like I'm doing so. There also exist cases in which individuals flash gang signs and mean it that way, and in which white students are suspended because of their hand gestures. For example, after posing for a team photo in fall of 2013, three white female basketball players at Farmington High School in Illinois were suspended for at least two games after displaying an obscene hand gesture in the photo. At least one of the three students admitted to that intention on Twitter.[37]

Other examples are out there of justified and unjustified accusations or suspensions based on nonverbal decoding. I don't envy the job of school administrators who have to monitor such displays to enforce school policies and to minimize unsafe behavior by students. I am not claiming to know whether the majority of such suspensions are in error and due to the FAE. But at least some are.

In general, it's cognitively or emotionally difficult to do anything but assume the gesture maker means the gesture as you interpret it, even though unseen situational factors might be eliciting the gesture and thus revealing a different meaning. That is the trap of the FAE.[38]

OBSCENE AND OTHER "OBVIOUS" GESTURES

So OK, some nonverbal behaviors take on a different meaning when we consider the context. But come on. Aren't we justified to be really sure sometimes? Nodding the head universally means yes, right? Actually, in some cultures, it means no. What if we find ourselves on the receiving end of an obvious obscene gesture? Then this chapter might just seem silly. I'm not just going to stand there like a dope after someone has flipped me off, right? In such cases, we might ask rhetorically, "Well, what else could the gesture mean?"

Ask the Gesture Maker

One way to answer this question is to ask the gesture maker. That's where the role of words comes in. Humans have verbal language, but we don't often make full use of it. In fact, when verbal information contradicts nonverbal information, we tend to believe the nonverbal.[39] This strategy is the exact opposite of that recommended by Nicholas Epley, who thoroughly researched the issue and concluded that "reading people's expressions can give you a little information, but you get so much more just by talking to them. The mind comes through the mouth."[40]

I have not forgotten my own position in chapter 1, that even words from the mouth do not fully justify thinking you can read minds, but on average, talking to and looking at people leads to more accurate impressions than just looking at people.[41] Roger Axtell, author of *Gestures: The DO's and TABOOs of Body Language Around the World*, has also recommended talking to people. Axtel wrote that "in the world of gestures, the best single piece of advice is to remember the two A's—'ask' and be 'aware.'"[42]

If someone makes a gesture directed at you, what's the harm in *asking*, in gathering a little more information from the gesture maker? OK, if you read the gesture as offensive, then you might be upset and offended, and it might be hard to ask. Maybe it would feel like giving the benefit of doubt to a rude person and opening yourself up for further insult. But asking can lead to important information that can corroborate or reverse your initial interpretation. If you decide you cannot take the chance of getting offended again, I don't blame you, but then try not to be 100 percent certain about your initial interpretation.

And OK, in a one-on-one scenario, it could be embarrassing to have to ask what a gesture means. And if the gesture might reflect anger or contempt, then it might be safer not to inquire. But then realize that you were (understandably) playing it safe and that you still cannot be sure about the meaning of the gesture.

Last, even if you ask the gesture maker, gesture makers can lie. So to be sure you understand the gesture, you'd have to engage in lie detection, at which most of us are no better than fifty-fifty. If you don't ask the one making the gesture or don't trust the gesture maker's reply, Axtell suggested asking around in the local culture, which to me could mean that of a country, a part of town, or a sport like basketball. Maybe go to the internet and look up the gang signs for your city, but be sure to check a basketball website as well.

Asking around or doing such research can increase the likelihood that you make a valid interpretation. You might wonder who has time to do gesture research, but the smartphone actually makes it doable to do research first and get offended later. Unfortunately, though, even if you investigate or ask around, increasing the likelihood of accuracy still does not ensure accuracy. Finding the exact hand gesture on your police department's website under a particular gang does not guarantee that the gesture maker intended that gang sign. Even if someone tells you what a gesture means, that does not guarantee that the gesture maker meant the same thing.

Axtell has written several books on communicating in different cultures, and he acknowledged this general point several times. He wrote, "No two people behave in precisely the same way. Nor do people from the same culture all perform exactly the same gestures and body language uniformly." Upon learning a brand-new meaning to a gesture he thought he thoroughly understood, Axtell wrote, "Just when we believe we have correctly divined all of the various meanings of a particular gesture, we can be wrong."[43] Axtell also acknowledged that he did not write scientific texts, but to Axtell's credit, scientists have come to the same conclusions of caution.[44] And if it's a posed photo you're interpreting, keep in mind that there's a photographer who might have been calling the shots and choosing the angles.

Besides *asking* around about gestures, Axtell recommended being *aware* of the gestures you make when visiting another culture or another part of town or, in my contribution to this advice, when posing for a local newspaper photo. I certainly don't blame the Jackson brothers for what happened to them, but you never know when you might be mistaken for belonging to a gang or when you might be read as insulting an entire country.

Famous Examples of Unintended Insults

President George H. W. Bush accidentally insulted Australia when he visited there in the early 1990s. It happened when he was passing by some crowds while riding in the backseat of his limousine. He thought he was making the peace sign or victory sign, a *V* formed by the forefinger and middle finger. But somehow his hand rotated so that his palm was facing back at himself, which most every Australian "knows" is a nasty thing to say to someone. It reportedly means, "Up yours, mate." The photo ran in newspapers the next day under the headline "President Insults Australians."[45]

President Bush's life situation, being raised in the United States, very likely contributed to his mistake. Americans probably don't care about whether the *V* faces backward or forward. I don't mean to excuse gestures that make people feel bad, just because the gesture maker is from another culture. Visiting different cultures is a big deal, and visitors bear some responsibility for knowing something about the laws and norms of the locale. But a full analysis of President Bush's behavior needs to include cultural factors. Then it's up to individual Australian citizens to decide how they felt about President Bush's behavior.

My point is that not considering cultural factors in negatively judging President Bush constitutes the FAE. FAE researchers have not traditionally included this type of cultural disconnect in discussions of the FAE. But whether the relevant situational factors are in the room, on the road, or in the everyday social norms that a person has been exposed to over a lifetime, overlooking those factors clearly fits the definition of the FAE. Sociologist Dane Archer wrote, "When it comes to gestures, culture determines not only how one says something but even what someone might want to say in the first place."[46]

Bush was not the first American politician to nonverbally insult citizens of a different culture. Richard Nixon similarly insulted a Latin American crowd with an A-OK sign. American soldiers triggered a brawl at a nightclub in Italy with innocent "vertical horns" not even directed at those who took offense. An American was physically assaulted by locals on a road in Nigeria when using the classic hitchhiker's thumbs-up to nonverbally request a ride.

Americans can also feel insulted by those from other cultures. Japanese audience members rattled an American governor when they appeared to nod off and sleep during his presentation. Closing eyes and nodding apparently reflects the paying of respect and attention in Japan in that context—the audience members weren't sleeping but rather concentrating. Cool.[47]

PERSONAL SPACE

Among many other possible examples of the nonverbal divide between cultures, there is the case of personal space. Once, while I was in a conversation with a colleague from another country, he and I traversed two or three feet of floor space as he stepped continually closer to me and I stepped back. In an episode of *Seinfeld*, Judge Reinhold played this role, what the show coined a "close talker." Kramer actually fell over while backing away from this close-talking character.

Some might take offense at such in-your-face behavior from a close talker, but I knew my colleague was from a culture that had norms for closer personal space. My knowledge of that potential cause did not make it much easier to converse within those few inches, but I did not take offense.

On the flip side, close talkers could take offense at the actions of someone like me who steps back little by little. The close talker might wonder: What's wrong with this guy? Why does he keep stepping away? Attributing stepping back to something wrong with me represents the FAE because it underestimates the role of not only my culture but also the immediate behavior of the close talker. Perhaps it was still rude of me to try to squirm away.

An NPR article on personal space quoted Kathryn Sorrells, a professor of communications studies, as saying that "it's easy to misread what someone is actually communicating if you only come from your cultural perspective."[48] A woman posted an online comment for the NPR article in which she described a classmate who she was sure was flirting with her because he came so close to her all the time. But she asked around and figured out that this young man's culture simply "had a different concept of personal space."

By the way, cultural differences aside, it turns out we are pretty bad at knowing when someone else is flirting with us.[49] In fact, those of us who are above average in nonverbal sensitivity are no better at accurately detecting flirting and might even be worse in some cases.[50]

IN FAIRNESS TO NONVERBAL-DECODING EXPERTS

In fairness to nonverbal decoders out there who have great faith in their ability to read minds, whether teachers or law enforcement personnel or psychologists, let me note that some of us are more accurate than others in nonverbal decoding. And research-based or on-the-job training may exist that can improve your nonverbal decoding skills. Paul Ekman and colleagues reported that some law enforcement personnel and psychologists showed superior lie-detection ability.[51] I do feel bad if this chapter is wrecking anyone's feelings of control over their social surroundings, feelings that are based on your belief that you can read other people.

At the same time, being *more* accurate than others in nonverbal decoding certainly does not mean being very accurate in an absolute sense. Also, those groups thought to be more accurate than others (teachers, law enforcement personnel, psychologists) may show only a slight superiority. According to researchers Christian Meissner and Saul Kassin and many others, training or on-the-job experience typically yields only very small improvements if any, particularly in lie detection.[52] And most of us strongly overestimate our own accuracy in nonverbally decoding other people—especially the longer we know these other people![53]

So if during this chapter, your belief you can read people or your general feeling of control is dissipating at all, then bingo (and sorry)—my message is getting across. (Research on the limits of decoding just faces is discussed in the next chapter.)

Further complicating the decoding process, some targets of nonverbal decoding are harder to read than others. Even Paul Ekman acknowledged that difficulty in mind reading particular individuals.[54] In general, people are harder to read than they themselves think. Research shows there is an illusion of transparency, in which people overestimate how much their own emotions and mental states can be read by others. In a separate phenomenon, the spotlight effect, people overestimate how much they stick out or are noticed by others.[55] It makes sense that we overestimate our ability to read others if we ourselves think we can be read like a book.

In further fairness to a belief in accurate nonverbal decoding, the prolific cross-cultural author and traveler Roger Axtell did identify a few gestures that he described as universal, by which he meant very unlikely to mean anything other than the collectively assumed meaning. His main example was the finger, which is to extend the middle finger with an otherwise closed fist. The finger is invariably, cross-culturally, and historically meant as an insult. Easy to decode. Or is it?

It turns out that even this "obvious" insult can be meant innocently, including by those who use sign language in some cultures, such as Australia, Korea, and Japan. I found a Japanese sign language (JSL) tutorial on YouTube and saw firsthand a nice young woman from Japan flipping me the bird. She did it over and over with a smile. She even added some up-and-down arm motion, one of many colorful elaborations on the bird if you really want to insult someone. The bird in JSL means "younger brother." In a tutorial for the Korean sign for "brother," the signer flipped me off with *both* hands![56]

THE ONLY CERTAINTY IN LIFE IS UNCERTAINTY

Although it seems obvious at this point that some Sheboygan Falls community members and the school district overreacted to the hand gestures of Jordan and Juwaun Jackson, I concede that I cannot read the minds of these teens. The preponderance of available evidence indicates that the teens did not intend to use gang signs. But it's still technically possible that they knowingly tried to sneak gang signs into the photo for some reason.

Justified absolute certainty is rare in person perception, especially in nonverbal decoding. I have no black-and-white formulas to share for how to read other people. We're too complicated as a group. There will always be exceptions. As the saying goes, the only certainty in life is uncertainty. Certainty is the mother of fools. One of my goals in this book is to make you more comfortable with these adages.

As will be discussed in the next chapter, even well-done research on the decoding of faces—not just body language—rarely shows anything close to a 100 percent connection between certain facial expressions and certain meanings or intentions. But that doesn't mean we cannot function overall in our day-to-day interactions with one another. Go with the apparent evidence, ask questions, make your best guess, and consider apologizing if you get it wrong.

GAYDAR

I couldn't end this chapter without some mention of a popular form of nonverbal decoding in which we think we can tell whether someone is gay, lesbian, or straight just by looking at them. The ability to tell is often referred to as gaydar. Bring on the stereotypes.

Just as racism and racial stereotypes can bias our blink-speed decoding of the behaviors of individuals of certain races, so can stereotypes of gay and lesbian individuals bias our guesses about who's gay and who's straight. In fact, both gay stereotypes and sex stereotypes guide our guesses about someone's sexual orientation. The primary component of the gay stereotype is sex-atypical behavior, in that we expect gay men to behave or carry themselves in typically feminine ways and gay women to behave or carry themselves in typically masculine ways.[57]

It turns out that there is a kernel of truth to gay stereotypes. Gay men and women, compared to straight men and women, *are* more likely to behave in sex-atypical ways in how they move and speak and otherwise carry or dress themselves.[58] Thus, on average, sexual-orientation guesses based on stereotypes will be true more often than chance guessing. But there is a lot of room between chance guessing (fifty-fifty) and fair use of the label "accurate." Is 55 percent high enough to call gaydar accurate? 60 percent?

Amazingly, most researchers who study gaydar take an all-or-nothing approach. They call gaydar accurate for any result that is above chance, even, in one case, at 52 percent.[59] Correcting for random guessing, a 52 percent accuracy rate becomes a 4 percent accuracy rate. I wonder how we would feel if an air traffic controller or radiologist had a 4 percent hit rate in detecting problems.

Comedian Ellen DeGeneres got in on some of this amazement at the start of one of her shows. She cited a 60 percent accuracy rate for gaydar from a national study and astutely pointed out that it's just 10 percent above chance guessing. She then downplayed the study by claiming that 60 percent of the time, she also knows which Olsen twin she's talking to.[60] It's not just funny or concerning on the surface (if you agree that it's funny or concerning). Social scientists in the last few decades have come to care more and more about something called effect size: the actual size of the result (the percentage, in this case), regardless of whether the result is statistically significant (that is, occurring at a level above chance guessing). A statistically significant result with a tiny effect size doesn't get the importance it used to in social science.

Even if this relation between stereotyped behaviors and actual sexual orientation were true 100 percent of the time—that is, even if being gay always led to sex-atypical behaviors (which it doesn't)—does that mean that showing those behaviors implies that one is gay? In other words, is it true that A (sexual orientation) implying B (certain behaviors) means that B implies A? No, of course not. I hope this reasoning sounds familiar. As discussed in chapter 1, even if A implies B, to conclude A in the presence of B would be the converse error. There can be other causes of B, other causes of "gay" behaviors, besides being gay.

Jon Cryer, who played working-class kid Duckie in the 1986 movie *Pretty in Pink*, made a similar point in 2012 in response to a statement from his *Pretty in Pink* costar, Molly Ringwald. Ringwald publicly asserted that Duckie was secretly gay. Cryer astutely replied that heterosexual men can give off gay vibes or behave effeminately. He apparently spoke from personal experience in how others treated him, saying, "I've had to live with that, and that's okay."[61] According to the gay-o-meter on the website Gay or Straight at the time, the average gay rating given to Cryer by site visitors was 74 percent. But Cryer is reportedly not gay.

Like all behaviors, sex-atypical behaviors can be due to genetic predispositions or environmental influences. Some boys who are naturally feminine or have traditionally feminine interests, but who are not gay, may have parents who encourage their sons in whatever ways they like to behave. Alternatively, such boys may belong to an accepting peer group or culture in which sex-atypical behaviors are simply not *dis*couraged. These boys may grow up looking even more stereotypically gay than had their parents, peers, or culture been less accepting.

Even what a sex-atypical behavior looks like can vary by culture. Jaroslava Valentova and colleagues demonstrated that gaydar functioned worse when American men judged the sexual orientation of Czech men or vice versa, compared to men judging someone from their own country. To explain this "within-culture rating advantage," the researchers suggested that the "meanings of behavioral displays can differ between cultures" from "gay accents" to other "orientation-related nonverbal behavior."[62]

In sum, you might falsely attribute a behavioral display to being gay when it is actually due to being raised in a particular culture or by particular parents. Overlooking or being unaware of such factors in mislabeling someone as gay is yet another case of the FAE.

Now let's reverse it. Even if being *straight* always leads to sex-*typical* behaviors (which it doesn't), that does not mean that showing sex-typical behaviors reflects being straight. Indeed, many gay individuals naturally behave sex-typically or have learned or trained themselves to behave that way.[63] The *HuffPost* article titled "25 Celebrity Coming Out Stories That Shocked the World" illustrates that sometimes gay individuals, even those whose behaviors are scrutinized by the public, are misread as straight.[64]

The cause of trying to behave in a sex-typical way seems situational. Society or peer groups often behave badly toward individuals who behave in sex-atypical ways. Similarly, behaving sex-typically can be conditioned by childhood same-sex peer groups independent of sexual orientation. Research shows that individuals who are gay but pretend to behave straight or more sex-typically are indeed successful, on average, in reducing the accuracy of observers' gaydar.[65]

So yes, there is a kernel of accuracy in gaydar. But as always, try not to be certain. Even based on carefully conducted research that concludes that gaydar is "accurate," there is sometimes a 48 percent chance that you would still be wrong. And one of the reasons for being wrong is the FAE, when we underestimate situational influences on orientation-related nonverbal behavior. Gaydar based only on viewing faces will be discussed further in the next chapter.

CHAPTER 4

WHAT'S IN A FACE? PHOTOS CAN LIE

Many of our conclusions about a person's character, attitude, or intentions based on first impressions of their facial features later turn out to be false. . . . A possible way forward is to abandon the assumption that faces have any essential meaning that applies without reference to the context of their use.

—Brian Parkinson, social psychologist

I have all the emotions that everyone has; it just appears that I don't.

—Steven Wright, stand-up comic

You never had a camera in my head!

—Truman Burbank,
main character in *The Truman Show*

In the previous chapter, I highlighted a photo of innocent hand gestures, the interpretations of which included gang signs, sports signs, and just being goofy. These gestures generated controversy when the young black men who used them were suspended from their basketball team on apparent suspicion of gang involvement.

What about photos of facial expressions? Are they easier to interpret? Many researchers in nonverbal decoding draw a conceptual line between decoding body language, such as hand gestures, and decoding faces. Most of us think we can read faces pretty well. You may have heard that the eyes, in particular, are windows to the soul. But can we infer anything near that much? In particular, can we accurately infer people's traits, deception, or sexual orientation just from looking at their faces? The overall answers appear to be no, no, and a little, respectively.

THE IRIS AS A WINDOW TO TRAITS?

Academicians have nearly reached the point of fully disowning the ancient practice of physiognomy—inferring character from facial features. Under some conditions, better-than-chance accuracy rates have been found when judging a face for extroversion and trustworthiness, but even those researchers acknowledged how low those rates were, commenting in one case that "the face is a rather opaque window to the soul."[1] Some biological psychologists have been investigating whether features of the eye, particularly the iris, might say something about an individual's traits. Perhaps the last hope for that eye-soul thing to be true.

Although there is some mixed evidence that eye color reflects something about how extroverted or sociable you are (darker color links to greater extroversion), that relationship is limited to toddlers. Among adults, more recent research has looked at features of the iris called crypts, contraction furrows, and pigment dots. The statistical evidence is shaky, but a few potential links have been found. For example, more contraction furrows may indicate greater impulsiveness. But alas, even if the evidence were stronger, these features of the iris are too small to count with the naked eye. For everyday nonverbal decoding, assuming you don't carry with you a strong magnifying glass, eyes per se do not give an accurate picture of traits.[2]

DETECTING DECEPTION FROM FACES

In a famous meta-analysis, psychologists Charles Bond Jr. and Bella DePaulo carefully considered hundreds of studies and reported an overall accuracy rate of about 54 percent for deception detection (for both non-experts and, surprisingly, experts), slightly above the coin-flipping 50 percent. The authors appropriately reported that people are "not good" at deception detection and that "people can barely discriminate lies from truths." And as low as that overall accuracy rate was, it was based on studies that included the reading of body language and vocal cues. Just looking at faces did not allow for better-than-chance accuracy.[3]

Bond and DePaulo made several suggestions for why people are so poor at deception detection. Among them was an argument that included the FAE. First, although most of us lie with some regularity, we judge the liar more harshly than we judge ourselves. When *we* lie, we tend to see a high-stakes need in the situation, but when others lie, we see a strong moral failing. Thus, we tend to assume that these other liars would feel ashamed or guilty for their moral infraction, and we keep an eye out for those emotional expressions in looking for deception. But liars, who usually see the situational need to lie, don't feel those emotions and so are misread as telling the truth. The authors' point was that we typically underestimate the power of context behind others' lies (this underestimation is the FAE).

FACE-BASED GAYDAR

As for sexual orientation, I return to an example from the previous chapter in which researchers Rule and Ambady reported that face-based gaydar was "accurate" based on a mere 52 percent rate of correct judgments. This result is only 2 percent higher than flipping a coin. And the faces used were from Facebook photos of men whose profiles indicated that "they were interested in other men for romantic or sexual purposes."[4]

Rule and Ambady acknowledged the possibility of a selection bias, in which men who are comfortable advertising themselves this way might look or present themselves as more stereotypically gay. Many gaydar studies similarly use internet-based photos. So it was not surprising to Jaroslava Valentova and colleagues that when they avoided the internet and instructed male participants to convey neutral expressions, there was no gaydar accuracy.[5]

Rule and Ambady also acknowledged that typical gay men might try to conceal their sexual orientation and thus be harder to read. Indeed, Ambady's own previous research showed that the sexual orientation of gay men who tried to pass as straight was correctly discerned only 43 percent of the time, failing to surpass the coin-flipping 50 percent.[6] Rule and Ambady did not cite Ambady's earlier research and surprisingly framed the issue as an open question, as if there were not yet any research on the topic.

To be clear, the gay men in Ambady's earlier research received instructions to try to pass as straight. The participants who misread these gay men as straight committed the FAE by overlooking that external influence. Put another way, the participants apparently assumed that the men's nonverbal cues looked straight because the men were straight. Oops. To be fair, the participants didn't know about the instructions to conceal, but some gay men in America do feel external pressure to conceal their sexual orientation in day-to-day life.

Despite the limitations of Rule and Ambady's 52 percent result, let me add that the only information the participants had was static faces that were flashed for one-twentieth of a second. Moreover, the hairstyles on the faces were digitally removed, to avoid providing cues with sex-typical or sex-atypical hairstyles. Under these conditions, it was a big deal to find better-than-chance accuracy rates. And overall, across multiple studies, accuracy rates in determining sexual orientation based on faces are generally above chance. When researchers add videotapes of body language and vocal cues, accuracy rates rise even a little higher.

Anecdotally, within certain communities in certain cities, there may be more reliable cues to being gay that gay members of the community have sort of agreed to adopt, such as wearing a different number of earrings in each ear or cutting one's hair a particular way. Notice the role of culture in these cases, whereby culture can interact with sexual orientation as the cause for one's appearance. As Roger Axtell advised in the previous chapter, we might need to ask around the local culture to be able to discern the meaning of certain purposeful nonverbal cues, whether they are everyday hand gestures or communications of sexual orientation through facial appearance.

Rule and Ambady did overstate their 52 percent result. It's not indicative of "accuracy" in an absolute sense. But Ambady conveyed a more balanced perspective elsewhere when she concluded that some individuals are easier to read than others, that some observers are more accurate than others, and that even 60 percent accuracy is "far from perfect."[7]

In sum, we have difficulty inferring people's traits, deception, and sexual orientation just from looking at their faces. Among several reasons, I've highlighted a few cases of the FAE. We overlook or underconsider the context behind facial features and expressions.

READING EMOTIONS FROM FACES

The bigger and more complicated question in facial decoding is whether we can accurately infer how people are *feeling* based on their facial expressions. Most of us think the answer is a simple yes. We take for granted that a facial expression is a readout of emotion. But the literature in which the question lies is truly massive and complex. And there have been some heated academic debates surrounding this question. It turns out that even defining an "emotion" is riddled with issues. I try to capture some of this complexity.

One of many counterexamples to the idea that faces equal emotions is deadpan humor. Stand-up comic Steven Wright is known for his dry delivery, but he has explained that his emotionless appearance does not mean he doesn't have regular emotions.[8] To look at his face and infer emotionlessness would overlook the situational comedic role that earns him a living. Many of us have learned how to control or fake our facial expressions when we want to hide what we're really feeling. Experimental psychologist Brian Parkinson put it lightly when he wrote in 2005 that "since the 1990s, the familiar view that faces directly express emotions has come under increasing scrutiny."[9]

There have been debates within popular culture as well, surrounding certain high-profile snapshots of famous people. In the infamous case of the selfie of President Obama at Nelson Mandela's memorial service in South Africa in 2013, the world pounced in varied displays of the FAE while making judgments. Lauren Collins of the *New Yorker* tried to convey the message of misinterpretation or overinterpretation by calling the story "the Obama Selfie-Face-Gate" and the "week's leading event of real-fake-news."[10]

THE FACE OF THE FIRST LADY

In this selfie story, there was one widely publicized photo of three dignitaries smiling while taking a group selfie (including President Obama) and of Michelle Obama's unsmiling face pointed elsewhere. (The previous and next few endnotes provide links to this photo.) Based on this photo, many reporters, bloggers, cable news hosts, and others on social media made strong dispositional attributions for behaviors of both the president and First Lady, despite the presence of situational and cultural factors. For example, many called the president disrespectful. But apparently smiling or having fun at a memorial service is not considered disrespectful in some African cultures (even if you're a world leader).

In other words, the immediate and cultural context at that memorial service could elicit different behavior than what might be expected at a typical American memorial service. At the least, those present who were in a position to feel disrespected very likely did not feel that way, because the president's behavior matched their own and definitely fit the situation. Americans can still feel that their president should behave more solemnly at any such event, but if such Americans ignore the specific context in explaining the president's behavior, that represents the FAE.

But let's focus on the First Lady's face. Many people thought she was angry about something. Confident interpretations of her face ranged from "not amused" to an "icy glare" and "rage." One reporter commented that the First Lady was "making 'the face' at her hubby while he was making eyes" at the Danish prime minister.[11] But according to the photographer who took this most discussed photo, Roberto Schmidt, these interpretations were way off.

Photos Can Lie

The photographer, Schmidt, was so aghast at the common misinterpretation of Michelle Obama's face that he thought he had better step up and say something. So Schmidt publicly explained that "photos can lie." Schmidt referred to the First Lady's facial expression as random or "captured by chance" and explained that "just a few seconds earlier the first lady was herself joking with those around her," including the Danish prime minister.[12] Just as closed eyes in a photo don't necessarily mean that someone is sleeping, other momentary facial movements caught on camera can be misleading.

Mrs. Obama did seem to be staring at something. But even if that were true, there was much to see at this event. And occasionally staring into space would be understandable when the event had already lasted more than two hours. Our smiling muscles do need rest. Yes, there was a selfie activity happening in the photo, but just because this activity made it into the photo doesn't mean it was the activity that was influencing

Mrs. Obama's face. The problem in interpreting someone's behavior in any photo is that only so much of the context can be captured within the four sides. To see more of the context, it would help to be there, like the photographer was.

In other words, there can be something beyond the boundaries of the photo that is influencing the facial expression. The observer of the photo is understandably less likely to consider something that cannot be seen. The observer may understandably be completely unaware of it. But being understandable does not make the judgment any less the FAE.

The biggest challenge for people in avoiding any form of the FAE is not the challenge of giving appropriate attention and weight to visible situational factors, though decades of research show we're not very good at that. Rather, the biggest challenge is being open to the possibility that there are situational factors in play that are *not* visible. And that invisible obstacle to accurate facial decoding is especially present in viewing snapshots because of the automatic absence of the majority of the environment, including the facets of any *recent* situations of the observed individual, even from just a second or two before the snap.

Even when the context is visible and we give it our full attention, we can still bungle our facial judgments. When the context is visible and causes us to read a particular emotion from a neutral face—that is, a face without an underlying emotion—it's called the Kuleshov effect. A clever group of researchers led by Hillel Aviezer took it even one step further. They showed that context can bias our interpretations of obvious faces as well—that is, faces that are usually interpreted as reflecting a particular emotion.[13]

Aviezer and colleagues selected a photo of a facial expression that is commonly identified as disgust and then digitally placed that exact face on four different bodies in four different contexts. In the disgusted context, the actor was holding a pair of crumpled underwear in two fingers and away from his face. In the sad context, the actor stood near a gravestone. Two other contexts depicted anger and fear. Although the face itself supposedly reflected disgust in every case, a significant portion of the participants misidentified the facial expression as sad, angry, or fearful in the photos that contained those contextual cues.

I'm not saying that the First Lady actually had a disgusted face that was misread as anger because of certain cues in the photo (although that's possible). I'm saying that people can misread a face even when they do consider the context. So without the context, it's not surprising how many times we misread faces. The conclusion from Aviezer was that faces don't necessarily have meaning unto themselves and that accuracy typically improves when we have context. The context contains clues as to what the face is reflecting.

Mind Reading, Racism, and Sexism

So was Mrs. Obama angry at her husband in the photo? Not likely. I previously discussed the potential role of racism in mind reading, such as seeing a gang sign in the innocent basketball hand gesture of a young black man. In writing for *Salon*, English professor Roxane Gay suggested that attributions of anger to explain the First Lady's face reflected not only racism but also sexism. Gay conveyed grave concern over the negative stereotype of a black woman as angry and territorial, and as evidence, she pointed to photos of the First Lady smiling and laughing with her husband and the Danish prime minister that were not publicized as frequently.

Gay also brought attention to a barely noticed photo of Laura Bush's icy glare from years earlier. The former First Lady's face was actually just an unsmiling face staring off somewhere at a public event, but it could have been an icy glare if the Obama-selfie reasoning were applied. Laura Bush's facial expression was captured while President Bush had a conversation with a young woman sitting behind him. I suspect we could find such fraction-of-a-second examples of supposed icy glares for many other presidents' spouses at public events.[14]

But to the possibility of racism and sexism for why people misread Michelle Obama, let's add ratings and politics. One of the messages of chapter 1 was that shock jocks or tabloids might say things for ratings and not because they really believe it. And political partisans might have been biased or might have knowingly overstated their interpretations for political gains.

Of course, everyday people who saw anger in the First Lady's face need not have any prejudice, ulterior motive, or political bias. It is very common for people to see emotions in facial expressions. Whether the emotion is actually there is a harder question, because behind-the-scenes context unrelated to the inferred emotion might cause the face to look that way.

Mea Culpas and Doubling Down

Some news organizations published updates to their original Obama-selfie stories. They wanted to incorporate the photographer's information about the context. And a few rare bloggers and social-media commenters acknowledged initial mistakes. But at the same time, others doubled down on their initial interpretation. It is truly difficult for some of us to cognitively separate an observed behavior (even a fraction-of-a-second facial expression) from a perceived disposition. That is the FAE trap.

Doubling down can also be about ego protection and defending our initially expressed feelings or views. As thoroughly described by Carol Tavris and Elliot Aronson in *Mistakes Were Made (But Not by Me)*, once we are caught in a mistake, we will often fight the impression that we made a mistake, in presenting to others and even in our own minds.[15]

In an online update, the *HuffPost* announced that the "world media had a skewed interpretation of the snapshot" (citing Roberto Schmidt). But in response to that headline, some commenters defended initial interpretations.[16] One wrote, "Really, then where are the photos showing the first lady happily involved in the celebration?" Another wrote, "Mrs. Obama's facial expression looks pretty real to me." The forgone conclusion is that facial expression equals emotion, but as I will discuss shortly, such a one-to-one connection between face and emotion has been debunked by contemporary emotion researchers.

Thank You for the Context

After the photographer shared what he saw, a few commenters did voice the avoiding-the-FAE message of this book. One commenter wrote, "Perhaps folks should slow down and read what the man who took the photo had to say. You would realize you are jumping to false conclusions."[17] Indeed, slowing down is a primary way to reduce the FAE (see chapter 10).

Another wrote directly to the photographer, "Thank you for giving the context!" Another wrote, "Don't trust photos! Poor Michelle Obama stops smiling for a moment and she is on front pages all over the world, depicted as the jealous spouse."[18] The phrase "taken out of context," usually meant for verbal communication, strongly fits here in a nonverbal way.

Of course, in some of our interpretations of a face in a photo, we're correct. But we're wrong much more often than most of us think. And a lot of people guessed wrong in this famous presidential case. The belief that even fraction-of-a-second facial expressions must mean something about underlying emotions is untrue. But it makes for good headlines.

THE ACADEMIC DEBATE

Contemporary researchers in nonverbal communication regularly recommend caution in thinking we can read minds or emotions from faces. José-Miguel Fernández-Dols explained that the "pioneering" ideas of Paul Ekman that connected certain facial expressions to certain emotions across cultures "fit into researchers' and the public's commonsense assumptions" and "constituted the most important and popular chapter in the study of nonverbal communication." But these same ideas "are actually grounded on problematic empirical evidence."[19] Alan Fridlund wrote simply that "facial expressions are not readouts of 'emotional state'" and that "one important determinant of our facial behavior is our social role with respect to our potential interactants."[20] What these researchers were coming around to saying, or saying outright, was that many of Ekman's original ideas were wrong or overstated in the big picture of emotions.

It can be so interesting and informative, and a little unsettling in a don't-know-which-side-to-believe way, to watch academics duke it out in published articles. And perhaps it can be boring for some—I do my best here to be brief. But I don't want to give the false impression, as some authors do, that research results always provide clear or simple bottom lines. In *Blink*, Malcolm Gladwell famously provided only one simplistic side of this facial-decoding debate, the side from Paul Ekman. Research results do sometimes provide clear and simple bottom lines, and they usually lean to one side of an argument or another. But large research areas can also be a bit messy (by which I mean complex). And the literature on facial decoding is especially large and especially messy.

In such debates in journals, there is sometimes a series of three articles: the critique, then the response, and then the rebuttal. The earliest and strongest outright facial-decoding debate was in 1994–95. The critique came from James Russell; the response from famous nonverbal-decoding expert Paul Ekman, and the rebuttal from Russell again.

I could tell the debate had become heated when Ekman appeared to call Russell a liar. Ekman wrote things like, "It is hard not to believe that Russell deliberately sought to create a false impression about my views."[21] (Notice the apparent mind reading undertaken by Ekman here in inferring intention.) Russell responded by writing that "any such implication is false, but I cannot think that Ekman meant what he said."[22] (Notice the apparent attempt to avoid the FAE by Russell here by *not* inferring intention.) Not bar fight material, but pretty serious for a journal.

This exchange between Ekman and Russell reminded me of a moment in the American Western film *The Big Country* when Charlton Heston called Gregory Peck a liar. Heston's character was a ranch foreman who was smart but quick to judge, and Peck's character was a sea captain who was smart but laid-back. I'm suggesting that James Russell is the academic version of Gregory Peck's character. Like Peck, Russell did not get defensive about being called a liar but did stand up for himself. But Peck and Heston took it one step further in their big fistfight scene over the matter the next morning. It was a big "Would you care to step outside?" moment. Both turned out to be respectable men. (The fight had no clear winner.)

Here is an extremely brief summary of those three 1994–95 articles from these two accomplished theorists and researchers, Ekman and Russell. For any reader familiar with the literature, please forgive me for what might seem like oversimplifications. For any reader overwhelmed with boredom, please forgive me for what might seem like excruciating details. But I would like to provide just a flavor of this early and complex debate. Then I will bring us up to date. Most of the issues introduced in that debate are still in play today.

The Basics

It might help you while reading the debate summary to know that in the area of emotional expression, there were two extreme positions and many in between. The two extremes were basically nature versus nurture. At the nature extreme, emotional expression was innate, biological, universal, and easy to interpret. At the nurture extreme, emotional expression was socially learned, culture specific, and difficult to interpret, depending on the context. Ekman's theory lay near the nature and universal end and so carried a higher risk of the FAE in underestimating or undervaluing the social, cultural, and immediate contexts. Russell sort of played devil's advocate in suggesting that Ekman's evidence could support any number of theories in between the extremes on this continuum.

More specifically, Ekman originally believed (or wrote) that there are seven basic emotions that are innately expressed in particular ways and can be accurately inferred from facial expressions by anyone from any culture: happiness, sadness, surprise, fear, anger, disgust, and contempt. Many readers who have taken an introductory psychology course might recognize some of these emotions as the so-called universal ones. Contempt eventually fell away, leaving six that still receive attention in introductory textbooks. Ekman had pitted this universalist view against many of his predecessors in the mid-twentieth century who supposedly believed that all emotional expressions were socially learned and culture specific. But Russell questioned Ekman's position on several grounds. I discuss three.

1. Who Believed What?

Critique

In a section titled "A Partial History," Russell suggested that Ekman oversold Ekman's theory. Russell suggested that Ekman and colleagues had overstated the uniqueness of their position compared to earlier views. In particular, Russell suggested that Ekman and colleagues misrepresented these earlier views as more opposed to the idea of universality and more entrenched on the side of culture than they actually were. Russell cited passages from earlier works to support his position.[23]

Response

Ekman wrote a section titled "Russell's 'Partial History' Is Biased." Ekman maintained that he had brought a very new perspective to the area of emotion. Ekman wrote that Russell was the one who misrepresented earlier views. And just as Russell supported Russell's own position, Ekman cited passages from earlier works to support his own position.[24]

Here is one of those unsettling don't-know-which-side-to-believe feelings in reading debates like this one. I mean, who has time to read dozens of books and articles to settle this disagreement for ourselves (though I've read many of them)? I am writing this book and would like to give you a bottom line on who's more right, but maybe that would just be *my* take. I am certainly not accusing Ekman or Russell of misquoting. There are quotes on each side. But Ekman wrote that "this is not a matter of honest disagreement. Russell's reporting is biased. He omitted what did not fit his agenda." The same could be reasonably said of Ekman's reporting, though Russell did not say it. I don't mean to wimp out here, so let me weigh in. Based on my reading, my take is that Russell was more right than Ekman.

Rebuttal

As a beginning to Russell's rebuttal points, he apologized if his writing had made anyone uncomfortable, and he emphasized how important Ekman's contributions to the field had been. But Russell proceeded to provide more quotes from earlier works to support his historical interpretations.[25]

Interestingly, Russell took an avoiding-the-FAE approach by identifying possible situational factors to explain why Ekman and his predecessors might have sounded more extreme than they actually were (as opposed to calling anyone a liar). Russell suggested that Ekman's predecessors might have sounded like cultural extremists because they thought they were up against a pure universalist audience. So these predecessors occasionally wrote in ways to try to convince universalist readers of a middle ground. You know, if you're speaking to a tough crowd, you might sometimes feel the need to speak emphatically and maybe even stretch an argument or two (not that I condone argument stretching).

And perhaps the relative universalist, Ekman, thought he was up against a pure *culture* crowd. And so maybe Ekman occasionally overstated the uniqueness of his universal-but-also-cultural theory to try to convince culture readers of a middle ground. Ekman might have been thinking, Who's going to read my stuff if the bottom line is "nothing new to see here"? One of the cultural parts of Ekman's position was that culture contains display rules that could sometimes influence how certain emotions are expressed.

2. Are Facial Decoders Accurate or Not?

Despite the importance that each author gave to the historical issue of who believed what, I found myself thinking that the bigger issue is what the data indicated. Are we accurate or not when we try to read emotions from faces? Russell and Ekman disagreed on this issue. But didn't the studies produce accuracy rates? Hard numbers to point to? Yes, but please read on.

Critique

Russell acknowledged that the average observer could usually infer the six particular emotions at statistically significant rates—that is, above levels of chance (or above levels that would reflect random guessing). However, that didn't mean the accuracy rates were high in an absolute sense. And that didn't mean the accuracy rates were as high as Ekman's theory predicted. Russell basically suggested that the rates were not all that strong and were in fact low enough to allow for several interpretations of the data besides Ekman's interpretation.

Response

Ekman asserted that the accuracy rates were strong enough to support his universalist view and that 100 percent accuracy was never predicted. He declared that all that should matter was "whether the amount of agreement was statistically significant"—that is, above levels of chance.

Rebuttal

Russell wrote that "statistical significance alone does not guarantee that the effect observed is large or meaningful." This statement represents a position that has become a tenet of social science. For countless statisticians and scientists over the last twenty years (since this 1994–95 debate), statistical significance is clearly important but is not enough.

Stereotypes of Facial Expressions

To the story of statistical significance not being enough, let me contribute the example of boys versus girls in math performance. It is one of many cases of a statistically significant difference with an effect size that is so small that the difference is almost meaningless to discuss. Depending on the precise content of the standardized math test and the ages of the students, the average difference between boys' and girls' actual scores has nearly reached zero, though boys, on average, still slightly outperform girls beyond what would be expected by chance. In other words, there are so very many girls out there these days, more than ever, who can outperform the average boy on a standardized math test. Therefore, pointing to a particular girl and assuming she is less capable in math than most boys is more likely to be wrong now than ever before, even if your chances of being right are still slightly above a flipping-a-coin guess.[26]

Using stereotypes in judging people from two groups is always risky. Using stereotypes is especially risky when the actual difference between the two groups is near zero, even if it's still statistically significant. Statistical significance reflects the "kernel of truth" in many stereotypes but does not justify judging a particular individual based on group membership.

So judging a certain facial expression as reflecting a particular emotion might have a kernel of truth. We have stereotypes (or evolved conceptions) for how people should look when they feel a certain way. But how accurate are such stereotypes? How large is that kernel of truth? Russell

123

argued quite simply and correctly that the lower the correlation between a certain facial expression and emotion, the smaller the kernel, and so the more wrong guesses that will be made. It's not that facial decoding is either accurate or not. It's not that facial decoding is either statistically significant or not. In both cases, that would be a false dichotomy.

The actual question is on a continuum. *How* accurate is facial decoding? To what *degree* is it accurate? Russell argued that the answer was much less accurate than that conveyed by Ekman and most of those who cited Ekman's research at that time. Accuracy rates were low enough to allow for interpretations other than universalist ones.

3. How Was Accuracy Measured?

Accuracy rates are kind of meaningless if there were problems in how accuracy was measured. Were there substantial methodological or measuring problems in Ekman's research?

Critique

Russell said yes, there were. He identified several potential problems in how Ekman and colleagues conducted their research that might have skewed the results. Russell provided evidence that correcting these problems led to even lower accuracy rates. For example, one problem was in how researchers obtained the facial expressions used as stimuli. The facial expressions were highly preselected, sometimes from thousands of posed photographs, and thus were not representative of facial expressions in general. Amazingly, in a highly cited 1971 article by Ekman and Friesen, some photos were included for use only if 70 percent of a panel of judges (or more) could correctly identify the emotion being posed.[27]

Just to be clear, this panel of judges looked at the photos *before* showing the (best-posed) photos to actual participants in the famous 1971 study. That's sort of like showing students the exam questions ahead of time, or using exam questions that 70 percent of students answered correctly the previous semester, inevitably leading to a higher average on the next exam. Without such preselection, according to Russell, accuracy rates could drop to 30–40 percent (just slightly higher than chance levels in multiple-choice guessing).

The fact that these facial expressions were mostly posed and not spontaneous constituted a separate problem. It was as if I asked you to show me a look of anger, and then I snapped a photo of you. Then I showed your photo to others and asked them to decide which of the basic emotions you were feeling. Notice the situational factor that caused your facial expression. You were not feeling anger. You were doing what you were asked, and probably in a way that would be commonly understood. But what if you were not asked to pose? Would your natural "anger" face still look that way? Not especially. Using spontaneous expressions (verified to have arisen from particular emotions) yielded accuracy rates as low as 13 percent and sometimes no higher than chance levels.

So if someone looked at such a photo of you in which you were posing anger and guessed that you were feeling anger, that would be wrong and would represent the FAE. It may happen sometimes in daily life that you do pose emotional expressions without really feeling the emotion, depending on where you are, whom you're talking to and why, what the social scripts might be, or who's taking the photo and why. In general, the presence of an observer and other contextual factors can elicit an expression without the emotion that many would perceive in it. Contextual factors can also inhibit expressions despite the presence of an emotion.

Response

Ekman questioned the validity of Russell's statements. In particular, Ekman wrote that he hadn't been preselecting faces that would get the best accuracy results per se but rather faces that fit a set of "a priori specified facial configurations." The point was that Ekman's theory was more narrow than Russell led us to believe. Ekman wrote that he and his colleagues did "not maintain that every expression will be universally understood" and that "we had theoretical and empirical reason to expect that certain expressions would be universal, and of course, we selected just those stimuli."

Rebuttal

Russell disagreed that he had misled readers about Ekman's theory. Russell suggested that what Ekman said *now* about the theory was different than what Ekman had said in the past. Basically, Ekman was never a 100 percent universalist, but according to Russell, Ekman now claimed to be more middle-ground than his writing had shown him to be in the past. Russell wrote, "Of course, positions evolve, and Ekman like anyone else can change his mind."

But I can tell you that introductory textbooks still largely follow Ekman's pre-1994 conclusions. That is part of why discussing this 1994–95 debate is still relevant. It's not just that I wanted to provide a small taste of academic debate, which some readers might find fascinating. It's also that this debate is not over, that many textbooks and popular press authors don't even let you know there *is* a debate, and that if anything, Ekman's side might be losing this debate. In the broad field of emotion, Ekman and Russell probably agreed on more than they disagreed, but the disagreements were heated.

Summing Up the Debate

So there's a little bit of soap opera in academics. I didn't even mention the disagreements between Russell and Ekman on who said what in personal conversations prior to the publications. The bottom line was that the powerhouses of emotion research were in disagreement. Reading about Ekman's work in Malcolm Gladwell's *Blink* gave the opposite impression, that there is an accepted and simple reality in the research of reading emotions from faces. No. Not only do the emotion researchers disagree, but they can get quite personal about it.

When submitting my manuscripts to journals for consideration, I've had my fair share of reviewers who commit the FAE and get personal. These reviewers seem to think they can read my mind when they make negative judgments as to my motives and intentions. It is an unfortunate behind-the-scenes possibility in the anonymous peer review process. But to see such personal exchanges in actual publications is relatively rare. I highlight this issue to convey how serious and not-agreed-upon the issue of facial decoding was and still is.

UPDATE: SITUATIONAL CAUSES OF FACIAL EXPRESSIONS

Since the 1994–95 debate, most of Russell's concerns have received additional evidence, and most emotion researchers are giving those concerns credence. For example, spontaneous facial expressions continue to yield much lower accuracy rates in facial decoding compared to posed facial expressions. And just as multiple-choice exam items are harder when there are more choices, and short-answer items are harder for most students than multiple-choice items, emotion researchers have found lower accuracy rates in facial decoding when participants are given more emotions to choose from or are given no preset choices at all.[28]

And new evidence-based concerns have emerged from Russell and others that further detract from a universalist view of facial expressions as emotional readouts and further point to the importance of context in reading faces. The number of articles and book chapters pointing this direction is overwhelming.[29] I will highlight a few points in the space that remains.

Let me be clear. For the average person, I believe that some emotions do lead to particular facial expressions, and some facial expressions do reflect the assumed emotion. There is this evolutionary kernel of truth, and the accuracy rates in facial decoding are often above levels of chance (especially when the faces are posed and not spontaneous). But there are many more counterexamples than suggested by Ekman and other emotion researchers from that time. And accuracy in facial decoding is much lower than most people thought. Newer studies with improved methods show even lower accuracy rates.

What I am adding to this emerging picture is how the FAE is involved. One of the reasons facial decoders get it wrong is because facial decoders sometimes overlook the context and underestimate the role of situational factors. Even if you believe that strong emotions are expressed facially, recall the point of logic from chapter 1: A implies B does not mean that B implies A. Even if emotions did produce certain facial expressions 100 percent of the time (which they don't), that does not mean that certain facial expressions necessarily reflect the assumed emotion. In other words, situational factors (and not just internal emotions) can influence someone's facial expression, so facial decoders become less accurate when they commit the FAE and overlook those factors. What are the primary situational factors that can influence someone's facial expression?

Mimicry and the Role of the Observer

As you observe someone's face and try to infer the emotion being felt, a common situational factor that can be overlooked is you yourself, the observer. You are part of the situation of the individual you're observing. Humans are social animals. We hang out with each other, and we influence each other's behaviors, even if we're just watching. In general, we try to present ourselves to each other in socially desirable ways, even if it's not how we usually are. We also tend to automatically mimic certain behaviors, including some facial expressions—it's called the "chameleon effect." Someone's foot tapping or shaking, for example, might not reflect nervousness but rather the fact that they saw your foot shaking first.[30]

In decoding the face of someone who can see you, if you infer emotion based solely on someone's facial expression, then you overlook the potential effects of your own presence and your own face. Your own facial expressions can cause similar facial expressions in others. In particular, individuals tend to smile in response to your smile without necessarily feeling happy. Angry faces can lead to angry faces without underlying anger.

In at least some cases, this mirror response is even run by its own set of neurons, called mirror neurons. And individuals often mimic your face automatically and without conscious awareness. Facial mimicry is so automatic that individuals even mimic faces they don't realize they've seen. Studies have flashed images of faces too fast to consciously register, and facial mimicry still results. In sum, you might smile without realizing you're smiling in response to a stimulus you don't realize you've seen. Theoretically, two individuals can each smile at each other without feeling happy, knowing why, or realizing that they have smiled.[31]

And facial mimicry itself can be influenced by other situational factors, such as your relationship to the person you're observing, whether the situation is one of cooperation or competition, and how much power you have relative to the person you're observing. In particular, you are more likely to mimic someone with whom you share some group membership. For example, we are more likely to mimic the faces of political leaders who share our political attitudes. So if people show a happy or angry face in photos from a campaign rally or town hall meeting, it might not be because they are happy or angry but rather because there is a nearby politician who is wearing such a face. If the politician is not captured by the photograph, then we would be unaware of a relevant situational factor in judging the people who are.[32]

Social Motives and the Role of Other People

Even before the Russell-Ekman debate, Alan Fridlund held a very different perspective from Ekman called the "behavioral ecology view." Fridlund and Ekman did not have an outright back-and-forth debate within a journal like Russell and Ekman did, but Fridlund believed Ekman was wrong. And unlike the Russell-Ekman debate, which seemed to get missed by the popular press, the Fridlund-Ekman debate eventually got noticed. In 2000, the *Toronto Star* conveyed Ekman's basic view that a happy face reflects a happy person and then announced that "Fridlund turns Ekman's argument on its head."[33]

Fridlund suggested that facial expressions reflect not emotions but rather social motives triggered by and directed toward other people in the situation (beyond mimicry). As such, facial expressions are social tools or communications to facilitate interaction with these other people. A sad face can elicit concern and concessions, an angry face can get enemies to back down, and a smile has too many potential purposes and non-emotional causes to list here. Fridlund's overarching point was that facial displays depend on the social context and the social role you're playing. Among many supportive results is that bowlers typically don't smile upon making a spare or strike until they turn and exchange glances with fellow bowlers. The faces for tasting salty or sweet foods, or for smelling good or bad odors, are nonexistent or indistinguishable while we are alone compared to with other people. Even babies' smiles toward their mothers depend on whether the mother is looking in the baby's direction.[34]

In 2006, Fridlund and Russell even teamed up to highlight these points and to convey the importance of social context in explaining facial expressions.[35] These authors suggested that automatically broadcasting one's true internal state (in one's facial expression or any behavior) would work against the survival of one's species. Thus, the idea of facial expressions being natural emotional readouts might feel like common sense but is naïve. Fridlund and Russell painted a broader picture of humans as seeing emotions everywhere, behind the actions of even nonhuman entities, even inanimate events such as the "angry storm." This concept of anthropomorphism often enters my mind during high-stress traffic when others with me personify cars, as in "That car is stupid" and "What does that car think it's doing?" People are often inclined to see traits and internal states even when they cannot exist.

Some researchers who have compared Fridlund's and Ekman's theories have shown there is at least as much support for Fridlund's theory as Ekman's.[36] Very recent studies have added support for Fridlund's views, including an article titled "Weep and Get More," which outlined the strategic use of expressing sadness in negotiations.[37] However, Fridlund's theory doesn't fit our common sense. His theory specifies a role for context and communicates an avoiding-the-FAE message to pay more attention to the context, whereas Ekman's theory of seeing emotions in faces fits the FAE nicely. I suggest that the counterintuitive message in Fridlund's and Russell's work is partly why it does not get the same popular press attention as Ekman's.

Among Ekman's responses to Fridlund, Ekman contended that people's smiling behavior while alone disproves or limits Fridlund's theory. How can we be sending a social signal in our smile when there's no one else around to see it? But Fridlund and others have shown what social psychology has stated for decades—that people can be influenced by not only the real but also the imagined presence of other people. People need not be in the room with you to influence your thoughts and behavior, especially your smile.[38]

The Role of Culture

As discussed at length in the previous chapter, nonverbal behaviors can be shaped by one's culture. Even Ekman acknowledged that there are different display rules in different cultures for expressing emotions, although Russell has suggested that maybe Ekman relied on display rules as an after-the-fact rescue from low accuracy rates in decoding faces from some cultures (as opposed to Ekman predicting particular display rules ahead of time).[39]

Aside from known differences in how people express emotions in different cultures, many researchers have shown that there is an in-group advantage in facial decoding, meaning we are better at reading emotions from faces when the face belongs to someone from the same culture as our own. This research strongly reflects the causal role of culture in facial expressions. So you could attribute a particular emotion to someone based on a facial expression and be wrong by overlooking or being unaware of the culture of the individual who is making the face.[40]

The Role of Random Context

When Michelle Obama was accused of showing anger in a split-second photograph that went viral in 2013, the photographer Roberto Schmidt had to get online to assure everyone that the First Lady's face was "captured by chance" and did not reflect anger. In a more recent viral photo, Beyoncé was accused of shooting a contemptuous side-eye at a man two seats away at a professional basketball game. After captions started popping up like "Never Look Beyoncé in the Eyes, You Fool," this man quickly cleared it up in a tweet. He wrote that Beyoncé was "beyond polite." Another overreaction to a celebrity's face in a photo.[41]

Photographs necessarily allow for such random fraction-of-a-second facial movements to give the wrong impression. People also have to blink regularly, and so some portion of photographs randomly catch the eyes closed, but that doesn't mean the poser is sleeping, tired, or dopey. In fact, it might be the flash of the camera that caused the badly timed blink.

There are so many possible random or miscellaneous factors that can influence a facial expression. Are they tears of joy or tears of sorrow? It depends on the context. In a rare introductory psychology textbook, the authors went beyond Ekman and showed an out-of-context photograph of this classic puzzle, the face of a sobbing man. The photo was labeled "Two emotions, one expression," and students were asked to guess which emotion. Seeing the picture with fuller context on a later page no doubt surprised many readers. I once watched a YouTube clip of a small girl

132

receiving her first puppy. She bawled and bawled—heart-wrenching and depressing, were it not for that little fact of the puppy that caused her so much joy. Another introductory textbook showed former Senator Jim Webb screaming with a scowl, but the fuller context showed that he was enthused and happily pumping up the audience at a political rally.[42]

In general, researchers have varied social contexts and observed changes in facial displays independent of underlying emotions. And there are, of course, some general patterns that have emerged concerning the effect of situation on facial expression. For example, it turns out that a more intense situation makes facial reactions harder to recognize. Sofia Wenzler and colleagues wrote that "emotional responses during extreme situations diverge from standard basic emotion" and that their and others' findings "demonstrate the ambiguity of extreme facial expressions and highlight the critical importance of context in emotion perception."[43]

IN SUM

When I began preparations to write this book, I knew the FAE was part of why we misread nonverbal behaviors, but I had little idea how enormous the nonverbal-decoding literature had become and how much facial-decoding researchers had come to focus on context. I had been a product of classic psychology training, meaning that I was taught that Ekman's FAE-prone theory ruled. So I decided I had to include at least one chapter on what I learned from the nonverbal-decoding literature, which quickly became two (packed) chapters. It's not enough. The importance of context goes beyond what I have conveyed. And Ekman's ideas have evolved since his classic work in the 1970s, including in his current work on microexpressions. But I have tried to lay out the basic sides with a few details in between.

In my view, since the 1990s, the research has moved away from Ekman's ideas and now resides at a middle ground. Some introductory psychology textbooks are finally showing some signs of this move. In 2000, the *Toronto Star* got it right in stating that "many researchers are now occupying the middle ground, agreeing that expressions are somehow connected to the emotions being felt, but at the same time admitting that the connection isn't as tight as Ekman has argued."[44]

Emotion researchers have stated that facial expressions can be about emotions or can be about something outside the person, but there has definitely been a shift to outside the person. In a recent article titled "Context Is More Powerful Than We Think," Russell and colleagues concluded by saying that "the facial expression may be emotionally relevant (a frown might indicate a negative situation) or it may not be (a frown might be the result of it being too sunny outside)." The data from this study did not particularly support Russell's own developing theory of emotion, leading him and coauthors to suggest the possibility that "a person's facial expression alone most reliably tells you that the person is reacting to something in the situation; thus, the message is that the situation is worth investigating."[45] This is as clear an avoiding-the-FAE message as I could state myself.

Fridlund's main contribution to the understanding of facial expressions has been his focus on our social role with respect to other people. My next chapter focuses on social roles.

SOCIAL ROLES: POPES DON'T BOUNCE

All the world's a stage, And all the men and women merely players; They have their exits and their entrances, and one man in his time plays many parts.

—Shakespeare, playwright

I am not Spock.   —Leonard Nimoy, actor

We've begun to raise daughters more like sons . . . but few have the courage to raise our sons more like our daughters.

—Gloria Steinem, journalist and activist

Why don't we see more grown men cry? Why don't elementary school teachers curse at their students? Why is it newsworthy that Barbra Streisand, Amanda Seyfried, Laurence Olivier, and several other top actors and comedians have stage fright or extreme shyness?[1] Why was there such interest and shock when people learned that the head of the Catholic Church, Pope Francis, had worked as a nightclub bouncer? (And he owned a Harley or two!)[2]

The likely answer is an ever-present but largely invisible social force that affects people's behaviors every day. That force is social roles. Big boys don't cry. Teachers of children have teacherly rules to follow (even if unspoken). Top actors must be communicative and expressive and must act (in front of people!) to make their living. Popes don't bounce (or ride

Harleys), or at least we don't expect them to. In the world of social roles, people behave in expected ways.

There are gender roles, family roles, work roles, and others. Specific roles include those of man, woman, friend, significant other, spouse, daughter, son, mother, father, doctor, nurse, janitor, banker, monk, store manager, salesperson, math teacher, principal, Apple Store genius, cashier, truck driver, student, patient, customer, police officer, firefighter, neighbor, and bystander. Some social roles are much more defined than others, and some individuals' dual or multiple roles can conflict (such as mothers who work).[3] But all roles can affect behavior through social norms or expectations—sometimes unspoken understandings and other times outright rules. Most of us conform to these rules. Consciously or unconsciously, through observational learning or conditioning, most of us go along with how we're *supposed* to be as part of certain roles.

Even our facial expressions are not immune to this process, as discussed in the previous chapter. Alan Fridlund took on Paul Ekman in claiming that facial expressions are caused not by emotions but rather by our social roles and social interactions with other people. James Russell more explicitly wrote that "society provides rules about appropriate facial behaviour in different situations (downcast eyes during a funeral, whether sad or not), and we try to conform to those rules."[4]

Fulfilling some roles is not always about simple conformity—it's how society functions. Parents can more easily get jobs compared to young children. Salespeople make more money if they're nice to the customer. Police officers and firefighters are better trained for emergencies compared to most bystanders. Math teachers know more math than their students. And we expect parents to pay the bills, salespeople to be nice, trained professionals to help in emergencies, and math teachers to teach the math. It's part of their roles, and it's just how things work. A major theory for sex differences says they're not primarily caused by evolution or biological differences but rather by the "differing restrictions and opportunities that a society maintains for its men and women"—that's gender roles.[5]

So we generally try to fulfill roles and expectations in our job, our family, our gender, and many other contexts. We "look" sad at funerals, even if we're not. We're nice to customers who spend money at our business, even if they are difficult. Men tend to keep their tears to themselves (at least in many cultures). Teachers watch their language in the classroom. Actors ham it up.

But when we see people fulfilling their roles, it's hard to separate the role from the person. We can't see a perceived obligation or the felt pressure from social norms. All we see is the behavior that, not coincidentally, fits the role. Thus, these social roles can bias and oversimplify our impressions of these other people, so that we commit the FAE—we underestimate the influence of the role and overestimate how much these people personally possess role-consistent traits or intentions. The man who doesn't openly cry at a funeral might be perceived as less emotional than he really is. Teachers might be perceived as more refined than they actually are. Actors might be perceived as more extroverted, and popes as more popely.

A recent viral photo illustrated how the female cashier at a bar might be perceived as more "nice" (that is, sexually interested in male patrons) than she actually is. In an effort to reduce the number of male patrons who hit on female workers at a bar called Beer Cellar Exeter, a sign was put up at the register titled "Why the female cashier is being nice to you." The two choices were "She is uncontrollably sexually attracted to you" and "Because that's literally her f------ job you cretin." The box in front of the latter choice was filled in as the correct answer. Her boss wanted her to behave that way. An effective approach to educating patrons about the FAE.[6]

Psychologist Mark Alicke and colleagues designed a study in which a school principal similarly had to do what his boss expected of him. The principal organized a 1996 symposium on the topic of hiring gay teachers. Faculty, staff, and community members submitted numerous speeches on both sides of the issue, but the principal only selected speeches on one side (pro- or anti-gay). In one condition, the principal made these selections of his own accord. In another condition, the school superintendent insisted on those selections. Even in the latter following-orders condition, participants still assumed the principal was pro-gay after selecting pro-gay speeches and anti-gay after selecting anti-gay speeches.[7]

So we tend to behave in ways consistent with our roles (or as ordered), even if customers, students, or other observers don't see it right away. A side effect of this whole process is that social-role violations can be surprising, funny, or newsworthy, as in the story of a pope who was a bouncer. In the animated film *Shrek*, Princess Fiona regularly violated parts of her gender role to comical effect, as when she single-handedly beat up Robin Hood and his men. Rodney Dangerfield's history professor in the comedy *Back to School* violated his teacher role when he cursed and screamed in students' faces (this professor was played by comedian Sam Kinison, known for his angry preacher-style rants).

Don't get me wrong—I'm not saying that Pope Francis is not popely. I'm saying that Pope Francis and many other public figures may be more complicated than they appear in public. One man in his time plays many parts (as does one woman). All of us are probably more complicated than we appear on the immediate surface, but when our behaviors are being influenced by an established role, it's even harder to see beneath that surface. Shrek spelled it out for Donkey: ogres are like onions.

Of course, some of us try harder to fit our roles than others, and some of us feel the role constraints more strongly. So some of us might be especially misunderstood. Maybe it's because we're conscientious about meeting perceived responsibilities, or maybe it's because we're insecure and eager to please. Maybe in the case of work roles, we logically see the benefits of every member of an organization doing their part, or maybe we're just desperate to keep our job to provide for our families or to pay for school. Maybe in the case of gender roles, we simply went through stronger gender conditioning as we grew up, or maybe we experience greater punishment from those around us for stepping outside our role (more true for men than for women). We may take our role very seriously, or we may just project an image very consistent with our role. In all these cases, we would publicly follow role-based expectations more strongly.

And for some roles, it's not about trying to fit the role but rather about the freedoms or opportunities the role affords. Men and women have different opportunities in most cultures (men typically have more opportunities than women).[8] As I will discuss, there are many self-identified shy actors and comedians who are outgoing in their jobs, sometimes outlandishly so, but only under the spotlight because they say the stage provides a freedom. But for the most part, social roles act as constraints or strong guides for behavior.

THE FACULTY ROLE

As a teacher, one of the constraints or influences I feel is on my language. There's growing pressure in universities to avoid words that can be taken as microaggressions (see chapter 2). I also try very hard not to swear in the classroom (who am I kidding—I never swear in the classroom). The same goes for my behavior during department meetings and when I sit down with deans and chancellors. I perceive my at-work role to be a well-mannered professional.

During class participation, students sometimes swear or use vulgarities, and when I summarize or paraphrase what they said for the rest of the class, I usually insert the nonvulgar equivalent. When I do occasionally repeat the student's exact words, there is usually a small uproar from the class, so I am quick to point my finger at the student and claim that I am only repeating what he or she said (followed by a quick low-key apology to that student).

If I really want to emphasize a point, or if I want to refer to something that is untrue or stupid, then the word "crap" might occasionally escape from me. And in this one story I've come to tell about me and golf, I refer to that "damned" golf ball that I can never get into the air. Immediately afterward in such cases, I usually offer an apology for my language (partly serious, but partly to get some laughs and play into my role).[9]

Once my students and I have spent several class periods together, they might think they know me in this regard. My unspoken no-swearing-no-vulgarity rule might paint a picture of me as a polite and refined individual. Maybe other things I do or how I dress further contributes to such an image (I generally wear ties at the beginning of a semester to help establish my role). I'm relatively certain that most of my students have this refined, polite picture of me, based on a hypothetical I raise every semester in my social psychology course. In this hypothetical, after noting some constraints on a teacher's language, I suggest the possibility that outside the classroom, I could be a foul-mouthed troublemaker and a really good swearer. The burst of laughter is sometimes deafening. I'm not confessing here to being a covert potty mouth, but I could be, outside the classroom (and off university grounds!).

Although some faculty swear during class time (perhaps more likely among tenured than tenure-track professors), many, like me, probably perceive swearing as inappropriate or not ideal in their role as teacher, mentor, or department member. And even the instructors who are class-time swearers might swear more often, more loudly, and more colorfully outside the classroom or department meetings. I'm not saying that every faculty member should behave a particular way on school grounds. If you're a teacher, of course you can decide how you want to behave. But when we observe the behavior of others working within an established role, it's hard, if not impossible, to know for sure what they're "really like."

Under the question "Do Teachers Swear?" at Yahoo! Answers, some commenters affirmed that teachers "seem so perfect" and "sure they swear just not in school." One commenter's dad was a teacher who "swore like a trooper at home . . . in 2 languages." Another offered, "Wat do ya [sic] think the staff room is for." A self-identified teacher wrote, "We do in our heads more times than you'd care to think!"[10]

Faculty also have to evaluate each other as part of the faculty role.

Tenured faculty in particular evaluate tenure-track faculty based on established standards, and so this role of evaluator might make some tenured faculty seem overly critical, nitpicky, or even mean. Although some faculty may indeed be all these things, the role effect might bias or exaggerate such impressions. Bosses and supervisors everywhere might be misjudged as more critical or hard-nosed than they really are because of the role of evaluator. Duties can be confused for traits.

Elliot Aronson, famous social psychologist and author of *The Social Animal*, seemed to cite this evaluator role when he described a potentially common role conflict among faculty. He described a fellow professor and friend whom students thought was warm and fuzzy but colleagues thought was critical and mean. Aronson asked,

> Who has the right impression—the students or the professional colleagues? Is he really a tough critical person who is simply putting on an act in front of students? Or is he really a warm and caring individual who pretends to be tough when confronting other psychologists? These are the wrong questions. The fact is my friend is capable of a wide range of behaviors. Some social roles tend to pull behavior from one part of the spectrum; other social roles tend to pull behavior from a different part of the spectrum.[11]

For Aronson, students who think they know their professor based only on the classroom context, in terms of perceiving stable personality traits (usually consistent with the teacher role), are at great risk of the FAE. Faculty who think they know their colleague based only on work contexts are similarly at risk of the FAE.

In the introduction, I mentioned a soft-spoken professor I know who played on a big-city roller derby team. And there's the history professor who was an American Ninja Warrior. Among other real-life teachers who can surprise their students outside the classroom is the "baby whisperer" from California. Math teacher and Vietnam veteran Jim O'Connor is authoritative and "mean" in the classroom. He explained that discipline is necessary for learning in a "class full of 32 teenage boys." But he is known at a nearby hospital for his volunteer work cuddling sick babies. A nurse there described him as a "natural-born cuddler" because of his ability to "get the crabbiest baby to calm down." One of O'Connor's students happened upon his math teacher at the hospital during a school blood drive and was "amazed to discover his stern teacher's softer side." Word of the cuddling math teacher spread quickly through the school.[12]

THE SHY, EXTROVERTED, LEAD-ACTRESS MATH STUDENT

Reversing perspectives, how do faculty view their students? Are there student roles? I once had a student who sat in the back of my classroom and never spoke all semester long. This course was in mathematics and well before I received my doctorate in psychology (I was a math teacher first). To the best of my recollection, this student never raised her hand, never answered any of my questions posed to the class, and never chatted with classmates. I don't recall telling anyone that this student was a shy individual, but if someone had asked me for my assessment of her, I probably would have said as much.

So when I was attending a university play later that semester and saw my shy student in the lead role, passionately and dynamically professing and yelling and stomping on stage, I was blown away. On some level, I had committed the FAE. I had explained my student's lack of participation and talking in class as reflective of a shy and timid personality. Oops.

But who's to say. Maybe I was still right and this student was shy, and it was only on stage in this one situation that she was outgoing and dynamic. If I look at her onstage performance and now believe she is an extroverted and outgoing person, I could be at equal risk of the FAE. As I alluded to earlier, there have been famous actors and comedians who have self-disclosed that they are actually quite shy or socially anxious and that it's the role of "actor" that allows them the freedom to openly express a variety of traits.

Brad Pitt reportedly "likes to play outgoing characters to break away from his natural shyness." Jim Carrey became the class clown in high school precisely because he was extremely shy and the clown role helped him make friends. The parents of Alexis Bledel (from *Gilmore Girls* and *Sisterhood of the Traveling Pants*) enrolled her in theater programs when she was young precisely because of her shyness: "She admits to still being shy, but is able to rise to the occasion when necessary for her career." Carol Burnett "describes herself as a shy person who is able to perform only when in character." Barbra Streisand has used a teleprompter and anti-anxiety drugs to address her stage fright. Sonny and Cher were supposed to be just Cher, but Cher's stage fright led her to ask Bono along. Despite David Letterman's "relaxed and outgoing" appearance, he was "known for carefully planning and orchestrating his show as a way of coping with his own shyness." Maybe most top performers are extroverted, but when trying to explain a performer's onstage behavior, the FAE can reduce our accuracy.[13]

So I'll never know for sure what, if any, stable traits my shy, extroverted, lead-actress math student possessed. But based on my classroom experience with her, I wouldn't have guessed she could pull off an onstage lead performance. When covering the FAE in my social psychology class, I usually take the opportunity to tell my students that I don't make any assumptions about their traits if my only interaction with them is in the classroom context. "It's too risky," I tell them, at least in part because of this role effect, one form of the FAE.

Similarly, counselors and other clinicians only interact with their clients in therapy and probably in one office. What a tricky situation. Therapists are trained to read people. But beyond the risks in thinking you can nonverbally decode someone or detect deception, even if you're an "expert" (see chapters 3 and 4), reading someone with whom you interact in only one type of situation is categorically risky. Lee Ross and Richard Nisbett urge caution and humility even for professionals.[14] I'm not certain whether there are accepted rules for the role of "good client," but that doesn't mean there are no rules in the minds of individual clients.

According to clinical psychologist Ryan Howes, "good clients" pay on time, do their homework, respect therapy rules, and are "thrilled with every session." These clients try to be polite, nonconfrontational, and deferential to the therapist's expertise, all of which can result in not sharing how they really feel if they are confused or upset by the therapist's words or behavior. Howes cited research showing that a large majority of clients acknowledge lying to their therapist, especially through omission.[15] I understand that clinicians might need to make best guesses about their clients to administer therapy, but they're only best guesses at risk of the FAE. I will return to this topic in chapter 8 when I discuss victim blaming in psychotherapy.

And I understand that even teachers sometimes have to make best guesses about their students' traits, in deciding whether to call on a student or to nominate a student for a school committee or an award. However, for any teachers reading now, my advice is to be careful (if you are not already).

Just because a student seems shy in your class doesn't mean he or she cannot psychologically handle an in-class question, although I personally don't call on students who do not volunteer. I don't try to read my students in this regard (see chapters 3 and 4 about the risks in thinking you can nonverbally decode).[16] I have a no-forced-participation policy in my classrooms. Students decide when and if they want to participate (though I actively encourage and structure out-loud participation). And just because a student seems shy in your class doesn't mean he or she cannot handle a high-stress activity outside class or one that requires prolonged discussions with other people (or even one that requires acting on stage!).

And just because a student seems outgoing or laid-back in class doesn't mean that he or she *can* psychologically handle being put on the spot during class time or being picked for an in-class demo. I observed an instructor once who put an unknowing student on display at the front of class to demonstrate a psychological effect. Afterward, the instructor told me that this student was laid-back and that he could handle it. But the instructor did not touch base with the student afterward (as is standard in a psychology study as part of debriefing). Even normally laid-back students can have bad days or insecurities when it comes to public behavior, or they might just be playing a laid-back role for their friends in class.

THE STUDENT ROLE

The student role is complicated and evolving. There can be social norms to be cool and laid-back, to answer questions in class and shoot for straight A's, or to not talk at all and just get by. Different students feel pressure or freedom to behave in different ways. According to wikiHow, the first step for "how to behave in class" is to "follow the expectations," which includes the advice to "be quiet."[17] Shy-seeming students might be going for well-behaved. Indeed, teachers may encourage quiet to maintain order, though most think quiet students need to overcome their "shyness."[18] I had a student once who I knew was academically enthusiastic and talkative based on his visits to my office, but who was relatively quiet in class. He explained to me at some point that he was purposely holding back to let other students speak.

The wikiHow staff created another site for students to explain "how to be smart and cool at the same time."[19] Indeed, being academically engaged or performing well in school does not typically go hand in hand with being "cool" or popular. In fact, it tends to be the opposite, at least in American samples. High grades can lead to the unwanted labels of "nerd" or "geek."[20]

Researchers have shown that the student role can depend on a student's gender, race, or socioeconomic status. Mary Reda, author of *Between Speaking and Silence: A Study of Quiet Students*, asserted that "racism, sexism, and classism often work to silence some voices."[21] For example, girls typically feel less welcome than boys in high-level math and some natural science courses. They're in the numerical minority and know they're not expected to do as well. As one girl shared, they can be directly teased for just being in that classroom, as in "You're a girl. Girls can't do physics." This general sense of the female role in science can lead female students and female scientists to disengage from their work and even quit altogether.[22]

On the other hand, in an engineering program with only 7 percent women, twenty-four-year-old Rebeca Abrantes made lemonade from lemons and succeeded in getting five of her male classmates to be her bridesmaids at her wedding. She said that with so few girls, "it's not like [she] had a lot of choices." She and her male friends "hammed it up" at her bachelorette party—the photos went viral.[23]

For black students, engaging with school and performing well is sometimes criticized by other black students as "acting white." When poor white students perform well, it's "acting high and mighty."[24] Psychologist Claude Steele, who triggered an explosion of research in the 1990s on why marginalized groups underperform, suggested that many black students disengage from or disidentify with school because of group norms. Steele wrote,

> Once disidentification occurs in a school, it can spread like the common cold. Blacks who identify and try to achieve embarrass the strategy by valuing the very thing the strategy denies the value of. Thus pressure to make it a group norm can evolve quickly and become fierce. Defectors are called "oreos" or "incognegroes." One's identity as an authentic black is held hostage, made incompatible with school identification.[25]

Researchers actually debate how prevalent this anti-school pressure is for black students, because the large-sample evidence is mixed. But even Karolyn Tyson, one of the strongest critics of the concept, acknowledged that some black students do experience this pressure to underperform. In one study, Tyson and colleagues studied eight schools and found one with obvious examples of this pressure. One interviewed girl said,

The problem comes from society because it is ingrained in us that blacks must act, speak, dress a certain way and if you deviate from those expected norms your blackness is questioned. I question it myself. I'm being denounced and rejected by blacks and that's ridiculous. . . . I came in here timid because I am black, and I was the only black person in my honors classes.

That school's personnel also noticed the problem. One adult commented that in the school culture, it's not "cool for minority students to be smart." A school counselor said that some black students "did not like being in honors courses because often they were the only ones" and because they felt that other black students would "look at them as if they were acting white, not recognizing that you could be smart and black."[26]

Beyond this research area is a much larger literature on stereotype threat—largely credited to Claude Steele. Stereotype threat is basically the anxiety or discomfort felt by minority group members because of society's negative expectations about them. Stereotype threat, like some social-role pressures, can cause girls and black students to underperform. Observing these students and attributing any low performance solely to low ability would overlook this societal pressure. Although this mistaken attribution would constitute the FAE, the stereotype-threat literature goes beyond the scope of this chapter.

My point has been that we can commit the FAE in explaining people's behavior by overlooking the power of social roles. When we try to explain why girls drop out of their science majors or black students perform poorly in school, we might just assume these students don't have the ability. If a black student seems timid in an honors class, we might assume she is timid by nature or is underprepared.

When I ask my social psychology students why they might seem shy in class even if they are normally extroverted people, they usually come up with answers relating to the student role. They also note that quiet behavior might reflect low interest in school, low interest in that particular course, concern about current circumstances at home, or dislike of their instructor. Mary Reda wrote, "Let's face it: Sometimes students are quiet because they have a bad teacher."[27]

In the example of my lead-actress math student, maybe she didn't talk in class because it was a math classroom. Unfortunately, math anxiety is as epidemic as ever these days, especially for American girls. But math anxiety won't get in the way of an onstage performance.

THE ULTIMATE ROLE EFFECT

So knowing whether an onstage performer would be talkative or quiet in a classroom is hard to say. What about other personal traits of the actor? When inferring traits in actors more broadly, many viewers think the actor is like the character or role that the actor is scripted to play. I refer to this bias as the ultimate role effect, and it's another case of the FAE.

Alison Arngrim, who played the nasty Nellie Oleson on the television series *Little House on the Prairie*, has said that even years after the series ended, people seem to think she is a nasty person who hates Melissa Gilbert (the actress who played her onscreen rival, Laura Ingalls). According to tv.com, one of Arngrim's replies to such negative perceptions of her was as follows: "So you can stop asking me if I really hate her [Melissa Gilbert] in real life. Sheesh. It was a TV show, people. People still think I'm really Nellie, that I tease stuttering children and make fun of crippled people."

For the record, Arngrim has conveyed that she and Melissa Gilbert were close friends. Arngrim has also dispelled myths about Michael Landon, who played Charles Ingalls on the show. She said, "He wasn't at all like the character he played on TV."[28]

Perhaps it is high praise for the actor when viewers commit the FAE. The actor did such a good job pretending to be someone else that the viewers seemed to forget it was just a role. Some viewers might defend their impressions by reasoning that an actor cannot play a role so well unless the actor is already like the character. Well, it makes sense that actors who are like their characters can play those characters well. A implies B. But that doesn't mean that B implies A, that if you see a great performance, then the actor must have already been like the character. No, that would be the converse error. Indeed, some actors study their roles for months, and practice the mannerisms and accents, to convince viewers that the actors are somebody else. Makeup, wardrobe, and scenery of course add to the illusion.

Research has verified beyond anecdotes that typical viewers are prone to the FAE when describing actors. The FAE occurs even when the viewer has seen the same actor in both positive and negative roles—it is usually the more recent role that biases viewers. The bottom line is that most of us cannot disconnect the behavior we observe from the actor (literally) who engages in that behavior, even when it's on the stage or screen.[29]

Leonard Nimoy conveyed this lesson in his book *I Am Not Spock*, which began with an incident at an airport where a mother introduced Nimoy to her child as Spock. Nimoy went on to describe how he personally differed from his role, despite how much people thought of him as Spock.[30] Actress Aubrey Plaza, most known for her deadpan role from the television show *Parks and Recreation*, commented that "once people see you do a character like that, and if they haven't seen you in anything else, they tend to think that's who you are and that's all you can do."[31]

THE SOCIAL-ROLES PARADIGM: PERCEIVING THOSE IN CHARGE

The existence of such roles that people play at work, school, or home has given researchers ample material to test for the FAE. Underestimating the influence of social roles is sometimes called the social-roles effect. Asking viewers to describe the actor behind the scripted role is a very straightforward FAE test—viewers typically underestimate the influence of that role. Assessing voters' tendency to believe what their party's politicians say to them (see chapter 2), despite politicians' role that's almost all about self-presentation and getting votes, is another potential way to show this overlooking-the-role effect.

The teacher's role, as discussed earlier, is about courteous communication and avoiding profanities, but it's also about being smart. My students might think I'm smarter than I actually am. I mean, they're paying to learn from me, and I'm always talking about stuff and sharing knowledge. I also get to ask a lot of questions in class, and obviously I know the answers for questions that I prepare. I'm in charge in class. I have the lectern. The original social-roles paradigm tries to study the effects of this role advantage of having the lectern.

The Original Paradigm

This classic paradigm is more commonly known as the questioner-contestant paradigm or quiz-game paradigm. It is the second-most common way to test for the FAE, after the attitude-attribution paradigm discussed in chapter 1, and it may be more relevant to everyday life. This paradigm tests the degree to which participants overlook the effects of social roles in rating the knowledge level of a person asking questions compared to the person answering those questions.

Lee Ross and colleagues constructed the first questioner-contestant paradigm in 1977. The basic idea is to randomly assign individuals to the role of questioner or contestant (by drawing one of two cards). If you are assigned to the role of questioner, then you have to generate ten trivia questions based on your personal knowledge. These questions should be "challenging but not impossible," and the questioner is to avoid both easy and unfairly difficult questions. Because you can use personal knowledge, it is not likely that your ten questions would look anything like someone else's. The music and sports and movies you like are fair game for creating questions. The books and magazines you've read are fair game.

Then as part of the paradigm, the contestant tries to answer these ten questions. In the original study, the contestants answered an average of four correct. For each incorrect answer, the questioner supplied the correct answer before moving to the next question. Ross and colleagues wrote that they tried to "capture the essential feature of many real-world encounters: One participant defines the domain and controls the style of the interaction and the other must respond within those limits."

Participants observing this scenario typically attribute greater knowledge to the questioner than to the contestant. Scoring just four right out of ten is like an F. It's 40 percent. Major F. And the questioner knew all ten. Whoa—the questioner must be smart. But had the contestant been able to generate questions based on personal knowledge, the questioner probably would have just as much trouble knowing the answers. The questioner had a randomly assigned role advantage that observers seem to overlook. The contestant had a role *dis*advantage. Thus, attributing greater knowledge to the questioner than the contestant constitutes the FAE. Even the contestants themselves thought the questioner was smarter, and both contestants and observers rated the questioner as smarter than the average student.[32]

Replications and Extensions

Many FAE studies since then have used this paradigm. Stéphane Jouffre and Jean-Claude Croizet added a variable of power: In one condition, the questioner exerted even more control over the situation. Specifically, the questioner got to decide how to divvy up the money if the questioner-contestant pair were to win a lottery (a supposed incentive to which all participants had access). In that condition, questioners and contestants showed an even stronger FAE. They attributed even greater knowledge to the questioner and less knowledge to the contestant. The researchers cited a large literature showing how biased our perceptions tend to be toward the powerful versus powerless. But this study was the first extension of that literature to the investigation of the FAE.[33]

In another replication of the questioner-contestant paradigm,

Bertram Gawronski investigated whether observers noticed the difficulty level of the particular questions, and he found that they did. For example, when the questions missed by the contestant were objectively very difficult, the observers rated both questioners and contestants as more knowledgeable (questioners because it's harder to know the answers to very difficult questions, and contestants because not knowing the answers to very difficult questions is more understandable). So it's not like the participants were not paying attention.

Gawronski also found evidence that observers were more likely to take the perspective of the contestant than the questioner, probably because observers would try to answer the questions for themselves. In that case, when the questions are particularly difficult, observers might be more likely to notice the difficulty and to notice the lack of fairness for contestants who didn't get to create questions. So observers might become less prone to the FAE. If I'm losing a game to someone, I might naturally examine the rules of the game more closely. Gawronski's results showed that when the questions were particularly difficult, the observers did indeed commit less FAE, and it was largely due to more generous ratings of the contestants' knowledge level.[34]

Extending this who's-in-charge paradigm to business, Ronald Humphrey randomly assigned participants to the role of manager or clerk in an elaborate office context (three clerks to two managers per session). These participants carried out role-consistent tasks. Managers responded to letters from customers, calculated production costs, reviewed résumés, and trained clerks. The managers were in charge, though the clerks could see that managers had manuals to explain how to be managers. Clerks, on the other hand, fetched files for the managers, sorted mail, and did data entry. Demonstrating the social-roles effect and the FAE, both clerks and managers rated managers higher than clerks on positive traits consistent with the managerial role, even though those roles had been randomly handed out to participants (with manuals for managers!). These traits included leadership, intelligence, and assertiveness.[35]

Before the Role Has Even Been Played

Work roles are not usually randomly handed out in life, but neither are they always earned or based on job-related abilities. Family members of a business owner or company president are sometimes handed high-level positions based on that familial connection. Political leaders, even US presidents, sometimes appoint friends, political allies, or family members to high-level roles even if they have little to no relevant experience. Depending on the position, men and women are often hired or not hired based in part on their sex and regardless of job-related experience, especially for science and leadership roles (men are more likely to be hired than women, even with identical résumés).[36] Then once you're in that role, you might be perceived to have stronger role-consistent qualities than you actually do.

Janet Morgan Riggs took this scenario to a whole new level. She found that before you're actually in a work or family role, even if you're only anticipating taking on that role, observers can still misread you based on that role. Even if your anticipated role is not your choice, observers can misread you. Riggs designed a study in which a married and full-time-employed male or female parent-to-be was deciding whether they would stay employed or stay at home once the baby was born. In one condition, the decision was freely chosen. In another condition, the decision was forced by economic circumstances.

In both conditions (freely chosen and forced), observers rated the parent-to-stay-employed as having stronger traits of agency, such as independence, self-confidence, and assertiveness (compared to the parent-to-stay-home), whereas observers rated the parent-to-stay-home as having stronger traits of communality, such as nurturance, warmth, and selflessness (compared to the parent-to-stay-employed). These results occurred regardless of the sex of the parent-to-be, although male observers strongly approved of women who would stay home.

In general, women's behaviors are more communal and less agentic than men's and are especially perceived as such. As I noted earlier, longtime gender-roles researcher Alice Eagly explained these differences as caused by the different work and family roles that society encourages or allows women and men to play. To automatically assume that such sex differences are caused by inherent biological differences is the FAE. Riggs raised this issue as well.

Riggs described how Eagly and colleagues had shown that both men and women in caregiving roles are perceived as more communal and less agentic than men and women in breadwinning roles. But Riggs wanted to "push the limits" of Eagly's perspective by testing perceptions of men and women who only *anticipate* taking on such roles, even when explicitly forced to do so by circumstances. In Riggs's conclusion, she claimed very strong support for Eagly's gender-role perspective.[37] I concur.

GENDER ROLES

Riggs provided an incredible demonstration of the power of the roles of breadwinner and homemaker. And because men and women so disproportionately hold those roles, it makes sense that observers would misread men as more agentic and less communal than they really are and misread women as less agentic and more communal than they really are. In discussing the real-life extensions of the questioner-contestant and manager-clerk studies, Gawronski similarly noted that people "do not adjust their dispositional inferences to gender roles."[38]

But there is so much more support for Eagly's gender-role perspective. I discussed earlier how there is sex discrimination in hiring. Why men outnumber women or vice versa in some occupations is not just because of naturally developing differences in experience or ability or interest but also because of gender roles or stereotypes in the minds of those who hire. In hiring for a leadership role, even just the smell of male perfume on the résumé (versus female perfume) makes hirers feel more certain in their decision to hire that applicant, whether male or female.[39]

I also discussed how gender roles can bias our explanations for female students' and female professionals' behavior in math and natural science fields. In particular, we tend to underestimate girls' abilities in these domains. Part of this process is that teachers, parents, and peers treat girls differently than boys in some educational contexts.

Misperceiving Newborns

Even right after birth, male and female infants are treated differently, in gender-stereotyped ways. They're dressed in different colors, given different toys, talked to differently, and touched with different degrees of frequency and roughness. Infants are also *perceived* differently depending on their gender label. Even the infants' own parents think they can see differences that do not exist. In general, infants who are labeled "girl" are viewed as smaller, softer, prettier, less strong, less attentive, and less risk-taking than infants who are labeled "boy," even when it's the same infant.

This research is sometimes referred to as the gender-labeling studies. One of the first contributions was the 1975 Baby X study by Carol Seavey and colleagues, appearing in the journal *Sex Roles*. The researchers showed the same three-month-old baby to multiple adults but labeled the baby a different gender for some adults versus others. The adults treated the baby differently depending on the gender label. But the one baby used was female, so Laura Sidorowicz and G. Lunney ran the Baby X paradigm again five years later, using babies of different sexes but still varying the gender label with different adults. Many other similar studies followed, with similar results.[40]

What is notable about some of these studies is that they are true experiments and not correlational studies. They are not simply correlating a person's sex with a person's outcomes. Rather, adults are randomly assigned to conditions in which the same infant is labeled "girl" versus "boy." When the adults start behaving toward and judging this infant differently, we can confidently say the gender label *caused* those differences.

Correlation does not imply causation, but true experiments like these allow for a cause-effect conclusion.

Over time, male and female infants, treated differently because of their assigned sex, become young boys and girls who largely behave as expected. Then they become men and women who show differences in behavior and career goals, but these differences can reflect gender roles and not necessarily any natural biological differences. This process is part of the gender-role theory of sex differences that Eagly and others have supported over decades.

I could not conclude a chapter on social roles without highlighting this theory, but with these few paragraphs, I cannot do justice to the hundreds of relevant studies. The bottom line is that when we try to explain why males and females behave differently or achieve different outcomes, we tend to underestimate the varied influences of gender roles, and that is the FAE.[41]

Biology and Gender Roles Interact

To be fair, the results of the gender-labeling studies were not perfectly consistent. Though the majority of such studies showed at least some evidence of the predicted gender bias in how adults see and treat babies, not all the studies did. Some researchers suggested that the education level of the adult perceivers could make a difference.

To be further fair, there has been a debate as to whether sex differences are primarily caused by biological or sociocultural (that is, gender-role) factors. But to convey this issue in either-or terms is misleading, according to Alice Eagly, because she herself acknowledges a biological role *in addition* to sociocultural causes. It's both. In my view, her decades-long drive has not been to discount biology as much as to get others not to discount gender roles. In essence, she has been trying to reduce the FAE in explaining sex differences.

But it gets even more complicated than biology and culture both playing a role: the biological and sociocultural factors can *interact*, in multiple ways. These interactions are not very straightforward, thus leading popular press authors to often avoid trying to explain them. Eagly and Wood wrote that popular press authors "who write about the engaging gender questions of the day often fail to ground their answers in psychological research" and that even when such authors try to cite the research, they "provide highly condensed summaries of scientific articles, very often presenting mere snippets of complex research programs."[42]

Talking in snippets may be an occupational hazard for such authors, but let me try to give you a taste of an interaction. Among several interactionist models, there is what Eagly and Wood referred to as the "jukebox." It is not their favorite, but the idea is that through evolution and natural selection, humans have inside them many cognitive or behavioral tools or "songs" for specific threats. When such a threat arises in a particular environment, it triggers the song like pressing that button on the jukebox. In this way, different social contexts can hypothetically lead to different behaviors. Because men and women are treated differently or face different threats, they may play different preprogrammed songs.

Why men and women behave and turn out the way they do is indeed complex. Biology and gender roles can intertwine. But my advice is simple. Don't discount gender roles. To do so is inconsistent with the research literatures and constitutes the FAE.

How to Reduce the Power of Gender Roles

At the start of this chapter, I noted a recent line from Gloria Steinem that parents have become more comfortable raising their daughters like sons but are still afraid to raise their sons like daughters. Social science agrees. Some parents may not even realize it's happening, while other parents might see it and regret it but fear that their sons might be bullied at school if they show a feminine side. Journalist Claire Cain Miller discussed more of Steinem's view that it is not enough to open doors for girls. An equitable society needs to do the same for boys.

Miller specifically discussed the economic disadvantages of continuing to restrict the roles boys can play. Miller wrote that boys are not being raised to "succeed in the new, pink economy." Traditionally feminine skills like cooperation and empathy are "increasingly valued in modern-day work and school, and jobs that require these skills are the fastest-growing." Miller asked psychologists and other scientists how we can raise boys to develop beyond the boys-will-be-boys stereotype to foster the more feminine skills. Based on their responses, Miller provided a dozen suggestions to reduce the power of gender roles.

The first suggestion is to undo the adage that big boys don't cry—let boys cry. Before the age of five, boys and girls actually cry to similar degrees, so it's not like there's a biological cap on boys' tears. Another suggestion is to let a boy be himself, even if he likes pink. Color preference is not a biological thing. Apparently, before the mid-twentieth century, pink was for boys and blue was for girls. Wow, that is *Twilight Zone* material. To offset the gender-typed work and family roles I discussed earlier, Miller suggested that male and female parents share in the housework, childcare, and breadwinning roles. Children who see such sharing are less likely to follow gender-typed paths.[43]

I want to emphasize that it is of course up to the parents to decide how to raise their sons, based on their own ideals and depending on whatever circumstances exist for the family. At the same time, there are potential long-term economic benefits of not gender-typing our sons and daughters—of not overly ascribing sex-consistent traits to those who self-identify as man or woman. Beyond economics, there is also the promise of less sex-based prejudice and discrimination and perhaps even less violent crime against women. In general, reducing prejudice reduces intergroup conflict. My next few chapters discuss how reducing the FAE can reduce conflict in many other ways.

CHAPTER 6

DRIVING WITH THE FAE

The one thing that unites all human beings, regardless of age, gender, religion, economic status or ethnic background, is that, deep down inside, we all believe that we are above average drivers.

—Dave Barry, author and columnist

Today after class I was driving . . . and was cut off. Normally, I would step on the gas at an opportune moment; I would return the favor. But today, I thought of the FAE . . . I let it go. I also felt less stress, and I am sure that is healthy.

—anonymous student in a social psychology course

While sitting in a long stalled line of cars, waiting for what feels like minutes to enter a rotary (or roundabout), it may be hard not to get upset at the driver of the red Nissan at the front of the line. This driver is not taking any initiative whatsoever to enter the rotary. Yes, drivers are supposed to yield to rotary traffic, but come on. What an idiot. People have no business driving if they cannot handle a simple rotary. Right? And the mass honking against the rotary blocker begins.

Honking your horn may feel good in some ways. You're trying to take control over a frustrating situation and get Red Nissan to move. You're otherwise going to be late. Or maybe it's just an anger release, or being true to your anger. But part of what's happening is also the FAE, according to social psychologist Sam Sommers, author of *Situations Matter*.

This incident happened to Sommers, and it turned out there was a funeral procession legally barring anyone from entering that rotary. Sommers missed this situational factor until his young daughter brought it to his attention. Classic. I first mentioned this example of the FAE in chapter 2, but now we're in the driving chapter, so here's a little more information.

Sommers was a few cars back and may have been the first to start honking. "What kind of person just sits there with all these cars lined up behind him?" Sommers wrote. "What was he waiting for, an engraved invitation? What the hell, our horns wondered aloud, was wrong with Red Nissan?" Sommers's daughter asked about the noise from the honking. Sommers had to take a deep breath before explaining how stupid this driver was. As the seconds or minutes passed and there was no change, Sommers thought that this guy had an "impotent personality" and that he was a "lost cause," adding, "It's a miracle he's able to dress himself each morning." Sommers was sure that he and his daughter were now going to be late and that he was going to want those minutes back on his "deathbed."[1]

The reader can feel the anger building. According to social scientists who study driving, such frustration, anger, and negative perceptions of fellow drivers are all too common, and they can lead to interpersonal conflict and even road rage against the presumed idiot. That driver at the front of the line could then become a victim. He was already being honked at by several cars—that can be a traumatic experience for some drivers, especially when they are powerless to do anything to stop the honking. This driver seemed to be feeling the stress when, as Sommers described it, the driver started "gesticulating wildly, as if trying to defend the ineptitude through the medium of mime. Still, the honking continued."

Many examples of road rage start out like this story, in which a law-abiding driver is caught in the crosshairs of an angry fellow driver who feels blocked in some way. Although full-fledged road rage may be less frequent than implied by the media, it obviously does occur and receives regular attention from academic researchers and not just the popular press. Much less than blocking a rotary has triggered the wrath of another driver, which can lead to car accidents or direct physical assaults. According to some surveys, a majority of drivers have been a recent victim of road rage.[2] When we try to explain why powerless or innocent victims suffer their fates, whether in an abusive home, in a natural disaster, or on the road, a whole other literature kicks in on victim blaming, which is another significant version of the FAE.

Interpersonal conflict, victim blaming, and driving anger are all in their own right enormous literatures in social science with obvious applications to everyday life. And they all intersect here in examples on the road when the FAE leads to interpersonal conflict, anger, and even road rage, and then when an additional FAE emerges in blaming the victims of the resulting car accidents or assaults. We might blame victims for not doing more to avoid their outcome or even for bringing the outcome on themselves. The assailant or the person responsible for the car accident is especially likely to blame the victim, but so do many outside observers and a surprising number of jury members in resulting court cases (with some help from defense attorneys).

Indeed, the saddest part of this discussion, in my view, is victim blaming. Talk about adding insult to injury. Victims of random misfortune are blamed for their bad luck. The despised rotary blocker didn't purposely time it so that he would be first in that line of cars when the funeral procession arrived. We don't choose the drivers of neighboring cars before getting caught in a neighbor-caused collision. Innocent victims of shootings, especially by police, have been blamed for getting shot. Victim blaming occurs at all levels of seriousness, and the reasons for victim blaming may surprise you.

But first, I further describe how people drive with the FAE and with anger and aggression. I discuss the reasons people give for their questionable or aggressive driving behaviors, and then I provide a fuller list of known situational contributors to aggression. My general message is that thinking more about the situational factors and reducing the FAE can reduce conflicts on the road and even save lives.

Then, in the next chapter, I expand some of my discussion to conflicts off the road. And in the chapter after that, I follow up with a more thorough discussion of how and why we blame victims, whether as part of interpersonal conflict, while watching the news, or in everyday areas of our lives. Reducing this form of the FAE can increase willingness to help those in need.

DRIVING WITH THE FAE AND ANGER

When I discuss driving with the FAE, I largely mean driving with irritation or anger toward another driver. The FAE is one cause of anger, and there is a lot of anger on the road. Among drivers in the United States, researchers have found up to four hundred billion hostile exchanges per year, contributing to about half of all motor vehicle collisions and two-thirds of all resulting fatalities. Angry or aggressive driving increases the risk of collision by about a factor of ten, and the average driver is angry behind the wheel at least once a day. Anger while driving is more common than anger during most other everyday activities and has become a very common topic of study for psychologists.[3]

What exactly provokes the anger on the road? Based on inside-the-vehicle data from audio recorders, cell-phone reporting, or trained passenger-observers; questionnaires; national phone surveys; and driver diaries, common complaints about other drivers include cutting, tailgating, weaving, speeding, hostile gestures, erratic braking, refusing lane access, not using turn signals, stealing parking spaces, and slow driving. This list is by no means exhaustive, and we may each have our own pet peeves on the road. Whereas men typically report more anger over slow driving and police presence (such as speed traps or getting pulled over), women report more anger over traffic obstructions, hostile gestures, and lawbreaking (such as speeding or running a stop sign). Overall, men and women feel similar degrees of anger on the road, though men typically *act* more aggressively.[4]

When we face these driving issues that irritate or anger us, our common responses include muttering, name-calling, yelling, gesturing, speeding up, and honking.[5] And we commit the FAE. When other drivers engage in one of those discourteous or bad-driving behaviors, we usually don't let them off the hook. We mutter and gesture and blame them. We tend to see these drivers as bad or incompetent people, feel certain about it, and then get even more angry.[6] The high frequency of driving anger, the anonymity provided by the enclosed cab, the inability to communicate clearly with other drivers, the absence of accountability for our attributions, the growing traffic congestion in many cities, the competing demands for our attention while driving, and the exaggerated belief (especially among younger drivers) that we are better drivers than those around us all increase the likelihood of the FAE on the road. It's quite a convergence of factors, almost any one of which can lead to the FAE on its own.[7]

Don't get me wrong. Sometimes that other driver who engages in bad driving is an idiot. Just as politicians sometimes believe what they say regardless of political pressures to say it. Just as teachers sometimes are just as polite and refined as they seem in the classroom. Sometimes behaviors can be taken at face value, just not nearly as often as most of us think.

And don't forget that explaining is not excusing. Even if there are situational factors in play that contribute to aggressive or dangerous driving, I'm not excusing the dangerous driver. In my view, whether to excuse is up to those whose safety was at risk, those who were hurt, or the judge and jury.

But regarding idiocy, the real issue is not whether other drivers are idiots or not. That would be a false dichotomy. There are several gradations between true idiot and perfect driver. The real issue is that observers of bad driving usually *overly* focus on the potential idiocy or other traits while overlooking potential circumstances. Few behaviors are caused solely by a personal or by a situational factor. It's usually a bit of both.

The idiot driver can be an idiot *in addition* to being affected by difficult circumstances. Indeed, idiots by nature are less cognitively equipped to handle difficult circumstances. Even extreme road ragers are often experiencing a last-straw break following one or more preceding stressful events in their lives (such as job loss or divorce), not that any of those events can excuse harmful behavior.[8] But when we feel offended or blocked or are physically hurt by another driver, we are often hard-pressed to acknowledge *any* role for circumstances.

(Bad) Winter Driving

I know there are idiot drivers among us, and I am sympathetic to drivers who have been run off the road or crashed into by one of them. It can be scary and stressful. But now I'm going to go out on a limb and suggest that sometimes it's not at all about idiocy. Sometimes in driving emergencies, the other driver is smart or skilled or making the best of a bad situation but still comes off as driving poorly.

In my one traffic accident ever (knock on wood), I was coming to a stop at a stoplight during an evening snowfall in December, and I was badly rear-ended. Despite my best efforts, I then slammed into the car in front of me. The driver I hit came out of his car quite angry *at me*. I'm not sure how smart or skilled I was, but I had done my best to keep my foot on the brake. But from his perspective, I was the idiot who slammed into him.

I explained to the driver I hit that I was rear-ended. I pointed back at the other car, and the anger from the driver ahead of me appeared to dissipate. Providing hard evidence of a situational factor can reduce the FAE. I felt a little dizzy but went to the driver who hit me and asked if she was OK. She stayed in her car and did not reply. The police and ambulance arrived, and I did not talk to her further. (I had my first ambulance ride that night—everything turned out fine.) I saw no car behind hers that slammed into her, and she received a ticket. But in retrospect, I might have lost an opportunity to gather further data about the situation of a real-life, real-time "bad driver." Was she distracted by something in her car? Did her brakes malfunction? Did she just come from a stressful event? Was she hurrying to an emergency of some kind? Was the road just too slippery? Or was she simply a bad driver with no concern about those in front of her?

Many winters later, I gave two media interviews about how to explain bad winter driving in the Midwest, especially at the beginning of winter. The premise seemed to be that people forget how to drive on the snow, and then they end up in a ditch or slammed into a tree or car. Why can't they remember what it was like just several months earlier and drive better? Every winter, the snow and slush come the same as the year before, and we have to adjust our driving—why don't people get that and just remember better?

Of course, that take on the bad winter driver sounds like the FAE, so I spent most of my interview time discussing our typical biased perceptions of each other. I discussed how aspects of winter driving make the FAE even more likely and how there could be multiple unknown factors behind any particular accident or slide off the road, even at the beginning of winter. The ice on the road could be abnormally slick, the kind on which even trained police officers lose control of their vehicles. Physics is physics when it comes to that friction thing. I once saw multiple cars including police cars slip, slide, and hit parked cars near the top of a hill, all within a few minutes. No one was flooring it. It was slow-motion disaster.

Or the driver could be distracted by passengers or an emergency radio broadcast or could be on the way to a different kind of emergency. Or maybe the driver was using cruise control, which is a little-known no-no on ice and water because it can lead to losing control. Even the assumption that the driver was driving last winter and so should know better could be wrong. Maybe the driver is sixteen and just started driving, or maybe the driver moved here from Florida.

Again, not that any of these possibilities are necessarily valid excuses for causing a collision. Being behind the wheel carries a responsibility not to collide with people. Stay off icy hills, at least until the salt trucks come. Increase the distance between cars. Slow down. Learn that no-cruise-control-on-snow thing. As I conveyed to one journalist,

> You can still beep and be upset at bad winter drivers, of course. I'm not telling you how to feel or act on the road. I'm just saying that there are usually multiple factors in play for most human behaviors and that most of us usually don't realize it.[9]

If you were the victim of a bad winter driver and feel like telling me, no, there are no multiple factors, no excuses—period—I get it. Even Florida-born drivers can technically educate themselves in preparation for their first Midwest snowfall, right? Unless they had to move here suddenly in winter for some reason. Sorry—my mind can't seem to help thinking of the "unlesses," but I still get what it feels like to be slammed into on the snow.

The article that quoted me concluded by citing a cognitive psychologist, who suggested that drivers can retrain their brain each winter, essentially do a little at-home practice on the snow to help them remember. It's good advice. Bad memory or arrogant overconfidence *could* be a major cause for early-winter car accidents, but how do we know for sure that's the cause when we pass by a particular accident on the snow? It's like a bad-winter-driver stereotype. Even if true on average (as some stereotypes are), it won't apply to every case. And we usually cannot just go up to the police or accident victim or ambulance driver to ask questions.

The person who rear-ended me that winter evening eventually appeared in court. I did not attend the court session because the accident had occurred out of state and I was already back home, and I couldn't stick around longer at the scene because the EMTs took me to the hospital. So I don't know what, if any, excuses she had. I am forever in a state of unknowing as to exactly why I got rear-ended that night. As I noted in the introduction, there is often an inevitable not-knowing why people act as they do. One of my hopes in writing this book, especially this chapter on driving, is that readers might become more comfortable with uncertainty. I discuss this goal further in chapter 10.

Driving and Giving Birth

The circumstances that some bad winter drivers or any bad drivers might claim in their defense may seem like pathetic excuses when we're the ones pushed off the road or hurt by their bad driving. But emergencies do happen that press many drivers to take some chances. One of the most outlandish excuses for reckless driving, the type of excuse that shows up in Hollywood movie plotlines, is that there is a woman in the car giving birth while the driver is speeding to the hospital. Sometimes the police officer who pulls this car over then leads the rest of the way to the hospital with siren blaring. Does that ever happen in real life?

I'm not sure about the police-officer-leading-the-way part—I think the police are actually trained to deliver babies, even in a car on the roadside. But for the rest of it, let me mention that my nephew's middle name is Ford. And he was so named because he was born in a Ford on his way to the hospital.

My brother received no driving award that night. His speeding and blowing stop signs might have made him look like a real idiot, and maybe some readers would still argue that he was, but there was also an emergency in play. Some pedestrians did in fact get riled and take offense at my brother's driving when they temporarily blocked his car as he neared the emergency room. I can't imagine my brother's or his wife's frustration. As for blaming the parents for not leaving the house sooner, my sister-in-law spoke directly to her doctor and received advice to stay home when she sensed it was time to go. Doctors aren't perfect, but it's hard to blame an expectant mom for listening to her doctor.

OK, so that's one story of bad driving actually being about a very pregnant passenger. Should this possibility now enter our minds every time we see a crazy idiot racing somewhere? Maybe. That's for you to decide. It does seem like an extremely unlikely possibility, but upon investigating I discovered it's a lot more common than I would've guessed. And that's how some journalists title their birth-in-car articles: "More Common Than You'd Think."[10]

Babies have been born in the front passenger seat (like my nephew), in the backseat, in Ubers, cabs, police cars, ambulances (of course), on highways and country roads, as well as in elevators, helicopters, airplanes, and hospital parking lots and lobbies. In some such stories, the driver pulls over and calls for an ambulance or 911, but in other cases, the driver decides to floor it, like my brother. These decisions can have multiple reasons, including once that the couple was following the advice, right or wrong, of the emergency dispatcher, who said to try to get to the hospital.[11]

Usually we just hear or read about these stories, but sometimes it's all caught on video from a police dash cam or the expectant father's smartphone. Go to YouTube and type in "baby born on way to hospital." In one case in 2015, the police pulled over an expectant couple for running red lights. The officers were nothing but helpful when they learned what was happening, and within about three minutes and caught on dash cam, there was some motherly screaming and the baby arrived. I don't believe the couple received a ticket that night.

And like my nephew, there have been many born-in-car kids who received names from their cars, such as Zafira, Jazz, and Lexus. One expectant mom who gave birth in a Camry gave her baby the middle name of Camryn. The woman said of her daughter, "If she's upset with me later, I'll tell her she's lucky she wasn't born in a Daewoo!"[12] Another baby received the first name of Kia after being born in a Kia Carens. Kia Motors heard the news, announced that it "proves the Kia Carens is a family car right from the off," and gave the family a brand-new Kia Carens.[13] Very cool. I don't mean to trivialize the scary parts of these stories. Either explicitly reported or implied, all these babies did arrive safely, with moms and babies in good health.

Of course, there can be a variety of other medical emergencies to explain reckless or speedy driving besides giving birth. During one of my conference talks on biases in which I used the high-speed tailgater as an example, someone from the audience described how she regretfully but severely tailgated another driver to quickly get to an injured family member at home. The tailgatee got so angry that he followed her home, stalked her for a few hours, and then sent her a scathing, name-calling letter pointing out how stupid and inconsiderate she was.

ATTRIBUTION-DRIVING STUDIES

So there are numerous stories from the news, social media, or audience members at social science talks in which aberrant driving behavior can have situational causes and angry fellow drivers miss the truth by over-looking or being unaware of circumstances. You probably have your own stories to tell. But these are just anecdotes, and many of the stories that make the news or Facebook are on the extreme side. Have research studies found systematic evidence that people make quick dispositional attributions against fellow drivers in the everyday? Yes.

First, though driving-anger studies rarely mention the FAE by name, they actually show substantial evidence for the FAE in the form of blaming that other driver. Anger triggered by another driver almost invariably involves such blaming, regardless of circumstances. Any provocation, whether on the road or elsewhere, involves identifying a human agent as responsible, and we don't pick ourselves.[14] The most frequent thought reported by drivers who are angry is that another driver is incompetent.[15] Psychologist James Averill, author of *Anger and Aggression*, wrote that "more than anything else, anger is an attribution of blame," and that "perhaps the most important fact about anger" is that "anger is a response to some perceived misdeed."[16] My emphasis is on "perceived."

At least as early as the 1970s, driving researchers more specifically reported that drivers tend to make unsupported and negative inferences about fellow drivers' motives and values. Drivers typically view accidents not as random or situationally caused but rather as caused by a driver's lack of skill or other personal traits, including accident proneness.[17] James Baxter and colleagues summarized some of this early research in a 1990 article titled "Attributional Biases and Driver Behaviour," in which they noted that committing the FAE can make us behave aggressively and be unforgiving toward these other drivers. Baxter and colleagues also noted the tendency for most drivers to think themselves above other drivers—specifically, to think they are less "aggressive, impatient, selfish and intolerant" than other drivers. I noted the above-average effect in the introduction—this is a driver's version and offers some justification for blaming that other driver.[18]

Baxter's own study regarded perceptions of tailgating and running stoplights. The researchers approached participants in or near their parked cars and asked them to read a story about one of these two infractions. Participants were randomly assigned to take different perspectives: that of having engaged in the infraction themselves or having seen someone else engage in that infraction. Participants mailed in their replies. The results showed that participants rated the other driver as more aggressive and less pressed for time than they rated themselves for the same infraction.

In 1994, Thaddeus Herzog videotaped staged driving behaviors from behind the steering wheel of another car. Then he placed his participants behind a mock steering wheel in a lab while they watched the videos. Similar to Sommers's experience of being stuck behind a stationary driver at a rotary, participants in one condition were (vicariously) stuck behind a stationary driver at a stop sign. I'll call the stationary road blocker Driver 1. After fifteen seconds, Driver 1 finally turned right, and then the participant, Driver 2, drove straight through the intersection. In another condition, Driver 2 had to swerve around Driver 1, who was backing out of a driveway. Herzog asked participants to "think aloud" their thoughts about Driver 1's behavior.

Herzog reported that participants "spoke freely and often, regularly inputting negative dispositional attributions" against Driver 1, such as "Look at that stupid driver!" or "What a jerk!" Herzog also administered rating scales. Participants gave stronger ratings for Driver 1's low ability and intelligence, compared to Driver 1's potential circumstances.[19]

Since then, several studies put participants through a similar drill of showing them infractions, asking them to read or listen to a story of an infraction, or asking them to recall a time when someone committed an infraction against them. Then participants had to provide an explanation for the infraction or rate the potential causes. The infractions included tailgating, cutting, weaving, honking, blocking, crossing a center line with oncoming traffic, not turning fast enough, shining brights in someone's face, hostile gestures, or doing whatever else the participants personally considered to be bad or risky driving. The other drivers were usually strangers but sometimes friends to the participant.

Although results sometimes varied for particular infractions, in general the participants cited the other driver's traits and intentions more strongly than circumstances, or in some cases just more strongly than they cited for themselves if they had committed the same infraction. Indeed, participants provided an array of situational factors when asked to explain their *own* infractions, so we know they could conceive the possibility of circumstances behind bad driving.[20]

I've asked my own students if they had ever engaged in some of the bad-driving behaviors studied by researchers, and if so, what their reasons were. Some students owned up to making poor decisions, others cited situational factors, and some did a bit of both. To justify tailgating, many students explained how they were late for work or school. Some tailgating students blamed the driver in front of them for going only the speed limit or five miles per hour over, calling the "slow" driver names like "Grandma" or "Grandpa." One student acknowledged that such perceptions of the law-abiding driver might constitute the FAE, while another student tailgated precisely to show the slow driver that their speed was rude.

One student self-identified as a road rager and called herself immature but said that swearing and making gestures at other drivers helped to relieve the stress from driving. To explain speeding, some students gave the classic explanation of keeping up with traffic, though one student explained it was because he had a fast car. Another had a pizza-delivery job and explained that more money can be made by driving faster. One student regretted an instance of passing two cars at once in a no-passing zone but explained that he was getting back at those two drivers, who had recently passed him.

To explain slow driving or pausing at intersections, students explained that they were in an unfamiliar place and unsure of directions, that they couldn't afford to get another ticket, or that they had been in a traumatic car accident that made them extra cautious. To explain slow turning, one student said she didn't want to spill a drink or cause her dog to fall over.

If we get upset at another driver for an annoying or aggressive driving behavior, I'm not saying it's incumbent upon us to put ourselves in the other driver's shoes and think about what our own reasons might be for the same behavior. That was the nature of my discussion with my students, but even if we had the mental capacity to do it in the moment on the road, it's your call. My point is that we are usually able to identify situational factors for negative driving behavior when it is our behavior—the possibilities occur to us or exist—and so not considering those possibilities when judging others can fairly constitute the FAE. And considering those possibilities can reduce anger and conflict and even save lives on the road.

SITUATIONAL CONTRIBUTORS TO AGGRESSION

These stories and studies identify numerous potential situational factors behind bad or aggressive driving. These are factors that most of us might relate to in explaining our own questionable driving behaviors without admitting to being aggressive or mean or stupid people. Especially being pressed for time, blocked, or provoked. But researchers of driving aggression and aggression in general have identified a number of other known contributors to aggression that may not occur to you as easily. They are not all good "excuses" when pulled over by a police officer (not that my student's "because I have a fast car" explanation was a good excuse either), but they are part of the potential context in explaining aggressive driving or aggressive behavior in general. And we tend to overlook them in committing the FAE against other drivers.

Combining the lists from driving research and the general aggression literature yields a sizable group of standard situational influences on aggression. Those influences include crowds, congestion, time urgency, provocation, bad weather, pain, heat, hunger, loud noise, unpleasant odor, alcohol (consumed or just alcohol reminders), culture, parent- and peer-based norms or values, watching media violence, playing violent video games, and a variety of other aggressive cues, including the mere presence of weapons as well as weapon pictures and words.[21]

Famous aggression researchers Craig Anderson and Brad Bushman have also identified incentives as increasing aggression. If there's something you desperately want, then you might be more aggressive to obtain it, part of the definition of instrumental aggression. Tailgating to get to work on time is a decent example of instrumental aggression while driving. Anderson and Bushman wrote that "the types of incentives that can increase aggression are as numerous as the number of objects that people want or desire."[22]

My main point is that knowing about these situational influences on aggression—and there are a lot of them—can reduce the FAE, not only during driving but also in any conflict where there is perceived aggression. A driver may not be able to say with a straight face that she tailgated you because there was an unpleasant odor coming from her backseat, but aversive stimuli like odor and noise do increase the likelihood of aggression, especially when the driver is provoked or running late. Would knowing about these stimuli in a backseat change how you felt about the aggressive driver who tailgated you or blew a stop sign to get to work faster? Maybe not. Unless perhaps you had to endure the odor yourself.

Some readers might wonder where an unpleasant prolonged odor of that magnitude might come from in a car. Among possibilities, my wife once lost track of a cellophane-wrapped cucumber in her trunk after a trip to the grocery store during the summer. She had wondered where that cucumber went and assumed it got left at the store. The odor slowly increased in the heat over several weeks until I discovered the green, molten plastic-wrapped jam in the corner of her trunk.

Driving blogs have also mentioned car odors of unknown origins. One blog query was titled "Smells Like Something Died in My Car," referring to an odor that smelled like a "combination of day old Burger King and rotten tomatoes." Helpful responders suggested checking for small dead animals, which had been discovered in tight places in other cars, but the culprit ended up being a small container of expired salsa lodged under a front seat.[23]

Social psychologist Dwight Hennessy, who conducted some of the driving research I've cited, also pointed out that "drivers can be changed by factors from outside the driving environment" such that "combinations of contextual variables may be conceptually limitless."[24] So anything that makes us angry or irritable before we get into the car can contribute to aggression while driving. That's quite a lot of potential situational factors.

I've already mentioned that road rage can be the end product of a series of other stressful or angering pre-driving events. One of my students described such a case. My student's male friend was apparently "always a careful driver" until the time when he had just found out his girlfriend had been cheating on him. He then became a hostile and reckless driver. In that car ride, my student didn't think his friend cared about my student's life or his own "because of his anger." Researchers have similarly identified cases of drivers who snapped on the road after a breakup or while going through a divorce but who were described by friends and neighbors as the "nicest man" or "a wonderful father."[25]

Sometimes domestic violence might even spill onto the road. A 1997 report noted 322 such incidents since 1990. The author of the report stated, "When love turns to hate, spouses and lovers are increasingly venting their rage on the highway." Estranged husbands and former boyfriends have used their cars as weapons.[26]

Most driving-aggression researchers, including Hennessy, do acknowledge a role for personality in aggressive driving, such that the neighbors' "nicest man" label would not really fit. For example, low conscientiousness, high sensation-seeking, and high trait aggression (that is, the predisposition to respond aggressively) strongly predict negative driving outcomes. General aggression researchers have added other traits, such as narcissism. Narcissistic individuals have high but unstable self-esteem and are highly prone to anger and aggression when their self-image is threatened.[27]

Hennessy wrote that "context factors are important to understand on their own" but went on to emphasize a theme of my book, that context factors "are best appreciated in interaction with personal factors."[28] As I've conveyed, behaviors are usually caused by a combination of personal and situational factors. Being high on trait aggression, in particular, makes a person much easier to provoke on the road and elsewhere. People who are already aggressive are more likely to see hostile intentions in others when the behavior is ambiguous, which is called the "hostile attribution bias."[29]

The fact that heavy crowds, unpleasant odors, loud noises, hunger, and high heat or humidity can put someone on edge and thus make them easier to provoke is probably not too hard for readers to believe. The fact that already being a hothead can make someone drive aggressively or be easier to provoke is probably very easy to believe. Some of the other contributors to aggression, however, may seem more controversial, such as watching media violence, playing violent video games, being in the presence of weapons, and experiencing alcohol-related primes. And yet the research evidence is plentiful and clear, especially for watching media violence.

Watching Aggression Causes Aggression

Hennessy argued that television and movies can cause aggressive driving because they tend to "glorify and promote speeding, risk taking, and dangerous driving practices as acceptable or even admirable." Hennessy reported results that watching even a short movie scene of dangerous driving did indeed increase dangerous driving behaviors in a driving simulator, including speeding and lane violations.[30]

But more generally, watching media violence and playing violent video games do increase aggression. There have been hundreds of supportive studies (true experiments and not just correlational studies), and there is broad consensus on this position among those who do the research, as well as medical doctors.[31] There are some caveats that I will still mention, but the cause-effect relation between watching aggression and behaving aggressively is not a myth, as some popular press authors contend. Quite the contrary. Even watching the aggression and verbal abuse on reality television can make us more aggressive.[32]

That said, there are still academic holdouts even among social scientists, especially regarding the effect of playing violent video games. These researchers are not convinced by the evidence, and some of them even suggest there could be benefits to violent video games. The debates between this minority of researchers and the majority are surprisingly heated. Based on my reading, many of the minority's arguments seem well-thought-out and research based and should not be dismissed out of hand. However, by and large, these researchers do seem to ignore or misunderstand the bulk of the evidence and to make straw man arguments in which they criticize the other side for conclusions the other side never or rarely drew. It's easy to call the majority view a myth if you first distort or misstate what that view is.

This minority of researchers is also more likely to resort to ad hominem attacks, characterizing the majority side as being driven by ideological values, dogma, or a moral crusade rather than by data. I can't help but see in these attacks the FAE, where conclusions that seem obviously based on hundreds of studies are attributed instead to the personal values and morals of the presenters. The debates are much more involved and technical than described here. I regret I don't have space to provide a more careful analysis.[33]

As for the aforementioned caveats, the negative effects of engaging with media violence apply mainly to younger viewers and younger video game players. These are basically children and teens, though there's some evidence for older participants. And even among these younger ages, the findings are still on average, as always. Not every younger participant is affected. In particular, it is individuals who are already aggressive for whatever reason who are especially likely to become more aggressive after engaging with media violence, not that the effect is limited to already-aggressive individuals.

In sum, there is no question in my mind that engaging with media violence causes aggression. Thus, media violence can be a situational contributor to aggressive driving. But the harder question is whether media violence is responsible for any of the high-profile shootings, road-rage assaults, or other extreme violence in society today. Just because media violence causes aggression doesn't mean it necessarily rises to the level of, say, a mass shooting. The most prominent media-violence researchers do not claim to know the answer to this harder question. These researchers acknowledge that there are multiple causes for extreme violence and that we cannot track down any single cause with certainty from case to case. But it would be illogical to completely rule out media violence as one of the possible contributors.

The Presence of Weapons

A cause of aggressive behavior much less discussed than media violence is the mere presence of a weapon. Of course, weapons contribute to violence in that weapons are instruments of violence just in terms of the physics, but what researchers have also known for decades is that merely the visible presence of a weapon can prime aggressive thoughts and make a person more aggressive or easier to provoke. This effect of a weapon is called the "weapons effect." Longtime aggression researcher Leonard Berkowitz is credited with the concept of the trigger pulling the finger.[34]

After the initial discovery, some studies looked for the effect and didn't find it, but researchers eventually learned that the effect does occur when participants don't suspect the purpose of the experiment. The weapons effect has been found in both American and European samples, with children and adults, and in both laboratory and field settings (including while driving in traffic).[35] In sum, reducing the availability of guns would reduce aggression not only by reducing opportunity to commit gun-based violence but also by removing some of the cognitive primes of aggressive thoughts.

Before I get much further, let me emphasize that this research does not automatically support greater gun-control legislation. As I tell my students, there is a right to bear arms in the United States whether or not reducing the number of guns reduces aggression. A family that lives in a bad part of town might want a gun for protection, even knowing the overall statistics about the effects of more guns (including the greater risk of tragic accidents in the home). Besides, not all gun-control legislation succeeds in reducing the number of guns, and sometimes just the anticipation of new gun-control laws *increases* the sales of guns.

That said, after a school shooting, when one side of the gun-control debate says that guns don't cause violence—people with mental health problems cause violence, the weapons-effect research does suggest otherwise. Even if mental health plays a role, the presence of guns cannot be ruled out as another factor. Extreme forms of violence have multiple causes, both situational and personal, so to explain gun violence by calling the shooter deranged or mentally disturbed and stopping your thinking there is yet another case of the FAE.[36]

Sometimes my students disagree that reducing guns reduces aggression by citing a report from somewhere that a gun-control law was passed in a city but violence levels did not change there. Isn't that proof against gun availability causing violence? No. Even assuming the gun-control law succeeded in reducing the number of guns, there are multiple factors that influence violence, and neither researchers nor legislators can control all these factors. Thus, reducing available guns might in fact be reducing violence in that city, but other factors might be increasing it at the same time. The net effect may be that violence stays the same.

Beyond the effect of seeing actual weapons, researchers have found more recently that even pictures of weapons or weapon-related words can prime aggressive thoughts and increase aggressive behaviors. So weapon-filled movies and video games would seem to apply. Interestingly, however, hunters are not adversely affected by seeing hunting guns, though they are by assault guns.[37]

Alcohol Cues (You Don't Have to Drink It)

To state that alcohol is one of the many contributors to aggression sounds like drinking can make someone aggressive or antisocial. Indeed, that's true, and common sense. But let me briefly add the more amazing result that just *thinking* you've drunk alcohol (when you haven't) can lead to the same effects. Even more amazing is that just as seeing a weapons-related word can increase aggressive thoughts and behaviors, so can seeing words that are semantically connected to alcohol. Drinking and driving is against the law. Apparently just thinking about drinking while driving might also contribute (to a lesser extent) to aggressive driving.[38]

Again, my main point in covering these situational influences on aggression is that knowing about them can reduce the FAE, not only during driving but also in any conflict where there is perceived aggression. In the next chapter, I cover other settings where aggression and interpersonal conflict can occur, and I highlight some of my motivations and challenges in writing this book.

CHAPTER 7

INTERPERSONAL CONFLICT: OFF THE ROAD

It is extremely beneficial, for personal relationships, to be able to recognize FAE because now I will be more likely to realize they probably didn't intentionally intend on hurting me.
> —anonymous student in a social psychology course

I can see where I should be more open to situational factors but sometimes, like when me and my girlfriend fight, it's so quick and heated that it becomes really hard to change thinking and consider situational factors when it's so easy to blame the person.
> —anonymous student in a social psychology course

An eye for an eye will only make the whole world blind.
> —Mahatma Gandhi

Do you know those people at the gym who don't do a good job wiping down their machine? Do you dread going to work because there's someone there who is disrespectful to you? Has the office microwave gone beyond gross (and you think you know the guilty party)? Do you have dings on the side of your car from coworkers or fellow students who park too close to you?

I spent a whole chapter on driving anger and aggression and the conflicts that can occur on the road, but annoyance, anger, aggression, and conflicts obviously can arise in many other interpersonal settings, more than I can cover. Interpersonal conflicts can occur in friendships, families, and romantic unions. Those in close relationships obviously know each better than two drivers who have never met. But sadly, we can be just as biased and aggressive, if not more so, against those we feel most close to. Conflicts can also occur among coworkers or colleagues, between employee and employer, and between consumer and provider.

Conflicts especially occur between groups, whether political, religious, racial, or national. It's part of the human crisis of intergroup prejudice. In the United States, racial tensions and political group conflicts have been spiking in recent years. When members of one group commit the FAE against members of another group in explaining negative group behaviors or outcomes, it has its own name—the "ultimate attribution error." It comes from research on prejudice.[1]

Although conflicts and prejudice can have multiple causes, I am focusing on the FAE as a cause. Sometimes conflicts occur or worsen because of misunderstandings about each other in which we overlook or underconsider situational factors. In particular, I want to focus on times when we see negative traits and intentions behind disrespectful, hurtful, or harmful behaviors where such traits and intentions may not exist. As discussed in the driving examples, such misunderstandings can lead to unnecessary anger, stress, and misguided retaliation, which are the makings of not only car accidents and vehicular assaults but also getting fired, quitting a job you need, divorce, domestic abuse, and even war.

So avoiding these misunderstandings might help to avoid those consequences. And it might even begin a more permanent life change, to an existence with less chronic stress or anger. Among multiple stories I can share, one student said she never gets angry while driving because she constantly thinks about the behind-the-scenes causes for other drivers' behaviors—which apparently frustrates some of her passengers.

Don't get me wrong. Sometimes other drivers are what they seem.

Sometimes a fitness enthusiast is rude or lazy when he doesn't wipe down the machine. Sometimes the coworker whose meal explodes in the microwave leaves the mess because she has zero respect for others. And someone who mouths off to us may simply be a hostile son of a gun.

So sometimes someone seems intent to disrespect or hurt us because she is intent to do so. And even if her hurtful behavior has other causes, I'm not excusing it. Maybe someone mistreats you because he's under a great deal of stress, but he shouldn't take his stress out on you! In general, I'm not advising that we necessarily ignore or walk away from conflicts in some charitable gesture, although we could. Nor am I suggesting that we necessarily respond aggressively. I'm just acknowledging that some conflicts are necessary to engage in, whether or not we understand why someone is behaving a certain way.

Coworkers have to work together to accomplish group goals, and so conflicts at work have to be addressed, as managers and department chairs know. Parents and kids who live together have to find a way to live together. Perhaps a customer who is mistreated can just go to another store, but (politely) complaining to the manager might prevent future mistreatment.

More serious, if a bully repeatedly hurts a child, trying to ignore it and have sympathetic thoughts toward the bully because the bully might have a bad home life might just lead to more run-ins. Victims sometimes need to engage the perpetrator (or ask the authorities to do so) to reduce the risk of future conflict.[2] If someone physically attacks us or our family or our country, we have the right to defend ourselves, even if the attacker is being driven by situational forces.

But to participate in an argument or altercation, if it comes to that, doesn't mean we can't look for situational factors at the same time. It doesn't mean we have to hold a unitary thought (at the expense of other thoughts) about how willfully evil the attacking person or country is. Yes, if they're physically attacking, that sounds evil. But if we stop our thinking there, then the explanation is probably incomplete, which is less helpful to a long-term resolution. If we stop our thinking there, it can lead to stronger and more prolonged anger, which can further bias our judgments in subsequent interactions. Some famous social psychologists might argue there's not necessarily *any* evil there.[3] That may be true, but let's not go there yet. Most behaviors are caused by a combination of personal and situational factors. Maybe there is a little evil within a large context of unpredictable and uncontrollable social forces.

In any case, whether to engage the disrespectful coworker or outright perpetrator is certainly up to you based on your circumstances or abilities. And as I mentioned, I'm not advising that we necessarily respond with force.

In Gandhi's words that "an eye for an eye will only make the whole world blind," the blindness metaphor has a double meaning for me (as perhaps Gandhi intended). It's not only about a cycle of violence that can spread out of control but also about how anger and automatic retaliatory aggression can cloud our judgment. It can keep us from seeing all the reasons for each other's actions.

THE ROOTS OF THIS BOOK

I mentioned in the introduction my hope that reading this book can literally bring more peace into the lives of those who wish they were less quick to get angry or defensive. The previous chapter and this one are where I really try to tackle this goal, first on the road and now in our other interpersonal relations. This goal is a large part of why I first decided to write this book. But I know that not everyone wishes they were less quick to anger. Some of us are perfectly fine with how quickly we get angry. If that describes you, this chapter is not as focused on you, but hopefully you might still benefit.

I realized at some point after years of social psychology training and teaching that some of the knowledge I learned and shared with others, or the way I understood and shared it, helped others to deal with conflicts. Not that you necessarily need a social psychology education to approach conflicts as I try to. I know there are individuals who don't get upset, at least not right away, at the bad behavior thrown their way. Their upbringing or experiences or neurochemical balances might be behind the calm. My goal here is to connect this less angry existence to attribution theory and other principles in social psychology, but also to my experiences with others. Others tell me the attribution stuff helps. And so this chapter is less referenced in terms of scholarly articles and books and more referenced to my and others' experiences.

As some of these individuals I've talked to would start to get angry at perceived mistreatment or misbehavior, they would remember something I said and find greater ability to step back or relax. This ability helped them to avoid or defuse a conflict, ignore a conflict without feeling slighted, or address a conflict more productively and with less stress and anger. While feeling less stress and anger, teachers I know have more easily calmed down disruptive students; coworkers have more quickly resolved in-office disagreements; and students have better handled disputes with teachers, significant others, and fellow drivers. And even if the conflict was not fully resolved, the stress or anger over the matter was less likely to linger. I don't have a single-line piece of advice at the moment, but it would have to include thinking about the context and the multiple possible causes for everyone's behavior.

One of my best stories is a driving example (borrowed from the first page of chapter 6). I had a male student who was ready to chase down and retaliate against another driver who had cut him off. My student told me that at that moment, he remembered our FAE discussions in class, took his foot off the gas, and felt less stress. Road rage averted.

I have a friend who had difficulty adjusting to a new job. Among the stressors, she felt mistreated by many of her colleagues. She asked why I thought these other people behaved as they did. My listening to her and our discussions about the possible causes for her colleagues' behaviors reduced her stress.

I had a female student who had an item that was stolen and whose boyfriend relentlessly got on her case about it, blaming her for not being more careful. Apparently they fought about the issue, and she was upset enough to talk to me about it after a lecture on victim blaming. After learning about the multiple causes of victim blaming and that victim blamers are not necessarily bad people (despite their perceived bad behavior), my student conveyed feeling a great sense of relief. Perhaps a breakup was averted.

I think there is great power in the ability to step back from a conflict and consider the multiple possible causes for everyone's behavior, especially the causes that hide in the context or behind the scenes. It's not easy, but considering multiple situational causes can reduce anger and reduce the risk of unnecessarily antagonizing the other person. The real challenge may lie in considering just the possibility of causes that you can never verify because, say, that other driver is speeding away from you.

Let me emphasize that I don't think it's your responsibility to step back and think about other causes. Maybe the thoughtless person who made a ding in your car in the parking lot should be the one doing some thinking. But if you are one of those individuals I mentioned earlier who wishes to be less quick to anger or who is looking for ways to find more peace in the day-to-day, then stepping back in this way or following some of my chapter 10 strategies can help. I hope the present chapter at least gives you something to think about.

I will focus on conflicts that happen in the workplace, between consumers and providers, and because of hunger. If these cases are not particularly relevant to you, I hope they can be generalized to the settings you care more about. The bottom line is that thinking about multiple situational causes and avoiding the FAE can minimize anger, prevent conflicts, or reduce conflicts more quickly and productively once they begin.

CHALLENGES

Despite my motivations, this chapter may be the most difficult for me to pull off. If you get upset at someone at work or in a close relationship after they mistreat you and you call them rude or vindictive or worse, my challenge is that I don't want to sound like I'm telling you that you're wrong and there's some situational factor you don't see. I don't know if that's the case, although it might be. I haven't spent years getting to know your significant other like you have, but as I mentioned in chapter 3, we especially overestimate our accuracy in reading other people the longer we know them. What I write about here is for you to think about. Let it simmer. You don't have to decide right now whether my points apply to you.

And you rarely have to decide right away how you feel about another's behavior toward you or what the cause might be. You can always get upset at the person later. Take some time. Gather more information. It may be easier said than done, but as I tell my students, there's no statute of limitations on getting upset at someone.

Situational factors behind others' negative behavior toward you can include childhood issues that get triggered when certain topics come up; your behavior toward others (whether misperceived or real); others' memories of your past behavior toward them; or any number of aversive stimuli, going back to my general list of contributors to aggression (see chapter 6). In particular, others might be dealing with stress from other parts of their lives.

I've come across a quote in multiple places from Robin Williams: "Everyone you meet is fighting a battle you know nothing about. Be kind. Always." I'm not necessarily recommending that you always have to be kind, though I can see some benefits there. However, that part about unseen battles is worth considering.

An ironic challenge in not getting angry at someone right away lies in the fact that some people get angry that they cannot get angry. Some of my friends and family have conveyed actual anger at not being able to get upset at some rude meanie at a store, at work, or while driving because of the possibility that there's more than meets the eye. Some of this anger is sometimes directed at me in that moment, because I planted the idea of multiple causes in their head, but their anger usually wears off by the time they tell me their story.

AT WORK

Have you ever felt mistreated by coworkers or a boss? Have people at work become angry at you and unfairly accused you of intentionally mistreating *them*? At-work conflicts are very common, their effects can be long-lasting, and managers are trained to address them.[4] On a run through the internet that included business magazines and university human resources sites, I found some common suggested tips for at-work conflict resolution. They include defining the problem and letting the employees express their feelings. Although such self-disclosure can reveal misunderstandings, the stated goal is more about employees letting off steam and feeling heard. These websites do not include any direct information about the FAE.

I acknowledge it is a risky tack to tell two upset employees that their perceptions toward each other might be biased, but I'm sure skilled managers can and do find less blatant ways to raise that possibility. One website at the University of Kansas did suggest to both sides of a conflict that they avoid early judgments and keep gathering information. Sounds good.[5]

I'm not trained in conflict resolution, and this chapter is not meant as management training. But as I've already conveyed, I believe knowledge about the FAE can be helpful for everyday interactions at work. Even the managers themselves can be mistreated or misunderstood in this way. It turns out that managers or company leaders often receive an unfair share of the blame for company failures or mistakes. They also tend to receive undue credit for successes. This bias toward leaders is another example of the FAE and part of what's called the "romance of leadership," in which observers overestimate how much personal control leaders have over company outcomes.[6]

The unclean office microwave is a modern-day example of the "tragedy of the commons," in which a broad social force is in play. Using appliances without cleaning them is less likely to occur at home. Something about the communal context is influencing this behavior. As noted by L. V. Anderson at *Slate*, "even offices populated by kind, lovely, diligent people often have run-down, amoral, even disgusting, kitchens." Office refrigerators where no one replaces the milk or other condiments might fit the same pattern. Even a CEO once "went ballistic on his staff because they didn't replace the milk."[7]

The historical reference to the commons is to a common area in a town to which all the residents or farmers have access, but few think about the collective effect of their individual uses, and the common area withers from overuse. As social psychologist David Myers describes it, individuals justify use of the area as driven by the needs of their situations, while they explain others' overuse as greedy or selfish. In the modern-day examples, I might think of my coworkers as slobs, but I myself might not clean a mess because I have to run to class or a meeting—that has to take priority, right? As Myers wrote, "Most never realize that their counterparts are viewing them with the same fundamental attribution error."[8]

When I'm using the copy machine at work and it breaks and I have to get to class, I ponder whether to leave the machine as is and risk someone getting irked at me or whether to be a little late to class to address the problem. It's sometimes a hard call. Usually I'll tell department staff about the problem as I run to class. Or I'll leave an apologetic note.

To address employee interpersonal conflicts, in which we might get unfairly or unduly angry at each other, a group of social scientists has developed a strategy called "social motivation training" (SMT). SMT involves rethinking why others behave badly. It's based on "attributional retraining" programs that communicate to participants that their attributions about *themselves* are incorrect or need to change. SMT, on the other hand, focuses on attributions about *others* and approximates the message of this book—that your attributions *might* need to change. In a major component of SMT called "mental simulation," participants are encouraged to consider the *possibility* of causes other than the obvious when coworkers commit transgressions. I created a website in 2014 that also carries this message, that I don't know if any particular person is biased, but we are all at *risk* of bias. The website is titled PARBs Anonymous, PARBs meaning "Persons at Risk of Bias."

SMT has been tested on participants with a variety of work experiences. In some studies, after this training, participants read a hypothetical scenario about a coworker's transgression. In other studies, participants were asked to recall their own experience with coworker transgressions. Then participants answered questions about how they saw the coworker. Compared to a control condition in which participants went through "job satisfaction training," and in some cases, compared to pretraining scores, SMT led participants to perceive less intentionality in the transgressor, feel less anger, and be less likely to hold a grudge.[9] Feeling less anger but still really wanting people to please clean that microwave is, of course, understandable.

CONSUMER VERSUS PROVIDER

Many of my students work in service and have stories about rude customers. And all of us have probably had to deal with rude or incompetent service providers from time to time. Are there that many rude and stupid customers, cashiers, and salespeople out there? Or can so many people's situations and lives really be that bad (causing these people to behave badly)?

Though the typical interaction time between customer and clerk might be short, people can still feel demeaned on both sides. Though we're usually strangers to each other, we might wonder, "What's wrong with him?" "What's her problem?" One of my suggestions is to practice rewording that common response. When Sam Sommers got stuck at the rotary (see chapter 6), he also asked what (the hell) was wrong with that other driver. Instead, try asking, "What's wrong with his situation?" or, "What's your life's problem?" or, "What's making you do this?" What if we said that in response to perceived infractions? It probably wouldn't sound right to us, and that might be part of why the FAE is so common. I will further discuss this rewording suggestion in chapter 10.

A number of researchers have investigated the attributions made by consumers and providers over negative outcomes or faulty products. Most of the results are not too surprising. When consumers explained a product failure as due to something within the company's control, they became more angry. They also were more likely to complain and want an apology. These results applied to products you can hold as well as to wait time at an airport.[10]

In the airline industry, staff can also negatively judge passengers. When I flew to California once, the plane was delayed in taking off because there was a man who was not taking his seat. He kept going to his overhead luggage. In between repeated announcements for all passengers to please be seated, I could hear the flight attendants getting very angry and describing this man as very conceited and self-important. I didn't talk to the man to get his story, but I did wonder whether he might be looking for something important in his bag, like medicine.

According to marketing researcher Elizabeth Cowley, customers waiting in line who observed a negative interaction ahead of them between a customer and service provider would usually blame the dispositions of the service provider (versus the situation or the customer). This result occurred especially when the soon-to-be-served customers expected to need something from that same service provider. Cowley suggested that such customers inferred dispositions to prepare for their own service encounters because people think traits are more helpful than situational factors in anticipating future behavior.[11]

Brad Tuttle wrote a piece for *Time* titled "We Hate You Too: Pet Peeves from Consumers—and from Retail Workers." A top pet peeve from consumers was "pushy sales reps." Top pet peeves from retail workers included customers who take an item from a shelf and put it back in some unpredictable place somewhere else in the store. Of this common consumer behavior, one employee said, "I have no idea why jerks have to do that." Another top pet peeve is customers "who rudely don't get off the !#@!*!@# cell phone at the checkout line."[12]

My cousin is an area manager overseeing several stores, and she told me a similar but more complicated cell phone story. When she first heard about this book chapter, she volunteered to share multiple examples of customers who didn't get along with her employees and vice versa. In one example, a customer got upset over waiting in line even though the staff attempted to direct her to an open register. The customer appeared to ignore or not hear the staff attempts because her head was down, attending to her cell phone. When her head surfaced and she reached her register, she was even more agitated about having to wait.

This manager said she talks a lot with her staff about how perception can differ from reality, how service providers need to try to see things from the customer's perspective, and how her staff should pause and slow down to listen to customers and each other. Indeed, slowing down is one of my suggestions for reducing the FAE (see chapter 10). In sum, she did not appear to get upset at the agitated customer. It might be because of an avoiding-the-FAE view. She said to me, "I think so many people are running around doing so many things at once and getting so worked up they don't see or hear what is going on around or to them."

HANGER

"Hangry" memes and GIFs have been on the rise in recent years. My students first informed me about the concept. In case you haven't heard, being hangry means becoming irritable and more quick to anger because you're hungry. This condition can contribute to conflicts at work, at a store, and especially, of course, at a restaurant. How many patrons act like jerks to their servers because they're hungry (and not just jerks)? In chapter 6, I listed hunger as a situational contributor to aggression, and there are many possible situational causes for not eating sooner. On the other hand, if someone doesn't eat all day because of laziness or bad time management, then I suppose hangry can amount to a trait. In that case, the server who gets angry at a hangry customer might not be committing the FAE, but servers are unlikely to know anything about the customer's day or traits.

Aggression researcher Brad Bushman actually published a study on hanger that got picked up by news sites. Bushman argued that "low glucose levels might be one factor that contributes to intimate partner violence." The recommendation is to eat before handling a difficult situation with someone else, though Bushman said to avoid high-sugar foods, which can lead to a sugar crash (possibly a literal one, if driving in traffic with a bunch of idiots).[13]

THE FAE AS A CAUSE AND CONSEQUENCE

For the careful reader who has been paying attention to my verbs, such as "causes" or "leads to," I want to assure you that I choose my verbs carefully. When I've said that the FAE can cause anger and aggression (in the previous chapter and here), I had consulted true experiments to back me up. Indeed, cognitive appraisals such as the FAE are well known to lead to emotions and actions.[14] It also turns out that anger and aggression can cause the FAE. As I noted in the introduction and attributed to Gustav Ichheiser, the FAE can be both a cause and symptom of the crisis of our society, which must include interpersonal conflict.

The fact that the FAE can cause anger and aggression makes it an important topic to understand to avoid or defuse conflicts. The fact that anger and aggression can cause the FAE may be even more important to know, because it shows how quickly a conflict can escalate. A hot day, a foul odor, or one too many red lights can make some of us angry, which can make us interpret others' intentions as hostile when they're not (FAE), which can then make us even more angry, which can then even further bias our interpretations of other people, and so on. This cycle can unfold at home or work or a store or wherever.

The driving-anger researchers whose studies I discussed in chapter 6 showed that dispositional attributions for bad driving strongly predict greater anger and aggression, and the more anger, the stronger the dispositional attributions become. And these researchers have often written as if dispositional attributions cause anger and vice versa. But in truth, most driving studies, at least the ones I cited, have used correlational designs. If you recall, correlation does not mean causation, though most of these authors did not note this limitation.[15]

But fortunately, there are true experiments (not just correlational studies) that support the cause-effect statements in both directions, that the FAE can be both a cause and consequence of anger and aggression in multiple settings. In these studies, researchers randomly assigned participants to different induced-emotion conditions and found that anger increased the FAE (while sadness decreased it). Researchers randomly assigned participants to different induced-aggression levels and found that greater aggression toward a person increases negative dispositional views of that person. Researchers most often randomly assigned participants to different attribution conditions and found that certain attributions (to traits or intentions) do influence emotion and action, including anger and aggression. I consider now just a few of these studies as examples.

Attributions as a Cause of Emotion and Action

I've already mentioned the SMT research that showed that thinking about multiple possible causes led participants to feel less anger toward a coworker. Other experiments have been more targeted in that they provided to participants specific attributions for a particular behavior or outcome to see the effects on participants' emotions and actions.

In one experiment, researchers set up a real-life pizza-delivery scenario in which actual customers received their pizzas later than promised. Then participants were given, via phone call from the pizza place, different reasons for the new delivery time: something to do with either the delivery person's traits (e.g., incompetent) or the situation (e.g., traffic conditions). The trait attribution caused lower tips compared to the situational attribution. Similarly, after an early delivery, a positive trait attribution (being hardworking) led to higher tips.[16] This research would seem to apply to wait times in restaurants as well.

In a large number of experiments, researchers provided information about an aggressor's intentions. Participants in these experiments were first provoked or harmed by an actor (presumed to be another participant). Then participants learned that the harm-doer either intended or didn't intend the harm. In the intentional condition, participants became more angry and retaliated more aggressively.[17] In a classic study by Kenneth Dodge, children's puzzles were messed up by another child, either intentionally or not. In the intentional condition, the young participants were more likely to mess up the other child's puzzle. A puzzle for a puzzle.[18]

Some of the mind-set research by Carol Dweck (author of *Mindset*) and colleagues also involved true experiments. These experiments showed that attributions (or beliefs about what causes what) can cause particular emotions and actions. In the fixed mind-set, the participant believes that traits are fixed, or not changeable. For example, we might think that a student is smart or not, and how much the student studies won't change that. In the growth mind-set, the participant believes that traits are malleable and that behaviors and outcomes are caused more by situational factors, including how much effort a student can devote to a course.

Many researchers over many years randomly assigned participants to different mind-sets in which participants were trained or primed to explain behaviors a particular way. Researchers instilled a fixed or growth mind-set by asking participants to read a persuasive article that supported that mind-set, to generate personal examples supporting it, or even just to read proverbs that effectively illustrated it. In all these studies, the fixed mind-set (akin to committing the FAE) led to more anger and retaliation against those who misbehaved.[19]

Attributions as a Consequence

When I described how angry Sommers got at that rotary blocker at the start of the previous chapter, I noted how honking our horns may reflect being true to our anger. Seeing that other driver as an idiot would also be true to our anger. What I mean to say here is that people like consistency, and so once the anger comes (whatever the cause), consistent cognitions or perceptions typically arise to justify that anger. Those perceptions include the FAE. Sommers's anger is more justified if that other driver truly is an idiot.

This emotion-precedes-thought idea is one of the lesser-known but important tenets of cognitive dissonance theory. Cognitive dissonance is a discomfort caused by inconsistency, and the theory has decades of support. Leon Festinger came to the dissonance idea after a 1934 earthquake in India. People near the affected area had anxiety and fear, and rumors circulated that worse disasters were coming. Festinger thought these people might have created and spread such rumors themselves to justify their fears. Festinger later conceptualized dissonance reduction as "making your view of the world fit with how you feel or what you've done."[20]

Similarly, I would argue, if we get angry at a coworker or significant other, we might (unconsciously) make our explanation of that person's behavior fit with that anger. Or we might be less willing to learn about the situational factors behind the behavior because such situational factors might undermine our negative dispositional inferences, particularly the inference of hostile intent. Indeed, some anger research to be discussed showed that anger caused participants not to take account of relevant situational factors, even when those participants were criminal investigators who were assessing a crime.

In multiple experiments, researchers randomly assigned participants to sad or angry conditions. A primary method to induce emotion was to ask participants to visualize as vividly as possible a sad or angry personal experience. In one case, participants had to describe their experience in writing. Another method asked participants to make facial expressions for sadness or anger. These methods had been verified as creating the intended emotion. Then, depending on the particular experiment, participants read a variety of scenarios in which there was a harm-doer and a victim or in which there was just a negative outcome. In another scenario, there was a storyline in which an individual's expectation for romance was thwarted.

The bottom line is that anger caused participants to think in more simplistic and punitive terms and to commit the FAE, whereas sadness caused the opposite (or led to more neutral responses). Compared to sadness, anger led participants to blame negative outcomes more on people and their dispositions and less on situational factors. Anger led participants to judge negative behaviors as being more intentional and to express greater willingness to punish the wrongdoer. Anger led criminal investigators to consider fewer situational factors in a criminal case, whereas sadness led to more thorough processing of all the information.[21]

And some people who act out their anger through aggressive behavior even blame their innocent victims and claim the victims deserved it. The next chapter covers victim blaming.

CHAPTER 8

VICTIM BLAMING

When individuals blame the victim for random acts of misfortune and insist that the world is just. . . . It is a confusion of what is patently outside the person—luck, chance, the fates, call it what you will—with some characteristic on the inside.
—Thomas Gilovich and Richard Eibach, authors of
"The Fundamental Attribution Error
Where It Really Counts"

We tend not only to hurt those we dislike but also to dislike those we hurt.
—David Myers, author of *Social Psychology*

In chapter 6, on driving with the FAE, I mentioned cases of road rage in which there is someone who gets hurt. In those cases, the assailant or the person responsible for the car accident is likely to blame the victim. On first look, this may be about avoiding legal culpability.

Then in chapter 7, on interpersonal conflicts off the road, I cited dissonance and attribution research showing that emotions can precede thought and that anger can literally cause the FAE and cause us to unfairly blame another. I also alluded to a line of research showing that aggressive or hurtful actions against an individual (often arising from anger) can cause the aggressor to make more negative dispositional attributions against that individual. Aggression against an individual can cause the aggressor to dislike that individual more than if the aggression had never taken place.

As social psychology text author David Myers wrote,

> We tend not only to hurt those we dislike but also to dislike those we hurt. . . . Harming an innocent victim—by uttering hurtful comments or delivering electric shocks—typically leads aggressors to disparage their victims, thus helping them justify their cruel behavior.[1]

It might sound pathetic, but cruel behavior toward another individual typically feels more justified if that individual is not a nice person. Our own cruel behavior can threaten our ego or feel inconsistent with our self-view (if we see ourselves as decent). So blaming the victim of our road rage may be more than just avoiding legal culpability. It can be about ego protection or avoiding the dissonance between seeing ourselves as decent and yet having caused harm to an innocent person. Oh, wait a minute—maybe this person is not so innocent. Yeah—that's it.

When aggressing against an individual causes the aggressor to disparage that individual, it's more than adding insult to injury. The injury actually causes the insult.

There are countless cases of victim blaming. The reasons for all of them fall into at least three categories to be discussed. The most subtle or counterintuitive of these reasons is illustrated here within an interpersonal conflict, in which the victim is someone *you* hurt (intentionally or unintentionally), and then by disparaging the victim, you feel better (not that all of us engage in this process). As I mentioned at the beginning of chapter 6, interpersonal conflict, victim blaming, and driving anger all intersect here. The present chapter completes this connection. But victim blaming occurs in many other settings besides on the road.

People can be blamed for being in an accident at home or work, being pickpocketed or robbed, being shot or killed (especially by police), being raped or sexually assaulted, being poor, being unemployed, losing their home to foreclosure, not having health insurance, having AIDS or other conditions or illnesses, being hazed or bullied (even if they're professional football players),[2] being caught in a mass shooting (such as the 2016 Orlando nightclub shooting),[3] and being caught in a natural disaster (such as Hurricane Katrina).[4] If children do something terrible or end up in a terrible outcome, and we can't bring ourselves to blame the children, we can always blame the parents—as when a toddler got into a gorilla enclosure, leading zoo officials to kill a beloved gorilla, or when eighth-graders visiting Washington, DC, didn't want to take a photo with the Speaker of the House.[5]

It's not that the blamed individuals in these outcomes are always blame-free. It's not that the blamed individuals bear zero responsibility. People may make mistakes at work that contribute to accidents. Maybe parents can do more to control their children. Maybe the fraternity member who gets hazed and injured knows full well that the hazing could get dangerous and makes the decision to risk it, independent of any conformity pressures (not that exerting his free will this way would justify the harmful behaviors against him).

But even in those cases, we often overestimate how much blame these individuals deserve, in that we typically underestimate the role played by circumstances. And ironically, if the perpetrator has not yet been caught or punished, if the injury or outcome is more severe or prolonged, and if the victim is especially powerless, then the victim blaming is greater.[6] Young children have been blamed for being sexually abused even if blamers had to go to the children's past lives to justify it.[7] Victims of natural disaster have been blamed for their suffering, their own deaths, and even the disaster itself, including because the victims were gay or supported gay rights.[8] Victim-blaming researcher Kent Harber and colleagues wrote that "blaming those most deserving of compassion may appear paradoxical if not perverse. Yet it can serve an important psychological function."[9]

I will not discuss all of these victim-blaming cases. There are many books solely about victim blaming that contain fuller discussions, especially regarding rape and poverty. And I am not trying to excuse victim blaming.

But I will describe the "psychological function" of victim blaming. Harber only mentioned one such function, the most commonly cited, but as I've mentioned, I think there are at least three possible reasons why so many of us (often unknowingly) utilize this form of the FAE.

Becoming aware of the reasons for victim blaming or learning more about it can help us to avoid victim blaming. In particular, if we're able to determine that our reason for blaming victims is ego threat, as in the road-rage example, then we can look for another way to protect or bolster our ego so we don't have to victim blame. Research has shown that alternative ego boosts reduce victim blaming. If the ego threat creates certain negative emotions, other research has shown that emotional disclosure can reduce victim blaming. Before deciding whether to blame the victim or not, share how you're feeling with someone.[10]

Reducing victim blaming is extremely important because if an innocent person suffers misfortune or physical attack and then, on top of that, is blamed for it, many negative consequences can occur. Such victim blaming reduces others' willingness to help those who are suffering and in need.[11] Victim blaming can increase victims' self-blame, self-silencing, anxiety, depression, and risk of post-traumatic stress disorder.[12] Self-blame is one of the few times we commit the FAE toward ourselves. It is ironic that others' FAE toward us can be responsible.

So I will refer to some of the cases of victim blaming and describe some of the relevant research as I go through each of the three reasons for victim blaming. Then I will discuss the case of people being blamed even for being unhappy, even when there are clear external causes for the unhappiness, such as disaster or divorce or death of a loved one. This topic is what I will call a gray area, because those you might feel are unfairly blaming you for your unhappiness may actually, in some cases, be trying to help you (and may even be clinically trained to help you this way!).

Particularly in the areas of sexual assault and child abuse, let me note that many therapists and victims prefer the label "survivor" over "victim." I know there are potential benefits in not accepting a victim role after suffering a traumatic event. I don't mean to treat the two labels as mutually exclusive. Being blameless in being attacked does not preclude having the power and resilience to recover from the trauma.

REASONS FOR VICTIM BLAMING

Personal Dissonance

In the road-rage example or other cases in which an aggressor hurts someone, the aggressor may feel dissonance between thinking oneself a decent person and yet having caused harm to someone innocent. Disparaging the victim helps to reduce that dissonance and address that ego threat. These aggressors may truly feel in the moment that the victim had it coming in some way.

In the classic research demonstrating this process, participants were given a cover story in which they had to deliver electric shocks to an actor playing the role of another participant. Participants were not overly pressured to deliver shocks because external pressure could provide an alternative means of reducing their dissonance, as in "the experimenter made me do it." Compared to a control condition or to pre-shock ratings, participants typically rated the victims after shocking them as less likable, less friendly, or less worthy of being the participant's close friend or roommate. (No shocks were actually delivered, but participants believed they were.)

In one such study, this victim-disparaging effect was only found when the participant expected no retaliation. This expectation can relate to the victim being more powerless, as in cases of domestic abuse in which abusers may say that the victims made them do it. In another study, the victim-disparaging effect was especially evident when the participants were first given positive feedback to boost their self-esteem. The researcher argued that having a positive self-image heading into the shocking stage increased the dissonance between self-image and hurting the victim. This result strongly suggested that this form of victim blaming is about ego defense.[13]

Road-rage and high-aggression examples may be rare compared to more everyday interactions in which we're responsible for someone else's pain. As Myers conveyed, even uttering hurtful comments can lead to blaming the person who gets hurt. Have you ever said the wrong thing to someone or come on a little too strong? Have you ever unintentionally made someone cry or feel bad? Thinking that the person who is hurt shouldn't be so sensitive or needs to grow a thicker skin may be a subtle form of victim blaming. It's at least worth thinking about if you've ever been in such a situation.

More common are instances of victim blaming when you are not responsible for someone's pain or suffering. Outside observers of road rage, as well as jury members in resulting court cases, often wonder whether the victims brought the situation on themselves or could have done more to prevent it. Observers of rape victims especially consider these possibilities. Defense attorneys for perpetrators may raise these issues. In these cases, victim blamers' own egos are not on the line. So victim blaming is not usually about ego protection or personal dissonance reduction. Why else do we blame victims?

Belief in a Just World

The reason for victim blaming that gets the vast majority of attention from researchers and popular press authors is that victim blaming allows the blamers to maintain a belief that the world is just. The reason victim blaming is an enormous literature is because of just-world theory, proposed by Melvin Lerner in 1980. In the just-world view, good things happen to good people and bad things happen to bad people. If something bad happens to someone who is good or undeserving of that outcome, then that worldview is threatened. And a threatened worldview, especially this one, can cause a great deal of distress. Put simply, seeing innocent people suffer is dissonant with just-world beliefs, and victim blaming reduces that dissonance.[14]

There is so much dissonance and stress for so many people when their just-world beliefs are threatened that people have developed many ways to reduce this stress. Lerner's 1980 book identified several strategies to cope with a threatened just-world belief. So it's not that people are necessarily eager to blame innocent victims. They have other options, both conscious and unconscious. If given the opportunity to reduce or stop suffering while it is ongoing, participants would do that before victim blaming. Participants also avoid victim blaming if they can convince themselves that "suffering builds character." But empirically speaking, victim blaming is an effective and common way to restore a just-world belief.[15]

Just-world beliefs are consistent with the common notions that you reap what you sow or that what goes around comes around. Interestingly, these adages might represent an A-implies-B problem. If you recall from chapter 1, I suggested that most cases of the FAE might boil down to a false assumption that just because A implies B, B must imply A. That error seems in play here, because even if sowing something bad or doing something bad always does come back around in the form of some negative outcome (A implies B), which is by no means agreed upon, that doesn't mean that a particular negative outcome necessarily reflects that you did something bad to bring it about. There are other possible causes of B besides A.

Research support for just-world theory lies in the aforementioned irony that if the perpetrator has not yet been caught or punished, if the injury or outcome is more severe or prolonged, and if the victim is especially powerless, then the victim blaming is greater. These conditions make the victim's outcome seem all the more unfair or unjust, and so they all represent greater threats to a just-world view and should indeed increase victim blaming. Research support for just-world theory also lies in the result that people who hold stronger just-world beliefs are more likely to blame victims.[16]

Need for Control

As I described in chapter 3 under "Motives That Drive the FAE," the FAE may be driven by a need to feel in control of our surroundings or by a desire to be able to predict or understand more than we actually can. I mentioned research that showed how reduced feelings of control caused greater misperceptions in which participants saw connections that did not exist. These connections included superstitious beliefs, such as that knocking on wood can somehow improve our luck at an important meeting.[17] I also mentioned the example of explaining an individual's unemployment or poverty by calling the individual lazy, because I probably don't see myself as lazy, and therefore I won't fear ever being unemployed or poor myself. Thinking I have control over this part of my future is comforting.

Many other examples of victim blaming can illustrate how fear of losing control of our livelihoods or lives can motivate us to connect a terrible outcome to some fault in the victims. In my view, being afraid that terrible and unforeseeable things can happen to us (triggered by the fact that such things happen to innocent others) goes beyond just a just-world belief getting threatened. The illusion of control is important to mental health,[18] and if we fear that uncontrollable factors can harm us at any moment, then that illusion gets shattered. Victim blaming keeps that fear in check.

Some just-world-belief researchers connect the need for control to just-world beliefs. But Melvin Lerner, who is credited with just-world theory, considered the belief in a just world a motive unto itself and separate from a belief in a "controllable world."[19] Others have argued that just-world beliefs can be subsumed under a general need for certainty. Some even raise the issue that the "belief" in a just world is not really the same as the psychological "need" for a just world.[20] So in explaining victim blaming, I'm separating the need for control or certainty, or the fear of losing control, from just-world beliefs.

This distinction between just-world beliefs and a need for control or certainty can be important because it can suggest other ways to reduce victim blaming. When victim blaming was caused by ego threat, I mentioned how researchers found that alternative ego boosts can reduce victim blaming. So it's possible that alternative ways to bolster feelings of control or certainty (besides victim blaming), such as religion, might similarly reduce victim blaming when people are faced with explaining human tragedies and feel a loss of control. Research has already shown that having "participants affirm their important values" as a means of boosting their "sense of security" precluded the typical misperceptions that arise from reduced feelings of control. These researchers speculated that an increased feeling of control provided by psychotherapy might similarly preclude a client from seeing negative intentions in others where they don't exist.[21]

Alternatively, if researchers can find a way to make people more comfortable with uncertainty, that should also reduce victim blaming. My own research has already found that people who naturally have lower needs for control and certainty are less prone to the FAE.[22] I will discuss this individual-difference research further in chapter 9.

GRAY AREAS

The real-life examples of victim blaming discussed thus far are relatively straightforward. But in day-to-day life, there could be many subtle or harder-to-interpret forms of victim blaming. I refer to some of these examples as gray areas because some readers might truly identify with the victim-blaming component here, while other readers might wonder what all the fuss is about.

The American Dream

Although Americans don't all agree that the dream is still alive, and not all politicians articulate the dream the same way, the American dream is basically the traditional view that if you work hard enough, then you will succeed and be rich. In logic terms, this statement can be rephrased (as the contrapositive) as follows: If you are not successful or well-off, then you did not work hard enough. This idea is classic victim blaming of those who are unemployed or poor—not that those who promote this version of the American dream mean to victim blame. In fact, it may be quite the opposite. Publicly espousing the American dream might be an attempt to motivate people or show patriotism.

Secretary of Housing and Urban Development Ben Carson seems to believe in the American dream. He uses himself as an example because he was born in poverty but became very accomplished. His views were in the news in 2017 for taking the idea up a notch and saying that poverty is a "state of mind." The backlash was swift, including from one Twitter commenter who said she would tell her landlord that she paid her rent with positive thinking.[23]

In fairness, the fuller quote from Carson is that "poverty to a large extent is also a state of mind." Carson also made some research-based suggestions for what people could do to minimize their risk of ending up in poverty. Some social scientists responded that correlations between mind-set and outcome are tricky to interpret, especially in a case study like Carson (who became successful and presumably had a positive mind-set), because poverty and the experience of deprivation can actually cause the negative mind-set that Carson said was the cause of poverty. Of Carson's view, one social scientist said, "I think he's got the relationship backwards."[24]

In further fairness to Carson, a Republican, those on the other political side also subscribe to the American dream. But in general, according to John Kenneth White, editor of *The American Dream in the 21st Century*, Democrats are more likely to support the government-run initiatives to increase opportunities for everyone to achieve the dream, whereas Republicans are more likely to emphasize the freedom in America to make the most of yourself on your own.[25]

Well-Intentioned Advice

Sometimes when we're going through a very hard time in a close relationship or at work, a close friend or loved one might try to be supportive by
making suggestions for what we can do to help ourselves: "Don't let yourself get down." "Don't let them make you feel this way." "I don't think you
should be putting this much pressure on yourself."

Some of us might hear only the support in words like these and feel better.
Indeed, these attempts at support may not even be meant as suggestions for
action per se but rather as simple expressions of sympathy. But some of us
might notice an implication that we're "letting" bad things happen to us, or
that we're the ones "putting" the pressure on ourselves. Maybe we are indeed
doing those things, and the supportive words help us to feel empowered and
to stop hurting ourselves. But maybe we feel unfairly victim blamed.

And who knows? Feeling victim blamed might not be just in our
minds. In the back of the mind of the supporting person, maybe they
believe that we did partly bring it on ourselves or that we are not doing
enough to help ourselves. It's hard for a close friend or loved one to watch
us suffer, especially if what's happening to us is not our fault and not
under our control. That's so unfair. Cue just-world theory. Things make a
little more sense or cause less distress for those watching us suffer if what's
happening to us is partly our fault or we're partly letting it happen.[26]

On Facebook, I've noticed several posts that I suppose are meant to
be supportive for anyone going through a bad day but that might rub
some people the wrong way if they're looking at the posts through a just-
world-theory lens. These posts are pieces of advice within those large
colored boxes, if you know the boxes I mean. Sometimes the advice is
attributed to famous people. "No one can make you feel inferior without
your consent." Or "There is no such thing as a bad day, just bad moments
that we *choose* [italics added] to carry around all day long!" I can envision
a Twitter commenter saying, "Thank goodness—I can just choose not to
carry around my injury from my car accident today."

Carolyn Gregoire, senior writer for *HuffPost*, titled her well-intentioned article, "This Is Scientific Proof That Happiness Is a Choice." She argued that "a large body of research in the field of positive psychology has shown that happiness is a choice that anyone can make." She cited a famous psychologist in saying that "the greatest discovery of any generation is that a human can alter his life by altering his attitude."[27] The research results are, of course, on average—it's not that "anyone" can become happy simply by following her strategies. But it's more motivating to say "anyone," isn't it? No, not for everyone. Some find it demoralizing.

Sandra Lee Dennis, author of *Love and the Mystery of Betrayal*, interpreted this view of happiness as coming from "a culture that is blind to betrayal and intolerant of emotional pain." Dennis went on to describe this approach to happiness as follows:

> No matter what happens to you, it is assumed that you have created your own reality. . . . The upshot of this perspective is that your suffering would vanish if only you adopted a more evolved perspective and stopped feeling aggrieved. . . . When you most need validation and support to get through the worst pain of your life, to be confronted with the well-meaning, but quasi-religious fervor of these insidious half-truths can be deeply demoralizing.[28]

Psychologist Barbara Held similarly referred to the "tyranny of the positive attitude in America," in which the emotional sufferer can end up feeling even worse after being blamed for not forging a better attitude.[29] Happiness researchers actually do know that attitude is not the "only" determinant of our happiness. But some popular press authors in the positive-thinking self-help movement go too far and oversimplify the message.

Another Facebook quote-in-a-box I found states, "When you think everything is someone else's fault, you will suffer a lot. When you realize that everything springs only from yourself, you will learn both peace and joy." Because of the all-or-nothing fallacy here (noted as a cognitive distortion by cognitive-behavioral therapists), there's not much room for your suffering to be anyone's fault but your own. But this line was credited to the Dalai Lama (which I have confirmed elsewhere). Of course, maybe this line was taken out of context from a lengthier or more subtle discussion, but there are philosophies and psychotherapies that promote the idea that all that matters is how you perceive things. Some Facebook posts are less gray when it comes to a victim-blaming message, such as "Some people create their own storms, then get upset when it rains."

Sometimes well-intentioned support groups and other organizations offer advice to help people to avoid *becoming* victims. In a report for the AAA Foundation for Traffic Safety, Louis Mizell suggested to refrain from "showing any type of bumper sticker or slogan that could be offensive."[30] I can see some people taking offense at the implication they are responsible for a road-rage attack because of their bumper sticker, not that Mizell meant to victim blame.

The advice to women to minimize their chances of being sexually assaulted includes "stay sober" and "use a buddy system." Such advice is not appreciated by all women and in fact can be seen as full-fledged victim blaming, according to Alexandra Brodsky, author of an article in the *New York Times* titled "Blame Rape's Enablers, Not the Victims." Brodsky wrote that such advice can "ease assailants' culpability by fixating on strategies survivors supposedly should have used to avoid assault."[31]

Psychologist Sherry Hamby, a founding editor of the journal *Psychology of Violence*, has conveyed that even therapists who work in prevention programs may unknowingly contribute to victim blaming by giving such advice. Hamby was quoted as saying,

> The absolute safest thing to do would be to never leave your house because then you'd be much less likely to get victimized. I don't think people have done a very good job of thinking that through and trying to say what the limits of people's responsibility are for avoiding crime.[32]

In the Clinic

So therapists may be at risk of victim blaming in the well-intentioned advice to women on how to avoid sexual assault. Other research has shown that therapists can blame rape victims even beyond giving preventative advice and can fail to consider the context from which clients come.[33] Of course therapists are not perfect. We are all at risk of bias. But therapists deal with clients at their most vulnerable, so discussing the potential for victim blaming or other biases in the clinic seems especially important. And of course, some therapists are at greater risk of bias than others, and not all therapists see things the same way.

Some therapists completely blame their clients for lying, or assume the client is just ashamed about something, while other therapists blame themselves and reflect on the office environment they've created.[34] And as I mentioned in chapter 5 on social roles, when clients lie about or keep secret their real concerns about the therapy or therapist, that can be due to the role of "good client" and not necessarily shame or a disposition to lie.

One therapist acknowledged that in his early years, due to embarrassment, he usually lied to his clients when they "accurately observed that [he] looked sleepy or stressed." He regretted undermining his clients' confidence in their own perceptions that were in fact accurate. He wrote how "sometimes, it can feel crazy-making, not to have your perceptions validated."[35]

This is one story. I'm not claiming that therapists lie easily. Far from it. But it is a real issue for clients to not feel their perceptions validated or to feel blamed for their suffering because they don't perceive things the right way.[36] As Sandra Lee Dennis conveyed, being told that "you have created your own reality" and that your emotional suffering can end by simply changing your attitude "can be deeply demoralizing." Most therapists who take this change-your-attitude approach are probably not that simplistic. And most of these therapists are probably trained to balance that approach with appropriate levels of other support. But some clients might still feel demoralized, perhaps especially if that balance is off and the therapist explicitly conveys the view that clients' problems are due solely to clients' inaccurate perceptions (even when the clients' circumstances are overwhelming).

Though I've read some of the clinical literatures, I am not trained in psychotherapy. So I will try to be brief in commenting that one of the tenets of cognitive and cognitive-behavioral therapy (CBT) seems to be that clients suffer from anxiety and depression because they do indeed think incorrectly or irrationally. In my view, that tenet might have victim blaming built into it, despite its potential to be empowering for many clients and despite therapists' good intentions. At least one practicing therapist has gone further than I in referring to a "'blame-the-victim' ethos that's inherent to CBT."[37]

David Burns, author of *The Feeling Good Handbook*, and many others who practice CBT do convey the principle that anxiety and depressive disorders are caused by cognitive distortions of reality. Of course, for many clients that may be the case, and therapy that tries to modify those cognitions can be helpful. But ironically, Burns and other therapists sometimes use cognitive distortions (even from Burns's own top-ten list of distortions) to try to change clients' thinking. In particular, Burns regularly encourages clients to realize that "it's not the end of the world."

In one case in Burns's book, a parent made a mistake that could have made a daughter sick. The parent got scared, but Burns's "rational" response stated that "it won't be the end of the world if she does [get sick]." After saying the world won't end, Burns sometimes continued with a life-goes-on assurance, such as "life goes on even if you're not successful all the time." I don't mean to cherry-pick from a very lengthy book. There are a variety of cases and different types of advice, many of which can be very helpful. Even the world-is-not-ending approach can be helpful for some clients. But most parents who fear for their child's health probably don't actually believe the world will end, even if their anxiety is spiking. For a therapist to exaggerate the parental concern to that level seems to be a distortion Burns calls "magnification." And pointing out that either the world will end or life will go on as normal seems to fit the distortion called "all-or-nothing thinking."[38]

Even if most clients' anxiety and depression are due to cognitive distortions or exaggerations, Burns and many authors seem to overgeneralize this possibility to all clients and cases. Moreover, many of those who support and practice CBT seem to ignore two big literatures that complicate the overall mental health picture: the literatures of depressive realism and the role of positive illusions in mental health.

Depressive realism refers to the findings that moderately depressed individuals have more accurate perceptions than nondepressed individuals. Indeed, depressed and sad individuals are less prone to the FAE.[39] The positive-illusions literature makes the case that certain biases, such as unrealistic optimism and illusion of control, are part of good mental health and even good physical health.[40] I will discuss these literatures further in chapter 10 and the epilogue. There are debates within these literatures. I'm not trying to tell you to stop seeing your cognitive-behavioral therapist. The therapy can be helpful even if your cognitions are not distorted, and some therapists effectively borrow parts of CBT in a broader or more varied approach.

But as a social psychologist, I consider it a red flag when I read books and articles about CBT and see no mention of these literatures. My concern grows further when I speak with those who teach or administer CBT and learn that they haven't even heard of these literatures.

CBT is often discussed as the best evidence-based treatment available for anxiety and depression, though not all meta-analyses agree. Success rates can vary between 25 and 60 percent, depending on various factors, including who the clients are. It does not work for everyone. And these percentages don't count clients who refuse to try the therapy.[41]

I wonder if one reason for the refusals or for why the therapy doesn't work for everyone is because of the demoralized feeling conveyed by some clients and acknowledged by some psychologists as due to victim blaming. I know other reasons can include that some clients don't do their "homework" and that some cases are just too extreme. But I also wonder if the therapy doesn't work for everyone because the cause of some people's anxiety or depression is not irrationality but, rather, accurate views of a truly horrible life situation.

Clients are not all the same. The next chapter covers individual differences further.

CHAPTER 9

THE INDIVIDUAL MATTERS TOO

We are not slaves to the power of situational forces. . . . In all the situations we have explored together, there were always a few [individuals], a minority, who stood firm.
—Philip Zimbardo, author of *The Lucifer Effect*

To be yourself in a world that is constantly trying to make you something else is the greatest accomplishment.
—Ralph Waldo Emerson, essayist and poet

In Stanley Milgram's famous obedience study, an authority figure in a white lab coat put participants under extreme pressure and ordered them to electrically shock another supposed participant to the point of screams and worse. Despite the pressure, 35 percent of participants refused to obey.[1]

In Solomon Asch's famous conformity study, five actors pretended to be participants sitting around a table and one by one spoke out loud the same wrong answer in several visual-perception exercises. The real participant knew the correct answer and was the last of the group to speak. Despite the pressure to go along, 25 percent of participants still gave the correct answer for all exercises—they never budged.[2]

In the well-known story, Kitty Genovese was murdered in 1964 outside a New York City apartment complex while thirty-eight onlookers did nothing to help. That is the power of diffusion of responsibility across too many bystanders, or so most reports said. But it turns out there was a bystander who shouted and scared the perpetrator away (initially), which allowed Genovese to make it into her apartment building.[3]

In the first bystander-effect study stemming from the Genovese story, John Darley and Bibb Latané staged a student's epileptic seizure over an intercom system for a participant to hear. When there were supposedly three other participants hearing the same thing (versus no other participants), 31 percent of participants still reported the emergency within a minute (compared to 85 percent of participants who thought they were alone).[4]

These examples are just a few of so many that illustrate that the individual matters, even in classic studies that showed how powerful the context can be in influencing our behaviors. The context didn't influence everyone. There were always some individuals who didn't fit the classic pattern and who were unaffected or less affected by the situational factors. Who are these individuals? Is there something about their traits that made them respond differently?

THE GLASS IS NOT TOTALLY EMPTY

So there are always a few individuals who stand firm. But for those who value individuality, I need to mention that this isn't a "Is the glass half empty or half full?" kind of thing. In these classic studies, the situation clearly overpowered most participants (not that I think those participants should feel ashamed). What I would say instead is that the glass is not totally empty.

Social science results are always on average. There are always individual differences. Strong situations won't usually overpower everyone, even if they overpower most of us. Some of us have traits, experiences, or goals that appear to make us less affected. Even when a situation does influence us, it might partly be because of something about us, not despite us. Some of us have traits, experiences, or goals that make us more suscep-tible to certain situational influences or more interested in going along. An easy-to-provoke person will respond more strongly to provocation. These cases amount to a type of interaction between person and situa-tion, in which the situational influence is there, but the individual's per-sonal factors can decrease or increase the degree of that influence.[5]

But aside from interactions, personal and situational factors can also simply be acting at the same time. As I've tried to convey throughout the book, people's behaviors or outcomes are usually caused by a combi-nation of personal and situational factors (in addition to interactions). Carrying out a harmful behavior can technically be caused by both situ-ational pressures, such as being ordered, and personal characteristics, such as being aggressive. A teen going along with peers in a questionable act can be caused by both conformity pressures and a lack of good judgment. Reckless driving can be part idiocy and part emergency. Losing a job can be part incompetence and part colossal economic forces.

We usually underestimate the situational factors like conformity pressures, economic forces, and unseen emergencies, but the personal factors can still matter. The individual is part of the equation—very often a smaller part than we think, but not necessarily at a zero level. Individ-uals' personal characteristics can (but don't have to) contribute to their behaviors or outcomes just as the influences from the context do.

LET'S NOT LOSE THE INDIVIDUAL

As a social psychologist, I was trained in a tradition that wants to teach people not to overlook the power of context. Most of us too easily and too quickly make assumptions about each other's traits and intentions. We overconfidently think we can predict the behavior of someone we know based on inferred traits. We overestimate our ability to read a per-son's facial expressions or body language. We think we can infer attitudes, prejudice, or negative intentions from a simple question someone asks us or even from a single word choice. "Whatever."

Politicians or media give us quotes out of context, and we react strongly without wondering about the full context or waiting for the quoted individual to weigh in. We think victims bring their fate upon themselves or at least could have done more to prevent it. We too easily blame others and get angry, and sometimes, as a result, we take misguided aggressive action. Oftentimes all we can see behind evil actions are evil people.

If we were more able to look past the individual and see the fuller context, then we would often realize that our initial assumptions were wrong or needed adjustment. If we could consider just the possibility that there *is* a fuller context and that there might be unseen situational factors, then we would be more willing to help victims. We would be less quick to blame and get angry. Saying "What's wrong with your situation?" versus "What's wrong with you?" can totally change the dynamic of the social interaction that follows a perceived transgression.

These are some of the messages I've been trying to convey so far in this book. I stand by all of them, even though not all of us fall into every one of these patterns.

But sometimes I've noticed that this important tenet and goal of social psychology might get taken a little too far. In the effort to increase the attention paid to context, the power of the individual can get a little lost along the way, at least in the minds of some readers and students.[6]

Sam Sommers, author of *Situations Matter*, has said that despite common beliefs about personality, "how we react to the world is actually driven by situations."[7] On the topic of romance, Sommers wrote that "attraction, like so much of daily experience, is all about the situation."[8] Other popular press authors describe the classic research by Milgram, Asch, or Darley and convey similarly black-and-white messages, like how "situations not personality dictate our behaviour" or how situations "trumped personal values."[9]

I once observed an instructor of an introductory social science course describe the Milgram obedience research. She described it very well and segued appropriately to a discussion of the Nazis during the Holocaust. But then she concluded that it was very unlikely that the Nazis did what they did because they were evil. This instructor seemed to take an either-or approach and landed on the side of the power of the situation to explain extreme wrongdoing. She is not alone in teaching Milgram's research this way.

In truth, if there were really only two choices—the situation or the person—then social psychology does typically put its money on the situation, but it's more complicated than that. The Nazis could have been evil in addition to being subjected to immense pressures against them and their families from superior officers and society. Without noting that complexity, and without reminding students or readers that explaining is not excusing, social psychologists sometimes come off as being in the business of exonerating wrongdoers (which is not the case). Research has shown that the simplistic message that context causes evil can undermine social psychology's credibility and make some people even less convinced that situations matter, especially when the evil has affected those people personally.[10]

Philip Zimbardo is sometimes criticized for going too far by writing a whole book on how context can make even good people do evil things. He titled it *The Lucifer Effect: Understanding How Good People Turn Evil*. And he even added another layer to the context by discussing the larger institutions or systemic influences that create the day-to-day situations that cause the evil. His book focused on his famous Stanford Prison Experiment, which showed how a strong enough system and situation could turn everyday students into abusive prison guards. Zimbardo held this experiment up as a primary example of how "certain very powerful social situations, settings, and structures can . . . suppress individual differences, and compromise deeply held values."[11]

But even the Stanford Prison Experiment turns out to be less clearcut. The guards showed many individual differences, and their personalities could have still played a role in their behavior. I will discuss the

Stanford Prison Experiment later in this chapter. And by the end of his book, even Zimbardo briefly highlighted the power of the individual, in a chapter on heroes—those who don't become evil or turn a blind eye even when the context encourages or demands it. Situations matter a lot, but the individual matters too.

I begin this discussion of the power of the individual by further describing the Kitty Genovese story and the bystander-effect literature. Not only did a bystander intervene and appear to save Kitty Genovese's life at the start of the incident, but a careful examination of the research reveals that victims have less to worry about in a large group of onlookers than social scientists have been saying. It's not just about clarifying the results. There was also, unfortunately, a mistake in a famous 1981 bystander-effect review, the correction of which has big implications.

I stumbled across the mistake myself in the late 1990s and eventually published its correction in 2008. Yet that mistake is still little known. I showed that as the number of bystanders increases, the likelihood that victims receive help from at least one bystander actually increases, if anything. Individual bystanders matter more than we thought, even against the forces of diffusion of responsibility. This finding is only slowly making its way into textbooks and bystander research, so I've been doing what I can to spread the word.[12]

THE TRUTH ABOUT THE BYSTANDER EFFECT

The Kitty Genovese story is often used to illustrate the bystander effect: how the more bystanders there are, the more the situation will inhibit helping behavior. It's one of those results that, although surprising and counterintuitive when first discovered, has probably begun to enter the American psyche as common sense at this point. Most of my students seem to recognize the bystander effect when I discuss it in class. So it's ironic that there are some common confusions or mistakes in how the research and Genovese story are reported.

No one supposedly intervened that night to help Genovese. It shocked the nation. But as I've mentioned, the story as commonly told has an error—in fact, multiple errors, the crucial one being that there actually was a bystander who intervened right away. This bystander saved Genovese's life in allowing her to make it into her apartment building. Unfortunately, the attacker did return and murder Genovese in a stairwell, which was not observable by most bystanders through their apartment windows, despite how the story is almost always told.

Even before Genovese moved out of view, the number of witnesses was apparently much fewer than thirty-eight, and not many of them had a direct or prolonged view of the initial attack, though they could hear screaming. In addition, there was at least one other bystander (and maybe others) who phoned the police right away. By the time the police arrived, Genovese was still alive, but she did not ultimately survive the attack.[13]

Even though two or more bystanders directly helped, some of us might think they could have done more. They could have run out there and walked Genovese to her apartment. They could have helped to fight off the attacker when he returned. But in life-threatening circumstances, in my view, it is hard to expect people to put themselves into harm's way. Maybe the average person is not brave enough, but there could also be situational reasons not to be a hero. Maybe some onlookers were single parents with kids who would be alone if something were to happen to their (heroic) mom or dad.

The first study following the Genovese story was the aforementioned staging of the epileptic seizure by Darley and Latané. Even though a greater portion of isolated participants reported the emergency compared to participants who thought there were three others, the authors noted that, importantly, the three other participants were not real. What if there were four actual participants who heard the emergency? In that case, how likely would it be that the victim would have received help from at least one of the participants? The authors were able to extrapolate an answer. They found that the probability of the victim receiving help was no different between conditions (though the help would come faster with fewer bystanders).[14]

Correcting a Computational Mistake

But this was a single study. Maybe other studies would show different probabilities. So even more important than a single study is a report that averages numerous studies. Such a report is called a meta-analysis. There was a 1981 meta-analysis by Bibb Latané and Steve Nida that considered more than fifty studies on the bystander effect.[15]

Latané and Nida concluded that victims are less likely to receive help the more bystanders there are. However, the authors made a computational mistake in their meta-analysis. In cases in which bystanders were under restricted communication with each other, such as hearing an attack from their separate apartments in the Genovese case, the authors miscomputed a mean. I noticed this mistake, corrected it, ran a few updated analyses, and authored a published article in 2008 to discuss the implications. I explained how under restricted communication, the results now showed that the more bystanders there are, the *more* likely the victim would receive help.[16]

This new result made sense, given the little-known truths about the Genovese case. Had only a few people heard Genovese scream, maybe it would have been less likely for one of them to be brave enough or empathetic enough to do something. The more people who heard the scream, the higher the likelihood that one of them would be sufficiently brave or empathetic. This pattern is just the raw power of numbers, but such a power would not lead to helping behavior unless there were an individual who wanted to and was able to help among the numbers. There are heroes among us for whom the situation does not matter. And the more bystanders there are, the more likely there will be a hero among them.

But the correction only applied to restricted communication. Under full communication, in which participants could see each other, the

224

authors' conclusion was still technically correct, that a victim would be more likely to receive help from a lone bystander. One explanation was that compared to restricted communication, participants under full communication might feel a greater risk of embarrassment to act when others could see them.

However, the authors conducted the meta-analysis by dividing bystander situations into two categories, situations in which there was one bystander versus more than one bystander. In other words, whether there were two bystanders or ten, those instances were lumped into one category. Such a lumping-together has since been criticized as not the best way to analyze such data, though it was not uncommon at the time to group this way. Since then, statisticians have strongly recommended conducting correlational analyses instead.[17]

I reanalyzed the data to assess more accurately what happened as the number of bystanders increased one by one. My correlational analyses showed, again, that in restricted communication, the more bystanders there were, the more likely the victim would receive help. In full communication, the number of bystanders did not matter—the correlation was statistically zero. Combining both restricted and full communication yielded a positive correlation—the more bystanders, the greater the likelihood of receiving help. In sum, overall, there appears to be some safety in numbers.

Another meta-analysis decision the authors made was basically to weight each study equally in averaging the effects. But some studies provided many more participants, so the authors also reported what would happen if they took sample sizes into account. In that case, their own results revealed that the likelihood of receiving help was greater when there was more than a lone bystander, consistent with my new findings. But the authors downplayed this outcome and stuck with their original weightings. Both approaches had justification at the time.

The Likelihood of Receiving Help versus Social Inhibition

The meta-analysis and my correction article are more complicated than I can fully convey here. But there's at least one more crucial point to make. The likelihood of a victim receiving help from at least one bystander is technically different from the probability that a single or average bystander would offer help. In other words, the probability of the average bystander helping could decrease in a larger crowd (think of a single rider on a subway car full of people), while at the same time, the victim could be more likely to *receive* help from at least one individual in that crowd. It just takes one bystander for help to be received.

What the meta-analysis and my study both confirmed was that the more bystanders there are, the lower the probability that the average bystander would help. This effect is called "social inhibition"—the average bystander is inhibited by a large group of bystanders. And yet, as I've reported overall, the more bystanders there are, the more likely the victim will receive help. Social inhibition is generally not strong enough to overtake the raw power of numbers, especially in restricted communication. It's a subtle mathematical point about the net effect of competing odds, but it's crucial to understanding what would happen to a victim in a crowd.

Unfortunately, many popular press and academic authors write about the bystander effect in ways that muddle the distinction between the likelihood of receiving help and social inhibition. In fact, several authors actually define the bystander effect as the reduced likelihood of receiving help, without apparently realizing the results they cite are for social inhibition. And I would argue that most people understand the bystander effect as the reduced likelihood of receiving help. As Latané and Nida themselves noted, the victim doesn't really care about social inhibition or the probability of the average bystander helping. What the victim actually cares about is *receiving* help—whether at least one bystander will do something to aid the victim.

226

Indeed, likelihood of receiving help must be what readers of tragic news stories care about as well. The reason bystander-effect research gets discussed in the news is because victims sometimes receive no help from anyone despite many onlookers, which is tragic and thus newsworthy. Or there are hero stories in which despite a large crowd, someone does step up and save the victim. But the hero story is unlikely to be titled "Child Saved by Hero in Crowd While Probability of Average Bystander Helping Plummeted."

People care about whether help was received, and probably not that average probability part. And based on my new results and even some of Latané and Nida's original results, the victim overall is more likely to receive help the more bystanders there are. In sum, the victim has less to worry about than we thought if there are many bystanders present.

Of course, there are still tragic stories in the news in which no one helps despite a large number of passersby. There could be multiple unique factors, and even with fewer bystanders, the same outcome might have occurred. So let me emphasize that I am not saying victims have nothing to worry about in a large crowd. If you ever find yourself in need of help in front of many people, the textbook advice is still good to follow. Point to or pick out one of the bystanders, if you can, and tell that person you need help. Following this advice can improve your chances to receive timely aid.

And if you are ever a bystander and hear a scream, I am not saying you have nothing to worry about. Hopefully you won't use my new results to assume some other bystander will help the victim. If you would have been someone to step up and help, hopefully you still will. In fact, learning about the classic bystander-effect research has made students more likely to help.[18] I myself probably benefited from this knowledge once or twice.

I lived in Milwaukee right after getting married, and one evening, my wife and I were in our apartment and heard a woman screaming on the street below. The scream came from around the corner from our window. A scream heard from one of dozens of apartments immediately rung of Kitty Genovese. I assumed others could hear what we heard, and I knew there was a risk that none of us would do anything or act quickly enough. So I fearfully headed outside to the street. I was grateful to find another guy running down the stairwell as I entered it. We quickly confirmed with each other the reason we were running. By the time we got outside, a purse snatcher had gotten away. The woman was OK. Others had reached her before we did. Maybe I would have run outside even without knowing about the bystander effect—I don't know—but I felt glad that I knew about it. Each bystander of course has to decide individually whether to take any risks in trying to help a victim.

In Cyberspace

In establishing the bystander effect or diffusion of responsibility as an easy-to-see phenomenon, *Situations Matter* author Sam Sommers wrote, "Look no farther than the ubiquitous mass e-mail to catch this process in action." He described his immediate deletion of such emails, such as when a recent mass email from a colleague asked if anyone could help a student with an internship question. Sommers guessed that each of his colleagues would similarly ignore the request, concluding that "being in a crowd—even a virtual, cyberspace one—permits inaction" and that the student would be better off contacting one faculty member directly.[19]

But according to my reanalyses of the data from the 1981 meta-analysis, the opposite should be true. Cyberspace is a pure case of restricted communication, in which individual respondents or bystanders cannot see each other (but know others are there), and my reanalyses had shown that the likelihood of receiving help increased with more bystanders in restricted communication. Therefore, the student should be better off sending a mass email—the more recipients, the better, even if each recipient knows how many other recipients there are.

At the end of my 2008 article, in a section titled "Online Requests for Help," I briefly summarized the results of my new analyses of three relevant cyberspace studies. In these studies, someone made an email or internet-based request for help from varying numbers of others. In each study, as predicted, the likelihood of receiving help increased as number of recipients increased, even when recipients knew how many other recipients there were. Social inhibition still occurred (in that there was a decrease in the average probability of a recipient responding), but it was not strong enough to overtake the power of numbers.

I later conducted a small meta-analysis and reported more fully on this cyberspace pattern. So even online, the more people you contact, the more likely there should be some individual willing or able to help you. If you're in trouble, then we can say the more people you contact, the more likely there will be a hero among them.[20]

Heroes

I attended a talk by Philip Zimbardo at a conference in the summer of 2007. I think the talk was for his book *The Lucifer Effect*, but what I most remember were his moving comments about heroes. He defined heroes as people who are somehow able to resist the situational pressures to do evil or the pressures not to act when someone needs help. I believe that was the first time I heard about Wesley Autrey, the "Subway Hero" who in 2007 faced a real-life version of Darley and Latané's staged epileptic seizure.

After a man had a seizure and fell onto the train tracks in front of a platform full of people in New York City, Autrey left his children with a stranger and jumped onto the tracks to try to pull the victim to safety. But there wasn't enough time because a train was coming. Autrey put his own body over the man's within a set of tracks, and the train passed overhead within an inch or so of Autrey's head. I later learned that as the man's seizure began, Autrey and two other bystanders "rushed to help." The man initially seemed OK but then fell onto the tracks.[21]

Why didn't diffusion of responsibility stop Autrey and the two other bystanders from acting? I don't believe it matters for my point. Even if there are strong situational factors pressuring people not to act, a few individuals may still act to help someone.

In Reflection

The first part of this chapter has focused on how the individual bystander is more important than most of us previously thought and how there are heroes who help the innocent even when the context pressures them to do nothing. But I know that I am also making a new scientific statement about safety in numbers. Before about fifty years ago, we assumed there was safety in numbers. Then after the case of Kitty Genovese, and dozens of studies, the idea of safety in numbers became a myth, one of the *50 Great Myths of Popular Psychology*, according to the 2010 book by that name.[22] And now I'm saying the myth may be partly true. We can go back, at least in part, to what we originally believed. In general, a victim is equally or more likely to receive help the more bystanders there are. In the least, we can discount the general notion that there is *less* safety in numbers.

Because of how long social science and the public have been calling the notion of safety in numbers a myth, I won't be surprised if there is some pushback on some of my assertions here. I welcome a discussion. I don't presume to know how a discussion might unfold, and maybe this issue will continue to go relatively unnoticed. But I hope that readers and reviewers will carefully assess my position, even review my data, take note of my caveats, and maybe begin to hold a slightly less pessimistic view of what happens when a large group of many individuals becomes aware of an innocent victim who needs help. Other researchers have also begun to argue for a more positive take on large groups of humans, specifically in how they can be helpful to a victim.[23]

THE STANFORD PRISON EXPERIMENT: WERE THE GUARDS ALREADY AGGRESSIVE?

Besides the bystander research, another classic study that is used to illustrate the power of the situation is the 1973 Stanford Prison Experiment (SPE) conducted by Craig Haney, Curtis Banks, and Philip Zimbardo.[24] In this study, university students played the roles of guards and prisoners after volunteering for a study on "prison life." Zimbardo played the role of prison superintendent. By most accounts, the mock-prison context and roles drove the guards to abuse the prisoners, leading Zimbardo to call an early stop to the study. But questions have been raised about the possible role played by the guards' personalities.

Among a few controversies surrounding the SPE, a later attempt at replication that screened out aggressive personalities yielded guards who did not give in to their roles in abusive ways. Even for the original SPE, later reports, including by Zimbardo, highlighted participants' individual differences—how there were both "mean and good guards" and how "both prisoners and guards challenged their roles not only at the start, but throughout the entire study."[25]

The study that failed to replicate the SPE differed from the SPE in several ways, so it's impossible to say whether screening out aggressive personalities was the reason the guards did not become abusive in the replication study. However, a 2007 study by Thomas Carnahan and Sam McFarland did demonstrate a real possibility that the volunteers for the SPE already had traits that might make them more prone to abusive behavior.[26]

Carnahan and McFarland wondered whether the phrase "prison life" in the advertising for the SPE might have skewed who was willing to volunteer for the experiment. So the researchers created two ads. Both were nearly identical to the original SPE ad, but one stated "a psychological study of prison life" and the other just stated "a psychological study." The results were astonishing. Compared to participants who volunteered for just "a psychological study," those who volunteered for "a psychological

231

study of prison life" scored significantly higher on measures of aggressiveness, authoritarianism, Machiavellianism, narcissism, and social dominance. The "prison life" participants also scored significantly lower on measures of empathy and altruism.

Carnahan and McFarland concluded that the reason for the SPE guards' abusive behavior might be more than just the powerful prison situation. The reason might also include the guards' traits because of a self-selection bias in who volunteered. In particular, the authors suggested that the situation and traits might interact to produce the abusive outcomes. The authors also made a case that there might be a similar interaction behind the real-life abuses in the Abu Ghraib prison scandal, which Zimbardo discussed in his book *The Lucifer Effect*.

In my view, Carnahan and McFarland worded their conclusions carefully and cautiously. They said "might" and "perhaps" and talked about both personal and situational factors in an interaction. They even acknowledged that their results did "not discount the power of a prison simulation, or of a real prison, to induce abusive behavior."[27]

But surprisingly, these qualifiers and acknowledgments did not seem to matter much when two of the original authors of the SPE, Haney and Zimbardo, defended their original interpretations of the SPE and heavily criticized Carnahan and McFarland's article. Haney and Zimbardo raised some important points but exaggerated Carnahan and McFarland's middle-ground position to be more extreme than it was.[28]

So there was the failed replication of the SPE, the individual differences documented among the SPE guards, and the possible self-selection bias in who volunteered for the SPE. These issues raise a strong possibility that the role of the individual was not completely muted by the power of the SPE situation. But unfortunately, few textbooks and instructors cover these issues or those references. For example, a recent survey showed that only a quarter of introductory psychology instructors mentioned the possible self-selection bias. Most students learn the classic interpretation of the SPE that leaves little room for the role of the individual.[29]

I truly cannot say how large the role of the individual is. I believe the role of the prison context is large. But I think more textbooks and instructors need to mention these potential problems in discussing the SPE. Let students know that reality might be more complicated.

INTERPERSONAL ATTRACTION: IS LOVE BLIND?

Besides these classic studies on victims in trouble and on prison abuses, let me briefly cover a lighter and more everyday topic: romance and interpersonal attraction. When looking at someone in love with someone else, how do we explain that love? Why does someone get drawn to that special other?

Most of us think it has to do with personal preferences and desires for a particular mate—he or she has to be special to us. But many authors suggest that we can become attracted to someone without really seeing their particular qualities. We can become attracted to someone just by sitting next to them frequently on a bus or in a classroom. It's called the "mere exposure effect." Proximity breeds attraction. Familiarity breeds attraction. It sounds a little like love can be blind (and not in the romantic way that the phrase is normally meant).[30]

There's also that classic scary-suspension-bridge study. It turns out that men can confuse their bridge-induced physiological arousal (such as elevated heart rate) for attraction to a woman who entered the bridge. It's a cool study, leading to the suggestion that you could take your date to a scary movie or on a roller coaster to increase your chances for love. Again, sounds a little like love can be blind if it can be tricked by a roller coaster.[31]

In sum, it's not very romantic to think you fell in love with someone because you sat near this person on the bus or because you misunderstood your fear of a rickety bridge. But such transfer of arousal does happen. As for familiarity, there is actually a debate about whether it breeds contempt or fondness.[32] As for proximity, there are many correlational studies showing how romantic partners had earlier lived or worked near each other, but as I've mentioned before, correlation does not mean causation. Co-occurring events, such as living near each other and becoming intimate, do not mean that one event caused the other. Proximity is a necessary component of falling in love, but it may not be sufficient. Are there any true experiments showing that proximity can cause human physical attraction? Not many.

The most commonly cited experiment is by Richard Moreland and Scott Beach. These researchers reported how sitting passively next to a female student in a classroom could cause greater attraction toward her compared to when she was not present or was present less often. But despite this conclusion about attraction, the main measure averaged ten traits, nine of which had nothing to do with physical attractiveness. The ten traits on which students rated the woman were these: interesting, attractive, unselfish, popular, unconceited, intelligent, warm, successful, honest, and sincere. Even more surprising, the participants included both male and female students, and the responses from the two sexes were statistically similar. I'm not an attraction expert, but inferring physical attraction seems questionable based on a measure on which male and female raters felt the same.[33]

Most authors who have cited this study did not go as far as using it to explain the "spark" of romance or physical attraction. Rather, they referred to a proximity-caused increase in preference or positive regard for someone. Although Sam Sommers had said that attraction is "all about the situation" and that the sitting-in-the-classroom study was evidence of "sparking,"[34] by the end of his love chapter, he took a more balanced position, in which individual preferences for a particular mate can matter as much as the situation. Consider a similarly balanced passage about friendship and love written by another social psychologist, Shelley Taylor:

> If he had not rented the apartment across the street, or if she hadn't decided to go skiing at the last minute, we would never have met, is

often the evaluation. Certainly these chance factors play an important role in relationships. But looked at another way, relationships are actively fashioned and constructed by the people who are in them. The world brings us into contact with many thousands of people, only a very few of whom become friends or lovers. From this perspective, it is easier to see how selective the friendship and mating process is.[35]

WHO IS MORE PRONE TO THE FAE?

So our individual preferences are part of the equation in romance. And there are individual differences in responding to powerful forces to conform, to abuse, or to look the other way when a victim needs help. The individual matters, just not as much as most of us think.

Just in case this chapter seems a bit confusing within the context of the entire book, let me repeat that the main message of this book is that most behaviors and outcomes are caused by a combination of personal and situational factors, but that most of us underestimate the power of the situation. The individual does usually matter too. Just, again, not as much as most of us think. This tendency to give undue importance to the individual and not enough importance to the context is the FAE. I'm sometimes concerned that well-intentioned social psychologists go too far and leave out any meaningful mention of the individual, but I'm definitely on board that most people commit the FAE, which can carry negative consequences for themselves and society.

Most of us commit the FAE. OK. So who are those few who don't? Or let me word it this way: who is more likely to commit the FAE? Just as there are individual differences in how much situations affect us, there are individual differences in who commits the FAE. Several studies, some of which I've already discussed, have identified some personal characteristics or traits that predict a stronger FAE. For example, I've reported that people who hold stronger just-world beliefs are more likely to blame victims.

I think there is great value in knowing the personality predictors of the FAE. Among several benefits, this knowledge can tell researchers who is in greater need of interventions or strategies to reduce the FAE. This knowledge might also help in the development of such strategies. I will discuss strategies in the next chapter.

For now, here is a nearly complete list of traits, dispositions, personal beliefs, or other characteristics that are predictive of greater levels of the FAE. If you self-identify with some of these characteristics, please know that I am not saying that therefore you must be one of those people more prone to the FAE. These results are on average. But if this section triggers some self-reflection, that's not necessarily a bad thing.

Those with Certain Traits or Dispositions

Those who score lower on measures of logical or scientific reasoning are more prone to the FAE.[36] These findings are consistent with my earlier suggestion that most cases of committing the FAE arise from a logical fallacy called the converse error. Perhaps relatedly, those who don't like effortful cognitive activities, meaning those who score low on "need for cognition," are also more prone to the FAE.[37]

As I've already mentioned, people who are more aggressive by nature are more prone to infer hostile intentions in ambiguous situations, a form of the FAE termed the hostile attribution bias. Perhaps similarly, people who score low on a mindfulness scale, and who are presumed to be quicker to defensiveness, are also more prone to this bias.[38] I also mentioned earlier the form of the FAE in which we think on-screen actors actually possess the traits that they portray in their role. Not surprisingly, people who feel more "transported" into the narrative while watching movies and television shows are more prone to this form of the FAE.[39]

I also mentioned how the FAE may be driven by a need to feel more in control, such that those who feel a greater need for control, closure, or structure should be more prone to the FAE. Individuals who score higher on a need-for-control scale have indeed exaggerated their dispositional attributions of others. There also are traits called "need for closure" and "need for structure," which both predict the FAE. Individuals who score high on these two traits also experience greater discomfort with uncertainty.[40]

Last, numerous FAE studies have investigated a trait called attributional complexity (AC). AC has several components, including high interest in explaining human behavior, the tendency to consider multiple causes, and the tendency to consider complex causes from inside the person and from the person's past.[41] High-AC people are considered socially smart, and the creators of the AC Scale strongly predicted that high-AC people would be less prone to the FAE. However, they found the opposite—high-AC people were *more* prone to the FAE.[42]

At this point, many studies have shown that high-AC people are more prone, but several other studies have found that high-AC people are less prone, as originally expected. I conducted a meta-analysis and found that high-AC people overall appear more prone to the FAE, but only slightly. One working theory is that high-AC people may be overconfident, especially when the attributional question is not difficult enough to motivate them to use their attributional skills.[43]

Those Who Hold Certain Beliefs

Several studies have shown that people who hold certain beliefs are more prone to various forms of the FAE. Some of these results I've mentioned in previous chapters. I will list them all here with the note that I'm not trying to pigeonhole anyone who holds any of these beliefs. A person is more complicated than a particular set of views. And as I said earlier, these results are on average. OK, people tend to be more prone to some form of the FAE when they hold stronger just-world beliefs, when they have a fixed mind-set (versus a growth mind-set), when they hold politically conservative beliefs (versus liberal beliefs), when they hold Protestant beliefs (versus Catholic beliefs), and when they hold something called a leakage belief (the belief that people's true traits and attitudes can leak from observable behaviors).[44]

Others

Although several studies show that Eastern populations are similarly prone to the FAE compared to Western populations, the overall evidence suggests that Western populations are somewhat more prone. This outcome seems due to the individualistic ideals more likely to be held in the West. People who think more individualistically pay more attention to others' traits than to the context.[45] Several researchers have also looked at age. Although the research is somewhat mixed, overall older adults seem more prone to the FAE than younger adults.[46]

A few studies have begun to find that upper- and middle-class individuals are more prone to certain forms of the FAE than lower- or working-class individuals. In particular, higher-class individuals were less likely to cite contextual explanations for socioeconomic inequality, job loss, and having poor health care. Although blaming the context for such outcomes might seem self-serving for lower-class individuals, higher-class individuals were also less attentive to the context in explaining people's emotional expressions, charity work, and criminal behaviors. They were also less likely just to notice changes in context from scene to scene in a visual-perception exercise.[47]

Last, ironically, happy people or people having a "good day" are more prone to the FAE, specifically using the classic attitude-attribution and social-roles paradigms. Apparently being happy reduces how carefully we process information from a situation (whereas sadness increases careful processing). Perhaps similarly, another study found that participants who were better adjusted emotionally were more prone to the social-roles form of the FAE. But interestingly, it is sad people who are more prone to victim blaming. I will discuss some of these findings a little further in the next chapter.[48]

Most of these individual-difference findings are correlational. For example, people with high need for control and structure are more prone to the FAE, but that doesn't mean it's the need for control and structure causing the FAE. But maybe it is. Maybe reducing these needs in people can reduce the FAE. In the next chapter, I will discuss many potential strategies to reduce the FAE.

CHAPTER 10

PROS AND CONS OF BEING BIASED: TO BE OR NOT TO BE

Ignorance is bliss.   —Thomas Gray, poet

Knowledge is power.   —Francis Bacon, philosopher

Fast is fine, but accuracy is everything.
    —Wyatt Earp, deputy sheriff and marshal

Dispositional inferences afford the observer a culturally acceptable way of gaining a sense of control over her or his environment, and feelings of control, however illusory, may ultimately yield greater psychological benefits than would logically impeccable inferences.
    —Daniel Gilbert and Patrick Malone,
    social psychologists

In the sixth Harry Potter film, Ron Weasley drank what he thought was "liquid luck" and then had the best Quidditch performance of his life. Liquid luck was a rare magical potion that made someone successful in everything they attempted. So of course Ron performed well. Except Ron never actually drank it. He only thought he did. Ron misperceived reality, and that misperception had great benefit. Even outside the world

241

of magical fiction, this type of outcome can happen. It's called the placebo effect.

PROS OF BEING BIASED

Misperception and bias can have both pros and cons, despite the common premise in books about bias that bias is bad. The placebo effect is one case of a pro, in which patients who mistakenly think they're getting a dose of medicine show signs of improvement as if they actually took the medicine. At a broader level, the placebo effect falls under self-fulfilling prophecy, in which expectations for a particular outcome can actually help to bring about that outcome, even if the expectations are biased. For example, expectations from teachers that students will do well in the classroom can lead to higher student performance.[1]

In the confirmation bias, avoiding evidence that contradicts our strongly held views can protect our ego. Feeling absolute certainty about our worldviews or our politics can prevent fear and anxiety, even if we're wrong in a provable way. Blind support for a political party can help its candidates to win elections. Overlooking the faults of those close to us and even failing to notice when they're angry at us can make for happier relationships.[2]

The Positive-Illusions Debate

Shelley Taylor wrote a book and many articles on the beneficial role of certain positive illusions. Taylor, her colleagues, and others amassed decades of evidence in hundreds of studies that unrealistic optimism, unrealistically positive views of self, and illusion of control are, in moderation, part of good mental health and even good physical health. Those of us who see ourselves and the world too accurately, and in particular who realize how little control we have in the world, are at greater risk of moderate depression, termed "depressive realism."

I sometimes think about J. K. Rowling when I think of unrealistic optimism. The manuscript for her first Harry Potter novel was rejected twelve times, but she persevered. Looking back, she wrote, "I wasn't going to give up until every single publisher turned me down." I don't know her exact thoughts or health indicators from that time, but her unrealistic perseverance has had many benefits for which she has said she is grateful.[3]

Case studies aside, there have been debates within both the positive-illusions and depressive-realism literatures. Most recent reviews of depressive-realism studies have concluded that the phenomenon is real (if not as strong as initially implied).[4] The broader debate about whether moderate positive illusions relate to better or worse health outcomes is harder to summarize quickly, but there is more evidence for better health outcomes. Most of the evidence is correlational, in that the positive illusions may contribute to good health, or good health may give people reason to be positive. But some of the evidence includes true experiments, including those that showed induced positive moods leading to positive health outcomes.[5]

To explain why some studies show negative correlations between positive illusions and health while many other studies show positive correlations, Taylor and colleagues have pointed out that the two sides of the debate typically use different measures of positive illusion. The negative-outcome side measures perceptions in more public or accountable contexts, in that those who exhibit positive illusions are more likely to be in the presence of contradictory evidence. On the other hand, the positive-outcome side of the debate measures more general perceptions when contradictory evidence is less likely to be present.

As an oversimplified example, looking at a blackboard and saying it's white is a more obvious illusion (and may predict negative health outcomes), compared to thinking the board must be white without having seen it, even if we know most boards in the building are black. A more relevant example for the negative-outcome side is when a neurotic or narcissistic individual "may think very poorly of themselves yet present

243

themselves to others in grandiose or narcissistic fashion." Such an individual does not actually hold positive self-regard and may lack social skills such as modesty, so it would not be surprising if they score lower on mental health measures despite their expressed positive illusion.[6]

Taylor has characterized the negative-outcome side of the debate as explaining positive illusions with stable traits like neuroticism and narcissism, whereas the positive-outcome side views positive illusions as "situationally responsive" in that "positive illusions are lessened as verifiability increases." Part of the idea from the positive-outcome side seems to be that mentally healthy people hang on to hope longer when an outcome is not yet certain. For example, research has shown that such positive illusions are more evident at the beginning of a project than the end, when project results start coming in. Positive self-perceptions are more evident "with respect to ambiguous personal qualities than with respect to concrete personal qualities with clear behavioral referents." For example, I might think I'm great at driving. Oh, you mean parallel parking? No, not so great, but I'm getting better.[7]

What I find especially interesting in Taylor's perspective is the idea that the negative-outcome side of the debate might be committing some form of the FAE against those who hold positive illusions by attributing those illusions to stable traits. On the other hand, the positive-outcome side describes the illusions as what would be most adaptive for a particular situation.

Pros of Committing the FAE

The potential benefits of just the FAE include maintaining the illusion of control or protecting against feeling a loss of control. As I mentioned in chapter 3, when people's sense of control is reduced or feels threatened, they're more likely to commit the FAE and to make connections or see patterns that aren't there. In chapter 9, on individual differences, I described how people who feel a greater need for control and structure are more prone to the FAE. In chapter 8, I described how victim blaming can help us not only to maintain a sense of personal safety and control over life but also to reduce the negative emotion and stress that can occur when we see an innocent victim suffering despite our just-world beliefs. Victim blaming can also reduce stress or dissonance and protect our ego when we are the ones who caused that victim to suffer (whether intentionally or unintentionally).

The FAE is also beneficial in everyday life because it's fast and efficient. Classic social psychology refers to the typical (biased) perceiver as a "cognitive miser" who's conserving cognitive resources. Gilbert and Malone wrote that "dispositional inferences are so economical."[8] Most of us don't have all day (or even ten minutes) to decide or investigate why that idiot cut us off on the highway. I often ask my students to time how long it takes me to commit the FAE. I set up the idiot-driver-cut-me-off scenario and then ask my students to start timing me. Then I say, "Jerk! OK, how long did that take?"

On the other hand, pondering and investigating the different possibilities can take much more time and might involve consulting friends, family, therapists, or even social science research or instructors (as my students sometimes consult me). And the brain can cycle back to this consideration of causes throughout the day or week or month. We might ask ourselves whether we should have reacted differently, and that determination depends in part on why the other person behaved as they did. Uncertainty is time-consuming (besides being uncomfortable). Finding one dispositional cause and being certain is fast.

CONS OF BEING BIASED

But then there are the cons of bias. Speed isn't everything. Even if Taylor is right and those three positive illusions typically relate to better health outcomes, they can still relate to negative health outcomes for some people.

And in fairness to cognitive therapy (about which I raised questions in chapter 8), negative illusions such as unfair self-blame and exaggerated feelings of pessimism or helplessness can play a central role in some forms of mental illness. Not all books on bias provide explicit lists of the potential negative consequences of bias, but I think those consequences are a large part of what motivates the authors to write these books. Here is a quick summary of potential negative consequences, drawing from some of my earlier chapters.

The negative consequences of the FAE and other misunderstandings (at least when others behave negatively or ambiguously) can include anger, stress, hostility, interpersonal conflict, prejudice, intergroup conflict, misguided retaliation and aggression, and even war, as well as a reduced ability to resolve conflicts or prevent their recurrence. The negative consequences of victim blaming include reduced willingness to help those in need and increased self-blame, anxiety, and depression in the victim. In therapy, blaming the clients can also reduce their motivation or ability to try to change their negative circumstances.[9]

More generally, many biases can result in just making poor decisions for ourselves, whether at work, in relationships, while driving, or in physical and mental health contexts. For example, overestimating our skill at something can cause us to take on a task we're not prepared for. The illusion of control can cause us to take excessive risks while driving. Too much optimism can delay necessary visits to the doctor. Taylor might say these levels of positive illusion go beyond moderate because they are not adaptive, but the positive-illusions results are on average—moderate illusions may not always be adaptive for some people.

If we are in charge at home or at work or in the government, then poor decisions caused by bias can negatively affect more than ourselves. Some disastrous decisions in history apparently arose from the phenomenon of groupthink, in which leaders and their loyal advisors committed the FAE in thinking their enemies were "too evil to negotiate with." Another groupthink-based example of the FAE is when people think that everyone else's head nodding about a terrible plan is due to support for the plan, as opposed to group pressures not to rock the boat.[10]

I've mentioned that positive expectations about students can lead to positive outcomes through the self-fulfilling prophecy, even if those expectations are biased, but the flip side is that biased expectations that students will do poorly can lower performance. I mentioned in chapter 5 the concept of stereotype threat, in which society expects certain groups of students to do poorly, such as black students and girls, and this expectation contributes to those groups' underperformance. Failing to notice a significant other's anger at us can be a blessing, but the flip side is that the anger can fester and later explode. Even the placebo effect has its opposite—it's called the nocebo effect, in which thinking you took a drug can lead to experiencing the side effects.[11]

Although avoiding evidence that contradicts our strongly held views can protect our egos (in the confirmation bias), that protection may only be short-term. If the evidence accumulates, some of us might feel even more dumb later for having held on to false views for so long, especially if we had spoken those views out loud or taken public actions based on them. Avoiding contrary evidence can also hamper successful problem-solving, whether the problem is in our marriage or job or of planetary proportions like global warming.

MANAGING OUR BIAS

Because there are both pros and cons to bias, my brief message for now is try not to reduce your biases all at once or too quickly (if you think you are biased), because you might start to feel a bit more helpless, less safe, less in control, or less positive about yourself or your significant other, which can contribute to depression. You might start to feel less certain about things that were solid truths for so long, which can increase stress, anxiety, and fear.

Being a little favorably biased toward yourself, your views, close others, and where you live can be a good thing. Quickly blaming others during anger, quickly blaming victims, and holding a superstitious belief or two can add to a feeling of consistency and control, also good for mental health. Indeed, FAE experts Gilbert and Malone went so far as to suggest that the pros of the FAE outweigh the cons, at least for the perceiver. They wrote that even incorrect dispositional attributions "may have few unfavorable and many favorable consequences for the observer."[12] So let's not necessarily beat ourselves up if we happen to become aware of a small degree of certain biases in ourselves.

However, some of us have more than a small degree of bias. In chapter 9, I outlined who is more prone to the FAE. And I think Gilbert and Malone might have overlooked the negative consequences of the FAE for those whom we unfairly judge and whose emotions and outcomes and retaliations can still affect us. In my view, the cons of bias outweigh the pros—if not just for ourselves, then for the others in relationships with us and for society at large. Because the FAE reduces help to victims, children in poverty and disaster zones can be affected. Because the FAE can cause conflicts, there can be victims of resulting violence. The recent spikes of prejudice, hate crimes, and political divides in America could also be due in part to the FAE.

I think most authors of books about bias would agree that the cons outweigh the pros. My students also seem to agree, even after learning about the potential mental health benefits of some biases. Specifically, after my students learned about the risk of depression if we become too accurate, I asked several classes of students to what degree they'd be "willing to sacrifice a little mental health to be more accurate." The average response was somewhat willing—it exceeded the midpoint of the scale (though not by much). Of course, you can decide for yourself if improved accuracy is worth the risk of depression.[13]

But for most of us, I don't believe it will come down to sacrificing mental health. I think there's room for improvement in most of us without a risk of depression or anxiety. In the epilogue, I will also discuss ways to offset that risk while reducing bias and becoming more accurate. For now, here are numerous research-based ways to reduce bias, especially the FAE.

LEARNING ABOUT BIAS: DOES IT REALLY HELP?

Many popular press books about bias suggest that learning about biases can help to reduce them. These books sometimes encourage readers to use their newfound knowledge to identify and reduce their own biases in their daily lives. Other times, the advice from authors is just implied: that by reading their books about bias, you will somehow become less biased. Does learning about bias really help to reduce it? Yes, but not as much as we would hope.

As noted by psychologist and artificial-intelligence expert Earl Hunt, "people are not robots; attempts to make them behave as if they were passive carriers of information are fundamentally mistaken."[14] What can happen is that people who learn about a bias translate what they hear into "This is what other people do, but not me." This phenomenon is part of the above-average effect, the tendency to think you are better than the average person. And research results do refer to the average participant and not everyone. That truth about social science leaves plenty of wiggle room for all readers to think they are smarter than the biased participants.

The above-average effect is why I advised in my introduction to try to be open to the possibility that you are average. If the majority of us can be open in this way, even if some of us are not prone to a particular bias, then on average, biases will reduce overall.

Social psychologist Emily Pronin and colleagues have conducted and cited numerous studies showing how difficult it is to look for our own biases. We see others' biases more easily than our own, which is known as the bias blind spot. And learning about the bias blind spot or the above-average effect not only typically fails to reduce these but can even increase them![15]

Another part of this equation is that we tend to trust our own perceptions as reality-based. This trust is sometimes called naïve realism. So when others disagree with how we see the world, we don't usually consider the possibility that we are the ones with skewed perceptions. Instead, we commit the FAE and attribute others' views to their personal politics or dispositions or biases. The greater the disagreement, the more we see the other side as biased, and the more we see our own position as reality based.[16]

So when others disagree with us or tell us we're wrong, even if they present research or facts for their side, the FAE can actually prevent us from seeing our own mistakes. The FAE is one way in which we might justify our confirmation bias, by attributing information that goes against our views not to reality but rather to the bias or bad intentions in those who provide that information, whether they are the news media, a political party, science, or particular individuals.

Fortunately, though, a number of studies (though barely a dozen) have shown that learning or taking a class about biases, including the FAE, can indeed help to reduce biases. As debiasing expert Scott Lilienfeld wrote, it's "some but not all studies," but at least it's some.[17]

Anecdotally, I have had many social psychology students over the years who shared experiences with me about avoiding the FAE after having learned about it. Students have become less angry at their classmates, significant others, relatives, and fellow drivers. Another student and her friends even created a game of regularly calling each other out on the FAE.

But social science education has limits. It won't reach every student and can sometimes backfire. As discussed in chapter 9, the best way to teach the FAE and reach more students is to avoid the all-or-nothing message that situations cause behavior without also mentioning that personal factors cause behavior too. This approach has the added benefit of being very true. Behaviors are usually caused by a combination of personal and situational factors.

Many psychologists, including Leonard Newman, Arthur Miller, and Philip Zimbardo, have documented a particular tendency in the American public to resist the idea that situations can be responsible for serious wrongdoing. Most people think bad behavior is caused by bad people, period. Specifically, when a social psychologist comments on a publicized crime or human rights abuse and says to be wary of the FAE because of the role of situational factors, people often falsely assume the social psychologist is excusing the wrongdoer. This assumption makes people upset and resistant to the situational information.[18]

Perhaps similarly, Vincent Yzerbyt and colleagues found that instructing participants not to think about dispositional factors in explaining a particular behavior did reduce the FAE for that scenario, but then it backfired. Compared to participants who had never been so instructed, the initially instructed participants committed the FAE even more strongly on the next scenario, when they were not instructed. The researchers called it a rebound effect. My takeaway is not to overly pressure others on what they should or should not consider as possible causes.[19]

My own research has shown that introductory students taking a survey became even more prone to the FAE when reminded about situational factors to explain aggressive behavior or bad driving, though students in a higher-level course became less prone to the FAE under the same condition.[20] Anecdotally, I have had a few students get visibly upset at the notion that situational factors play any role whatsoever in explaining terrorist acts against the United States. These students earnestly argued that there is no excuse for terrorism, even though I had just emphasized that explaining is not excusing. One student wrote, "Terrorists do not need to be 'explained' through situational factors. Their actions speak for themselves."

This resistance by some students is probably due in part to their FAE-based beliefs. This resistance is part of why I emphasize every semester that explaining is not excusing. Even if situations are part of why people commit crimes or terrorist acts, that does not excuse criminal behavior.

Some people wonder, why bother identifying situational factors if not to excuse? One answer is because better explaining bad behavior can help us to prevent it in the future.

Popular press books about bias usually don't discuss how to reduce biases besides by learning about them. At the same time, these books rarely acknowledge any limitations or difficulties in such learning. I am trying to fill these gaps. In the remainder of this chapter, I discuss additional research-based ways to reduce the FAE. I am not trying to tell you to do these things, but if your goal is to reduce the FAE, then these strategies are worth considering.

WAYS TO REDUCE THE FAE BEYOND LEARNING ABOUT THE FAE

1. Learning about the Situational Factors

It seems easy to understand how we can overlook a situational factor if that factor is unknown or invisible. If I giggle during a phone call because my dog is licking my feet, the person I'm talking to won't know that unless I tell them. My sister sometimes utters out-of-the-blue interjections during our phone calls. Initially I wonder if it was something I said, but it's actually one of her little dogs needing some immediate direction. More important is an example in which we may not realize the particulars of the economic or social forces behind cases of job loss, home foreclosures, or poverty. Or we may not see the stereotype threat that lowers minority group members' academic performance, or the conformity pressures that led to poor decisions, whether from teens or loyal advisors to a president. Going back to my introduction and chapter 2, we cannot hear the question about race asked by a 911 operator if the news organization only releases audio of the response, as in "This guy looks like he's up to no good. . . . He looks black."

As I discussed in chapter 4, any photo of an individual necessarily excludes a majority of the situation or physical environment, which is one reason it's so easy to misread the mind of an individual in a photo, even if they appear to be smiling or making an angry face. If a missing situational factor becomes known, perhaps by talking to the individual or photographer, then at least some observers would reevaluate the meaning of a face.

Nicholas Epley, author of *Mindwise*, similarly recommended not just looking at people to judge them but also talking to them. They can then share any circumstances that could explain appearances or questionable behavior. Roger Axtel, author of several books on communicating in different cultures, similarly recommends asking around in a culture before firmly deciding why someone is using a particular gesture. If the reason for a gesture varies from culture to culture, and you judge or get offended without knowing that, then you are at risk of the FAE. In general, learning about the context does reduce the FAE.

2. Slowing Down Our Judgment

But to follow Epley's or Axtell's advice to talk to people takes time. We wouldn't be able to make an immediate firm judgment. In their recent book *The Wisest One in the Room*, Thomas Gilovich and Lee Ross similarly concluded their section on the FAE by encouraging readers to slow down. They wrote,

> If you want to be the wisest in the room, discipline yourself not to rush to judgment about individuals until you know, and feel you truly appreciate, the situational forces and constraints that are making their influence felt.[21]

Malcolm Gladwell himself, author of *Blink* and then-champion of the FAE-prone blink-speed judgment, later acknowledged that such a fast judgment is "probably more often terrible than it is good." Gladwell also conveyed that writing *Blink* had taught him not to use his instincts in judging others.[22] The FAE does happen instinctually, automatically, and quickly, and many textbooks even define the FAE as an automatic or spontaneous dispositional judgment that doesn't receive enough adjustment even once situational information becomes known.

If we are able to wait to make a decision, we may not even have to spend that time gathering more information. Jerry Burger significantly reduced the FAE by waiting several days to ask participants for their attributions after running classic FAE paradigms.[23] Even if you don't think waiting a few days will change your mind, maybe it's worth giving a try. Similarly, victims of verbal or physical attacks are more able to consider the context after a few months.[24]

Of course, in some cases, decisions about someone have to be made right away. If you're at a bar or social event and someone you just met asks you out, you might have to make a quick decision. I'm not sure how it would go over to say you need time to gather more information (you can do some gathering on your first date before agreeing to a second date!). But if someone cuts you off on the highway or unfairly yells at you in front of coworkers, there's no statute of limitations on getting upset at this person. You can always judge and get upset later if you decide to think it over (even if you defend yourself in the moment). In the case of the in-office yelling, you can try to talk to the yeller one on one after things have calmed down. You can try to find out what their (situation's) problem is, if you think it's worth the effort.

Of course, the getting-upset part may not always feel under our control. It can be automatic, and as I discussed in earlier chapters, it can automatically trigger the FAE. So to slow a judgment might sometimes require slowing our anger first. Easier said than done. I discuss mindfulness practice later in this chapter—it is one of several strategies to reduce anger. But if we are able to postpone a judgment, extra time can also allow the anger to dissipate naturally, leading me to suggest that we not respond to nasty texts or emails right away if possible. Or we can go ahead and draft our angry replies putting the nasty senders in their place, and then decide a little later whether to click Send.

3. Reducing Cognitive Load

Research shows that adding cognitive load, or keeping participants busy with mental tasks, increases the FAE.[25] Thus, by removing tasks or distractions or reducing cognitive load during a judgment of someone, the FAE should reduce. If the cognitive load arises because it's a stressful or busy time, then waiting to judge someone (if possible) until the stressful or busy time passes should accomplish the same goal.

The FAE similarly increases when a video or audio recording of a behavior is visually or acoustically fuzzy, requiring extra concentration. Thus, if we're watching a live news story of a disaster or a posted video of some crime, we should be able to minimize the FAE by making sure the picture is sufficiently clear and the volume is sufficiently high. If the video quality is poor, see if someone else on YouTube has posted a better copy.[26]

4. Being Accountable for Our Judgment

If we cannot clear up the picture or postpone our judgment, we can at least try to justify our judgment. Accountability has been operationalized multiple ways, but the common element is to have an expectation that we will have to explain or justify our judgment to someone else. This expectation decreases a number of biases, including the FAE.[27] In raising children or teaching students, this approach to reduce the FAE may be easy to implement. We can require or encourage our children or students to please explain themselves. I sometimes write in exam questions to "please justify your answer." In trying to reduce our own bias, it might be harder to hold ourselves to this standard. We might feel certain that we're right and feel no need to explain to ourselves. Perhaps we can find someone else to tell, or we can keep a journal.

When people have extreme political attitudes and are very certain they understand the underlying political policy when they really don't, Steven Sloman found that something like accountability can reduce that overconfidence. Sloman asked participants to explain the policy—that is, "what it is and how it would lead to specific consequences." As a result, participants' attitudes and their sense of understanding became less extreme.[28]

5. Training in Logical, Statistical, or Scientific Reasoning

In chapter 9, I cited research showing that more logical- or scientific-minded individuals are less prone to the FAE. Although this research was correlational, at least one true experiment has supported the position that logic training reduces the FAE. Mark Schaller and colleagues trained participants in the logic of statistical analysis of covariance. For example, in one of multiple training scenarios, the researchers asked participants to compare two tennis players with win records of 40 and 60 percent respectively. Though it seemed like the latter player had superior ability, participants also learned of relevant situational factors, such as that the 40 percent player played more matches in a tougher league than the 60 percent player. These situational factors covaried or co-occurred with the different win records and indicated that the 40 percent player actually had superior ability. Compared to a control group, trained participants were later less likely to commit the FAE in ability and intelligence judgments in two new scenarios.[29]

6. Being Sad

As counterintuitive as it sounds, my own and others' research has shown that people made to be happy in the lab or movie theater become more prone to the FAE, and people made to be sad become less prone. Those who are already moderately depressed or having a "bad day" are also less prone to the FAE. The apparent reason is that sadness and moderate depression involve or trigger more careful thinking and more attention to the details of the environment.[30] I don't want to recommend making ourselves sad to reduce the FAE. But if you notice yourself very happy or you're watching a funny movie, perhaps you can postpone important judgments about someone else's behavior until your emotional state falls closer to neutral.

7. Being Happy or Self-Affirmed or Less Emotional

The glaring exception in the sadder-but-wiser FAE research is for the victim-blaming form of the FAE. Happiness increases the classic forms of the FAE (using the attitude-attribution and social-roles paradigms), but happiness reduces victim blaming. As discussed in chapter 8, watching an innocent victim suffer can cause negative emotions, due to wanting the world to be just or predictable, which motivate people to blame the victim as a way of restoring predictability and feeling less negative. It makes sense that happiness is a natural buffer against the sad reality of the suffering of innocents, and thus, happy people have less need to resort to victim blaming.[31]

To my knowledge, however, no author has yet directly reconciled how happiness increases most forms of the FAE but decreases victim blaming. Happy people pay less attention to the details of a situation, so why doesn't that cognitive deficit make them more prone to victim blaming like they are more prone to other forms of the FAE? It may simply be that the seriousness of a suffering victim overrides the tendency in happy people to pay less attention. Put another way, perhaps the situational reasons victims suffer catch the attention of happy and sad observers equally.

The bottom-line suggestion here is that before judging a victim, watch or do something that makes you happy. Call it a distraction if that helps, and then make your final decision about why something bad happened to someone.

Our happiness of course can have several sources beyond our activities or the movies we watch. Receiving praise from others, achieving a success, or reflecting on past achievements can also make us happy. Even just reflecting on a few positive aspects of ourselves can help. These reflections are called self-affirmations. Citing self-affirmation theory, Annemarie Loseman and Kees van den Bos showed that just writing down three positive characteristics of ourselves can indeed reduce victim blaming. They told participants it was a distraction task, but it was actually to influence emotions. The researchers did not cite the happiness-FAE research but rather suggested that self-affirmations can help us to better regulate or reduce unwanted emotions.[32]

Regulating or reducing negative emotions can also be accomplished by emotional disclosure. And as discussed in chapter 8, emotional disclosure can reduce victim blaming. Kent Harber and colleagues reasoned that watching innocent victims suffer causes negative emotions because such suffering is dissonant or discrepant with just-world beliefs. Then they cited discrepancy theory in explaining that sharing emotions with someone else can translate a disturbing event into "smaller, more easily parsed propositions," which can "realign" beliefs with events so that the negative emotions dissipate.[33]

So whether it's self-affirmation or self-regulation theory, discrepancy or dissonance theory, or just the raw power of happiness, there are a few suggestions here to reduce victim blaming that involve reducing negative emotions. Do something that makes you happy, or reflect on positive aspects of yourself, or talk about your feelings with someone you trust.

8. Being Empathetic

The idea that empathy or taking another's perspective should reduce the FAE is very intuitive. Being able to walk in someone else's shoes would allow us to see the other person's situation more clearly. Although having empathy for certain others may be easier said than done, many studies have shown that structured directions to take someone else's perspective have increased situational explanations for others' predicaments.

In one study, graduate students in a counseling program went through a role reversal, in which they watched a videotaped case of a client and had to imagine and articulate how they would feel in the client's position. Compared to a control group, these participants later showed reduced levels of the FAE in viewing multiple videos of clients with situation-caused problems.[34] In research on victim blaming, participants took the perspective of the victim of an electric-shock experiment (of the nature described in chapter 8). Compared to a control group, these participants showed less victim blaming.[35]

Perspective-taking instructions also seem to reduce the ultimate attribution error, a form of the FAE in which we underestimate the power of the situation in explaining negative outcomes of members of another group. Theresa Vescio and colleagues showed this effect in white participants who listened to a staged radio show in which an African American male student described his difficulties adjusting as a first-generation college student.[36]

Besides perspective-taking instructions, research has shown that just mimicking the physical movements of someone can increase empathy for that person. Mariëlle Stel and colleagues then showed that mimicking the behavior of a victim of a crime reduced victim blaming. The mimicry of that first victim even reduced the blaming of a completely separate victim in an unrelated crime scenario. The researchers argued that mimicry creates an empathy mind-set that goes beyond how we view just the mimicked individual. They noted that being around an actual victim of a crime might reduce a natural tendency to mimic, so they recommended that police officers, therapists, and others close to the victim purposely try to mimic the victim's behaviors and expressions while talking to the victim.[37]

Some readers might feel silly trying this at home. But the idea here is that purposely mimicking the movements and expressions of people to whom something bad has happened, whether on the news or in our social circles, has a chance to reduce victim blaming in general.

9. Being Reminded of Our Own Similar Behavior

So if the other person is a client with psychological problems or is a victim of a negative outcome or wrongdoing, empathizing with that person can reduce the FAE. But what if the other person is the wrongdoer and we are the victim? Is it realistic to think we can empathize with the wrongdoer? Would empathy be enough to reduce the FAE against the wrongdoer? What if the wrongdoer apologized first?

Seiji Takaku has investigated these questions. Takaku suggested that apologies are often not enough to reduce the FAE but that an apology plus empathy might work. However, the standard instructions to take the wrongdoer's perspective might not be enough to induce the empathy. Takaku suggested that we might have to be reminded of our own past transgressions. Moreover, this type of empathy induction might cause a feeling of hypocrisy or dissonance, in that we want to blame the current wrongdoer but know that when we had similarly transgressed, we wanted to blame somebody else or the situation. That would be double standards. The additional discomfort from such an inconsistency might then lead us to blame the current wrongdoer a little less, to reduce the inconsistency.

In one study, Takaku described a scenario to participants in which a classmate mistreated the participant and then offered a thorough apology. But first, Takaku instructed participants to visualize and write out a description of a past event in which they intentionally or unintentionally hurt someone else. Compared to a control group, instructed participants were less likely to make dispositional attributions for the classmate's bad behavior. In another study, Takaku used a driving scenario in which the transgressor cut off another driver. Again, when participants were made to think of their own driving transgressions, they were less likely to make dispositional attributions for the transgressor's behavior, even without an apology.[38]

Thinking of our own transgressions may be the most challenging way to reduce the FAE so far. But let me emphasize that the real transgressors in your life may be very bad people who acted with very little situational influence and that your own transgressions may in no way compare. And as always, you can decide how you want to think or act. Although Takaku did mention the FAE and did measure attributions, his focus was on forgiveness. Deciding whether to forgive is a very personal decision. But the bottom line here is that reflecting on our own bad behavior weakens the FAE. So if the goal is to reduce the FAE, this strategy is worth trying.

10. Being Mindful: The Raisin Task

Yet another way to induce empathy is through a practice called mindfulness. The practice or concept has been around for centuries in Buddhism and has been incorporated into multiple psychotherapies, including mindfulness-based cognitive therapy and acceptance and commitment therapy. The definition for mindfulness slightly varies across texts, but it is basically a process of attending to the present moment in an accepting or nonjudgmental way.[39]

Science has begun testing the effectiveness of mindfulness in helping people with a variety of psychological and physical problems. Among these researchers, many have argued that mindfulness can foster empathy.[40] Thus, because empathy can reduce the FAE, so should mindfulness. And as I mentioned in chapter 9, people who score higher on a mindfulness scale are less prone to the FAE.

Tim Hopthrow and colleagues conducted three experiments that showed a five-minute mindfulness exercise can indeed reduce a classic form of the FAE (using the attitude-attribution paradigm). They called the exercise the "raisin task" because it involves slowly and carefully touching, smelling, and eventually eating a raisin. Why the raisin task reduces the FAE is not certain. The researchers acknowledged that it might be because mindfulness can increase empathy. But they more strongly suggested that it was because mindfulness improves cognitive processing, including (but not limited to) attention to detail.[41]

Why mindfulness works is less important for the present chapter than the fact that it works. The five-minute raisin task might not be easy for everyone to try. In fact, there are some risks in mindfulness practice for some people.[42] But the raisin task is fast and well-known, with directions and videos at several websites.[43]

11. Becoming More Comfortable with Uncertainty

Yet another reason mindfulness might reduce the FAE is because mindfulness can make people more accepting of or comfortable with uncertainty. As I discussed in earlier chapters, a primary motive behind the FAE and particularly behind victim blaming is to increase feelings of control or certainty. This motive suggests two options to reduce the FAE. First, find a non-FAE way to increase those feelings. As I cited in chapter 8, researchers have discovered at least one such way, having participants affirm their important life values. Second, find a way to become more comfortable with uncertainty. As I cited in chapter 9, people who feel lower needs for control or certainty and feel greater comfort with uncertainty are naturally less prone to the FAE. Is there a way we can make ourselves feel less of those needs and more of that comfort?

There are entire books on this topic, including one titled *Comfortable with Uncertainty* by Pema Chödrön, which provided several tools to become more comfortable with uncertainty. One of those tools is mindfulness. In another book, titled *Nonsense: The Power of Not Knowing*, Jamie Holmes conveyed not only that it is possible to become more comfortable with uncertainty but also that we will gain a power in doing so. That power includes learning from our mistakes and solving puzzles.[44] I'm suggesting that power would also include reducing the FAE. There is an inevitable not-knowing why most others behave as they do. Accepting that and becoming even a little less certain about a dispositional cause would necessarily reduce the FAE.

Even if we want to try, it may be a long and challenging process to become more comfortable with uncertainty and with not knowing why others behave the way they do. Reading books like Chödrön's might help. Reading famous quotes about how foolish certainty is might help too, as in "Certainty is the mother of fools" and "Doubt is not a pleasant condition, but certainty is absurd."[45] In the literature about growth versus fixed mind-sets, reading just an article or relevant proverbs is enough to lead participants to adopt a particular mind-set, at least in the short term.[46] So perhaps researchers can similarly create an uncertainty-is-OK mind-set by exposing students to relevant readings and proverbs such as those cited here.

12. Playing Serious Video Games

Probably much less challenging than facing the truth of uncertainty in life is to play video games. Researchers have recently designed what they call "serious games" to reduce a variety of biases, including the FAE. These are basically educational games that simulate real-life decision-making with an avatar and thus represent hands-on learning. So far, these efforts have shown some success, but more so for biases other than the FAE. In one of two FAE studies, the serious games did reduce the FAE, but not to a greater degree than a less hands-on educational video.[47]

I'm optimistic that as these researchers further develop their games based on current results, the hands-on learning via video game will go further than traditional education in reducing the FAE. At the least, students would probably be more motivated to play well-designed games with scoring than to listen to a lecture. I envision an educational website where students can play these games for free. Of course, some instructors I know are very good at accomplishing hands-on learning even in a traditional classroom.

13. Adopting a Growth Mind-Set

The growth mind-set literature has been growing steadily as an educational movement to help students achieve. This mind-set allows us to believe that we can learn more and do better because our abilities and other dispositions are not fixed. Although most of the literature is focused on personal achievement, the early mind-set research established that the growth mind-set leads to fewer dispositional attributions for others' behaviors.[48] Thus, adopting a growth mind-set should help to reduce the FAE. In my endnote here, I provide a link for several resources to help toward that end.[49]

14. Using Non-FAE Language

Emotion researchers have found that forcing your facial muscles to form a smile (by holding a pen in your teeth or taping rubber bands to your cheeks and over your head) can cause positive emotion. So you're not truly smiling, but your brain somehow thinks you are and generates the corresponding emotion. Similarly, being manipulated into configuring your fingers in a way that "gives the finger" primes hostile thoughts and leads to greater hostile attribution bias. The general idea is that "acting 'as if' one feels something will result in that feeling."[50]

When I've discussed the potential effect of saying things like "What's wrong with your situation?" versus "What's wrong with you?" I've been thinking about this research. Going through the motions of a smile or hostile gesture can trigger feelings or thoughts as if you meant those motions. Can going through linguistic motions do the same? Instead of asking "What were you thinking?" or "What's your problem?" in response to bad behavior, we can try "What problem in your life made you do this?" Can using non-FAE language reduce the FAE? If not in ourselves, in those who hear us?

In the 2016 sci-fi film *Arrival*, the theme was that language can rewire the brain. In the film, it was an alien language, and the rewiring created psychic abilities. Obviously that goes too far, but linguistic and cognitive psychology have indeed found that word choices can influence our thoughts and memories. Gender-neutral language in referring to occupations, such as "firefighter" versus "fireman," can affect perceptions of those occupations.[51] Leading questions from therapists or detectives can affect memories.

In the classic leading-question study by Elizabeth Loftus, participants watched films of car accidents and were asked how fast the cars were going when they "smashed" versus "hit" into each other. Compared to the "hit" group, the "smashed" group estimated higher speeds and one week later were more likely to recall broken glass, even though there had been no glass. Leading questions can hurt eyewitness testimony.[52] Perhaps asking "What's wrong with your situation?" versus "What's wrong with you?" can act as some kind of prosocial leading question, not only for the respondent but also for the questioner.

In other research, describing someone's behavior with adjectives versus verbs leads to more dispositional attributions from listeners, as in descriptions such as "John is unintelligent" versus "John failed the course." Or "John was mean to me" versus "John yelled at me." The just-the-facts-ma'am approach in using verbs over adjectives can reduce the FAE, possibly even in ourselves.[53]

A more subtle effect has been found in the type of verb used. If we read about an interaction or relationship between two people, interpretative-action verbs such as "criticize" or "attack" lead to different inferences than state verbs such as "dislike" or "hate." In general, compared to state verbs, the action verbs lead us to infer that the relationship is less stable, that the specific interaction is less likely to recur and more influenced by situational factors, and that the person who was criticized or attacked was less responsible.[54]

I mentioned in chapter 1 how someone's use of a particular word does not necessarily reflect a personal view or bias. But using particular words has potential to create or reduce bias.

No one has yet specifically tested the effect of saying things like "What's wrong with your situation?" but over time and with practice, it may reduce the FAE in both the speaker and listener. We can consider modeling this kind of language and thinking for our children and students. Feel free to tweak these phrases to better fit your style or your relationship with these individuals. Instead of "What's wrong with your situation?" you might try a question like "Is everything OK?" You wouldn't be committing to a particular judgment. It's just how you word the question.

REDUCING THE FAE OF THOSE WHO ARE CLOSE TO US

The bias-blind-spot research shows that we can see others' biases more easily than our own. This research does not guarantee that we're correct if we think someone else is biased. Indeed, other research shows that our perception of bias can be biased. But what if we are correct? What if a family member, friend, significant other, spouse, or coworker commits the FAE (against us or someone else)? Should we try to address it?

If a person misjudges us by overlooking something in our situation that only we know about, then sharing that information with this person seems like a no-brainer (unless, of course, our personal information is none of this other person's business). Where I'd like to raise a few issues is for cases in which people come to us for support because they are upset about how they've been treated by someone else. I've been the listener in this scenario on many occasions, and over time, I've seemed to get better at the delicate task of reducing a potential FAE.

Let's say your close friend had a bad day at work. Her boss yelled at her or talked down to her about something that was not her fault. Your friend is visibly upset and says her boss is so mean or so stupid or has no regard for what the staff go through every day. Let's say you've heard about this boss before and have some basis to think there's something else going on, such as marital problems. So you might be tempted to raise the possibility of situational factors to explain the boss's behavior. But your friend is angry and crying and came to you for support. What should you do? Reducing the FAE can reduce her anger and stress. It might make her feel better. Should you go for it?

First, it's up to you. You know your friend. Your friend may be more or less able to handle certain responses from you when she's upset. And you may be more or less comfortable giving different responses, including head nodding, hugging, or direct advice. Here are a few general suggestions for your consideration if you decide to try to address a potential FAE.

Beware victim blaming. It's hard to watch a close friend suffer, especially if it was through no fault of hers. Wanting to tell her that she's overreacting to her boss or is overlooking something in her boss's situation might reflect victim blaming. Consider following some of the strategies in this chapter to reduce the risk of victim blaming so that you can consider your friend's situation while free of that temptation.

Be sure to communicate in some way that explaining is not excusing. You can decide how to do so. I don't especially recommend opening with "I'm not excusing your boss's behavior, but." When some people are upset and sense you're not going to agree with them, they stop listening after the "but." I even know some people who have acknowledged that they would think the exact opposite: that excusing is exactly what you plan on doing, even more so than if you had never raised the issue of excusing. Perhaps you can just assert that there is no excuse or that the boss should not behave that way. Let that simmer for a while before deciding whether to go for the "but."

In fact, it might be wise to wait to mention any situational factors until emotion subsides, for multiple reasons. Some of my clinician friends have told me to first acknowledge, if not necessarily validate, your friend's emotions, as in something like "How frustrating" or "I'm sorry." Looking at this scenario from your friend's upset perspective, the world may be black and white. People are either with her or against her, and you don't want to risk sounding like you're taking her boss's side in the against-her category. Taking the boss's side can feel like betrayal. Your friend's ego might also feel threatened if she thinks you're telling her that she's wrong.

By the way, as discussed in chapter 8, emotional disclosure can reduce at least one form of the FAE in victim blaming. Perhaps just letting your friend vent to you and validating her suffering can begin to reduce any FAE against the boss.

If you decide to raise the possibility of situational factors, word your thoughts as a question and not a direct statement, as in "Is it possible there's something else going on?" or "I wonder if there's something else going on." And avoid the all-or-nothing approach of thinking it's all situation. It's unlikely that it's all situation. And people in general have trouble accepting an all-situation explanation for wrongdoing.

Last, keep in mind the pros of the FAE. Yes, you want to reduce your friend's FAE-induced anger and stress, but as discussed, the FAE can also have psychological benefits, such as maintaining a sense of control. Perhaps something like "You know your boss better than I do" or "You know what you're doing at work" can help to maintain that sense of control before a discussion of possible situational factors chips away at it. Good luck with any such efforts.

In general, I believe the cons of the FAE outweigh the pros, but some people are at risk of depression and anxiety if they become too accurate. And your friend might stop coming to you for support if you sound like you're taking the boss's side. There's a lot to be said for head nodding when a friend needs support. In the epilogue, I will discuss the pros-and-cons issue further and make some final suggestions to try to offset the mental health risks of accuracy.

RATIONAL WELL-BEING

The truth will set you free, but first it will make you miserable.

—Mark Twain, author and humorist

We do not err because truth is difficult to see. It is visible at a glance. We err because this is more comfortable.

—Alexander Solzhenitsyn, novelist and historian

Sometimes the truth is easy to see. It's right in front of us, but it's still hard to accept. Those harmed by sexual assault and other tragedies are victims. Jobs hold contractual duties, though many of us still think people performing those duties are somehow showing us personal preferences or traits. A candidate whose rallies we attend may get caught in a big lie, though we still believe our candidate and criticize mainstream journalism.

Even when hundreds of studies and nearly 100 percent of scientists contradict our strongly held view, many of us find ways to avoid, downplay, or distort that information. At least initially. Our egos or political loyalties or feelings of control are on the line. We might need some time to come around, though some of us never will. In the Harry Potter series, the Minister of Magic was desperate not to believe that the Dark Lord, Voldemort, was back, but eventually he accepted it when Voldemort stood right in front of him.

But sometimes the truth is hard to see or is physically not visible, as when the context is withheld from us by a news organization or a political ad. When NBC played that audiotaped 911 statement, "This guy looks like he's up to no good.... He looks black," how could listeners know that something so crucial was left out? When we see a facial expression or hand gesture in a photo, we cannot see the context beyond the boundaries of the photo, even if the gesture matches a gang sign. When we see others driving badly or performing poorly at work or in the classroom, or when we hear the hurtful things people sometimes say, we also often cannot see what's going on in their contexts. Is the driver rushing someone to the hospital? Is the student who underperforms feeling stereotype threat? What stress might these people be enduring behind closed doors? Where did they pick up that hurtful word they chose to use?

We cannot assume there is a situational factor that would change how the behavior appears, but we also cannot assume there isn't. Was Robin Williams right when he said that everyone you meet is fighting a battle you know nothing about? If not, it might be very hard to discern who is and who isn't. The greatest challenge in reducing bias is being open to the possibility that there are situational forces in play even if we cannot see them.

But we can see our own contexts. We know if the 911 operator asked us for the race of the victim. We know whether we are rushing someone to the hospital. We know what battles we are fighting, even if they are unknown to others. Perhaps this is part of the truth that is easily visible in Solzhenitsyn's terms. We can see that our own behaviors and outcomes, especially when they're harmful or extreme, have situational causes. But it's so hard for so many of us to allow for this possibility in others. The truth in explaining behaviors and outcomes is this universal possibility that there's more than meets the eye, but in viewing others, it's more comfortable and less time-consuming to stick with the surface explanation.

In writing this book, I updated what I knew from many literatures, and I was blown away by some of what I found, in both quantity and concept. Over and over again, driving researchers have connected being angry on the road to blaming that other driver. Just-world-belief researchers have learned in greater detail the lengths to which we can go (and why) to avoid the truth that innocent victims are innocent. The more unjust the outcome, the further we'll go, and the more negative the consequences will be for the victim. Emotion and nonverbal-decoding researchers have focused more and more on context and culture in understanding expressions. Accurately reading an emotion is not as universal as we thought. Context is needed.

The context is indeed more powerful than most of us realize. Context is not just something we underestimate in determining a cause but also something that helps us to interpret someone's words, actions, appearances, predicaments, and emotions. It takes more effort and time to examine and incorporate the context. It can make us uncomfortable or embarrassed to have to undo our initial assumptions about a person, especially if that person has wronged us (and we retaliated). It can make us miserable or afraid to learn the world is less just and controllable than we thought and to hear evidence that disproves our long-held views.

The truth can be uncomfortable. It can make us afraid, anxious, and depressed. So it's not surprising that mentally healthy people typically hold a number of positive illusions and commit biases to support those illusions. Some research even suggests that antidepressants improve mood by first inducing positive biases.[1] Our well-being is not rational.

By committing the FAE, we can reduce feelings of uncertainty and increase feelings of control relative to the complicated and scary reality of multiple and contextual causes. Committing the FAE reduces the discomfort of cognitive dissonance by justifying our unfounded anger or by supporting our illusion of a just and safe world.

But committing biases, including the FAE, carries a number of costs as well, and the costs outweigh the benefits, in my view (see chapter 10). So reducing biases is the way to go. Can we do so without feeling anxious or depressed? Is it possible to reduce the FAE and other positive biases and maintain well-being at the same time? Yes. I believe people can be both rational and happy. I call this state rational well-being—having good mental health without committing the irrational biases to which so many mentally healthy individuals are prone.

As I said in chapter 10, I think there's room for improvement in most of us without a risk of depression or anxiety. For most of us, I don't believe a small reduction of bias will risk our mental health. But a greater reduction of bias or reducing many of our biases quickly might carry a risk. And for some of us, even small reductions might threaten our well-being. We might have to work at maintaining our well-being while becoming more rational.

THE SUGGESTIONS

What I've been promising for the epilogue are suggestions to minimize the risk of depression while reducing bias and becoming more accurate. See chapter 10 for suggestions on how to reduce bias. Now I provide suggestions to offset the risk of depression. If you are already accurate and experience moderate depression, hopefully this section might also help. I've shared these suggestions with my students at the end of my social psychology courses in case students have become less biased during the semester. For severe depression (if not moderate depression), I recommend seeking professional help from a doctor or psychotherapist.

I tell my students that my suggestions are antidepressants, but the kind I'm allowed to give without getting in trouble. They are essentially reminders. For example, I remind my students of all the benefits of being accurate (derived from all the cons of being biased). The benefits include making better decisions for ourselves, being better problem solvers, reducing the stigma felt by victims, increasing willingness to help those in need, getting along better with others, reducing intergroup prejudice, reducing stereotype threat, reducing unfounded anger and retaliation, and preventing or reducing interpersonal conflict and stress.

So my first suggestion to offset the risk of depression in becoming more accurate is to remember all these benefits of becoming more accurate. These are no small things. We can even review them out loud with ourselves. These reminders can make us feel good about accepting a difficult truth, and feeling good can offset depression.

In addition, these reminders are consistent or consonant with being more accurate, and consonant cognitions are a primary way to reduce the discomfort of cognitive dissonance. If you recall, one reason we commit some biases is to reduce dissonance. Accepting that good, innocent people can suffer horrible fates is dissonant with our just-world beliefs. Accepting that another's bad behavior toward us was due to extenuating circumstances is dissonant with the anger we felt and acted upon. Accepting negative information from journalists about our candidate is dissonant with our support for that candidate. Accepting evidence for climate change is dissonant with climate-change denial. Dissonance is part of the negative emotion and depression that can come from being accurate and accepting evidence. A common way we get out of this dissonance is to not accept that evidence and to be biased against victims, against the targets of our anger, against journalists, and against science. These biases underlie typical irrational well-being.

My point is that another way to reduce the dissonance in accepting a difficult truth is to add consonant cognitions. If you have avoided bias and are wrestling with a scary or sad truth, think about the benefits of accuracy. If we can reduce dissonance with these consonant cognitions—these reminders of the benefits of accuracy—then not only will we feel better, but we will also be less tempted to take the more biased routes to reduce dissonance. We can maintain our well-being in a more rational way.

My second suggestion to offset the risk of depression in becoming more accurate is to acknowledge that becoming more accurate means becoming more intelligent. It's a combination of book smarts and street smarts. It's something to be proud of. In other words, telling or showing ourselves that we are smart is a self-affirmation, and self-affirmations can reduce dissonance because dissonance is often a threat to self-esteem. Even if a self-affirmation doesn't directly reduce dissonance, it can still offset depression.

Certain famous quotes might help us in a self-affirmational way to equate accuracy with intelligence or with wisdom. Alexander Pope said, "A man should never be ashamed to own that he has been in the wrong, which is but saying in other words that he is wiser today than he was yesterday." Reducing our biases makes us wiser. Often attributed to Socrates, "The only true wisdom is in knowing you know nothing." Perhaps a bit overstated, but it sounds like that inevitable not-knowing why people act the way they do. It seems wise to accept.[2]

My third suggestion comes from a prominent theory in social psychology called social comparison theory. The tenet I highlight here is that people feel better about themselves if they compare with others who are worse off. Your drive to read this book and what you have learned here place you above the average person. It's true. I'm just saying. Compared to those who have not read social psychology texts or this book, you now hopefully know more about biases and how to reduce them. And this knowledge can lead to all those benefits of accuracy.

Social comparison research also shows that just comparing with others in the same boat as you can bolster self-esteem and offset depression. Knowing you're not the only one with a particular problem is part of why social support groups can help so many people. In particular, know that you're not alone in being at risk of bias. My PARBs Anonymous website draws on this support-group theme (PARBs meaning "Persons at Risk of Bias"). Because we're all at risk of bias, my website boasts having the most unofficial members of any support group on the planet.

Of course, clinical psychology has identified other reasons beyond social comparison processes that support groups can help people. And psychology at large has developed a multitude of interventions that can increase positive emotions. Some interventions are more helpful for certain people than others but may be worth trying in order to offset the risk of depression in becoming more accurate. A very recent review has identified the interventions that have strong support. They include imagining future possible positive events, remembering or writing about past positive events, forcing laughter (as in laughter yoga and aerobic laughter), and mindfulness practices such as loving-kindness meditation.

Especially relevant to this book, other interventions involve trying to influence our own context. These interventions are called situation modification or situation selection. Although clearly there are limits on what situations we can select for ourselves, research has shown that the average person becomes happier from socializing, exercising, being in nature, and performing acts of kindness, and not so much from working, commuting, and being on the computer. (Of course, some of us do love our jobs.) *How* we engage in some activities also matters. Strategies that maximize positive emotions include saving the best activity for last and spacing out an enjoyable activity over time.[3]

Trying to influence our own context to be happier reflects the broad message of this book: that our behaviors and outcomes are usually caused by both personal and situational factors. The individual and context both matter, but in explaining *others'* behaviors and outcomes, most of us can do better to recognize the power of context.

ACKNOWLEDGMENTS

I received a great deal of help to complete this book. Author and editor Susan Simmons was with me from the beginning to help me learn about the publishing process. She helped me focus my ideas, provided vital feedback on early chapters, and was always available for a question or social support. I gratefully acknowledge several others who read chapters and shared their expertise and experience. They include John Weaver, Lynda Warwick, David Havas, Heidi Berg, Julie McQuinn, Diane Knich, and especially my friend and fellow writer, Sherrie Yurk.

I thank editor Steven Mitchell and Prometheus Books for giving me this opportunity to share my message with the public. I thank Robert S. Baron and John Harvey, my mentors from graduate school who influenced me as a researcher, who never failed to find time to write a reference letter, and who gave me encouraging feedback when my book project began.

I thank my father, Robert Stalder, and late mother, Theresa Stalder, who were so supportive of my education at every stage. My mother would have been happy to see my book published. My wife and I lost other loved ones along the way, including my wife's great-uncle, Datta Patil, without whom my wife would never have come from India to Milwaukee, where we met. These losses were among many challenges in completing this project. My wife and I are very grateful to those who supported us during these times, especially my sister, Julie McQuinn.

I thank my father and siblings for confirming the details of the family stories that I shared in the book. I am appreciative of my sister-in-law, Anuradha Salunke, who so often went out of her way to ask about my writing and to express support. I am especially grateful to my wife, Shubhangi Stalder, who listened to my ideas, read chapters, encouraged me

ACKNOWLEDGMENTS

to break up my computer time with exercise, and supported me in many other ways. More than anyone, she had encouraged me to take on this project.

Finally, I thank the University of Wisconsin-Whitewater College of Letters and Sciences, which granted me a sabbatical when my book project began. And I thank my department colleagues who agreed to heavier teaching loads, without which my sabbatical would not have been granted.

NOTES

INTRODUCTION: SOCIAL JUDGMENT AND ERROR

1. Christopher Y. Olivola and Alexander Todorov, "Elected in 100 Milliseconds: Appearance-Based Trait Inferences and Voting," *Journal of Nonverbal Behavior* 34 (2010): 83–110.

2. Nicholas Epley, *Mindwise: How We Understand What Others Think, Believe, Feel, and Want* (New York: Alfred A. Knopf, 2014); Lee Ross and Richard E. Nisbett, *The Person and the Situation: Perspectives of Social Psychology* (London: Pinter & Martin, 2011).

3. Matt Philbin, "Shameless: NBC Never Tells Viewers It Smeared Zimmerman with Doctored Audio," NewsBusters, June 20, 2013, http://newsbusters.org/blogs/matthew -philbin/2013/06/20/shameless-nbc-never-tells-viewers-it-smeared-zimmerman-doctored-aud (accessed July 25, 2017).

4. In the social psychology literature, error and bias are not technically the same thing. Bias is a skewed perception independent of logic or evidence, but the perception is not necessarily always in error. As they say, even a broken clock is correct twice a day. But in this book, I will generally use these two terms interchangeably.

5. David Myers, *Social Psychology*, 11th ed. (New York: McGraw Hill, 2013); Daniel R. Stalder, "Political Orientation, Hostile Media Perceptions, and Group-Centrism," *North American Journal of Psychology* 11 (2009): 383–99.

6. Shelley E. Taylor, *Positive Illusions: Creative Self-Deception and the Healthy Mind* (New York: Basic Books, 1989).

7. Epley, *Mindwise*, 59, 63, 111, 119.

8. Christopher Chabris and Daniel Simons, *The Invisible Gorilla: How Our Intuitions Deceive Us* (New York: Broadway Paperbacks, 2009), 7.

9. Daniel J. Simons and Christopher F. Chabris, "Gorillas in Our Midst: Sustained Inattentional Blindness for Dynamic Events," *Perception* 28 (1999): 1059–74. Their article described a total of nine gorilla conditions, eight in the main procedure and one more at the end of the article. (In eight other conditions, an "umbrella woman" was used in place of the gorilla, and only about a third of participants missed her, perhaps partly why the book was not titled *The Invisible Umbrella Woman*.) Of those nine gorilla conditions, five mirrored real-life viewing. In the other four, the actors and gorilla were "partially transparent" (the researchers included these conditions to mimic an earlier study's procedure of superimposing separate displays). In the "partially transparent" conditions, about 70 percent of participants missed the gorilla. Makes

sense—the gorilla was partially transparent. Combining the partially transparent and real-life conditions together led to the result reported in Chabris and Simons's book that "roughly half" of the participants missed seeing the gorilla.

10. Trafton Drew, Melissa L.-H. Võ, and Jeremy M. Wolfe, "The Invisible Gorilla Strikes Again: Sustained Inattentional Blindness in Expert Observers," *Psychological Science* 24 (2013): 1848; Elizabeth R. Graham and Deborah M. Burke, "Aging Increases Inattentional Blindness to the Gorilla in Our Midst," *Psychology and Aging* 26 (2011): 162; Daniel Memmert, Christian Unkelbach, and Steffen Ganns, "The Impact of Regulatory Fit on Performance in an Inattentional Blindness Paradigm," *Journal of General Psychology* 137 (2010): 133; Aude Oliva, "Seeing and Thinking in the Mist," *Science* 329 (2010): 1017.

11. Janet S. Hyde, "The Gender Similarities Hypothesis," *American Psychologist* 60 (2005): 581–92; Janet S. Hyde, "Gender Similarities Still Rule," *American Psychologist* 61 (2006): 641.

12. Barbara Oakley, *Evil Genes: Why Rome Fell, Hitler Rose, Enron Failed, and My Sister Stole My Mother's Boyfriend* (Amherst, NY: Prometheus Books, 2007), 19. Dr. Phelps wrote the preface from which I took the quote.

13. Ross and Nisbett, *Person and the Situation*, 3, 7.

14. Ibid.

15. Maria Sciullo, "Pitt's 'Vampire Professor' Competes on 'Ninja Warrior,'" *Pittsburgh Post-Gazette*, August 2, 2014, http://www.post-gazette.com/ae/tv-radio/2014/08/03/Pitt-s -vampire-professor-competes-on-Ninja-Warrior/stories/201408030001 (accessed July 25, 2017).

16. "Yoga for American Soldiers: Yoga for Veterans and Service Members," Yoga across America, 2014, http://www.yogaacrossamerica.org/drupal-7.0/yfas (page removed).

17. Hal R. Arkes and Philip E. Tetlock, "Attributions of Implicit Prejudice, or 'Would Jesse Jackson Fail the Implicit Association Test?'" *Psychological Inquiry* 15 (2004): 257–78; Frederick L. Oswald et al., "Using the IAT to Predict Ethnic and Racial Discrimination: Small Effect Sizes of Unknown Societal Significance," *Journal of Personality and Social Psychology* 108 (2015): 562–71; Daniel R. Stalder, "Thinking We Can See Invisible Racism," PARBs Anonymous (blog), August 18, 2016, https://parbsanonymous.wordpress.com/2016/08/18/ thinking-we-can-see-invisible-racism/ (accessed August 18, 2016).

18. James Friedrich, "On Seeing Oneself as Less Self-Serving than Others: The Ultimate Self-Serving Bias?" *Teaching of Psychology* 23 (1996): 107–109.

19. Jamil Zaki, "Psychological Studies Are Not about You," *Scientific American*, September 5, 2013, http://blogs.scientificamerican.com/moral-universe/2013/09/05/psychological -studies-are-not-about-you/ (accessed April 6, 2014).

20. Ross and Nisbett, *Person and the Situation*, ix.

21. "Author Malcolm Gladwell on His Best-Selling Books," interview by Anderson Cooper, *60 Minutes Overtime*, November 24, 2013, video, http://www.cbsnews.com/news/ author-malcolm-gladwell-on-his-best-selling-books/ (accessed July 25, 2017).

22. Thomas Carnahan and Sam McFarland, "Revisiting the Stanford Prison Experiment:

Could Participant Self-Selection Have Led to the Cruelty?" *Personality and Social Psychology Bulletin* 33 (2007): 603–14.

23. Daniel R. Stalder, "Revisiting the Issue of Safety in Numbers: The Likelihood of Receiving Help from a Group," *Social Influence* 3 (2008): 24–33; Daniel R. Stalder, "Updating the Bystander-Effect Literature: The Return of Safety in Numbers" (presentation, Annual Convention of the Midwestern Psychological Association, Chicago, IL, May 5–7, 2011).

24. Taylor, *Positive Illusions*.

25. Michael T. Moore and David M. Fresco, "Depressive Realism: A Meta-Analytic Review," *Clinical Psychology Review* 32 (2012): 496–509.

26. "James A. Garfield," Wikiquote, 2017, https://en.wikiquote.org/wiki/James_A._Garfield (accessed July 28, 2017). The original source of this quote isn't entirely clear—it's been attributed to others as well as Garfield.

CHAPTER 1: SPEECHES AND TRAFFIC JAMS: FAE BASICS

1. Peter M. Rowe, "Let Those Shoulder Drivers Stew in Their Own Juice," *New York Times*, June 25, 1995, http://www.nytimes.com/1995/06/25/nyregion/l-let-those-shoulder-drivers-stew-in-their-own-juice-939495.html (accessed July 28, 2017).

2. Abraham Piper, "Car Drives on the Shoulder to Avoid Traffic Jam, Gets Proper Payback," 22 Words, September 12, 2012, http://twentytwowords.com/2012/09/12/car-drives-on-the-shoulder-to-avoid-traffic-jam-gets-proper-payback/ (accessed July 28, 2017).

3. The FAE is also known as the correspondence bias.

4. Gustav Ichheiser, "Misinterpretations of Personality in Everyday Life and the Psychologist's Frame of Reference," *Character and Personality* 12 (1943): 152.

5. Kurt Lewin, "The Conflict between Aristotelian and Galilean Modes of Thought in Contemporary Psychology," *Journal of General Psychology* 5 (1931): 141–77.

6. Floyd Rudmin et al., "Gustav Ichheiser in the History of Social Psychology: An Early Phenomenology of Social Attribution," *British Journal of Social Psychology* 26 (1987): 165–80.

7. Daniel T. Gilbert and Patrick S. Malone, "The Correspondence Bias," *Psychological Bulletin* 117 (1995): 23.

8. Ichheiser, "Misinterpretations of Personality in Everyday Life."

9. Rudmin et al., "Gustav Ichheiser in the History of Social Psychology."

10. Friedrich Nietzsche, *Human, All Too Human: A Book for Free Spirits*, 2nd ed., trans. R. J. Hollingdale (Cambridge: Cambridge University Press, 1996).

11. Fritz Heider, *The Psychology of Interpersonal Relations* (New York: Wiley, 1958), 54. The actual quote is "It seems that behavior in particular has such salient properties it tends to engulf the total field rather than be confined to its proper position as a local stimulus whose interpretation requires the additional data of a surrounding field—the situation in social perception."

12. Ichheiser, "Misinterpretations of Personality in Everyday Life," 152.

13. Lee Ross, "The Intuitive Psychologist and His Shortcomings: Distortions in the Attribution Process," in *Advances in Experimental Social Psychology*, ed. Leonard Berkowitz, vol. 10 (New York: Academic Press, 1977), 173–220.

14. Edward E. Jones and Victor A. Harris, "The Attribution of Attitudes," *Journal of Experimental Social Psychology* 3 (1967): 1–24. Jones and Harris actually reported similar results from two separate studies in that 1967 article, but in their first study, the results were unexpected. So the authors regrouped and designed a stronger second study, which is the one reported in textbooks and described here.

15. Gilbert and Malone, "Correspondence Bias," 22.

16. Bo Bennett, *Logically Fallacious: The Ultimate Collection of over 300 Logical Fallacies* (Sudbury, MA: eBookIt.com, 2012). Some readers might know this principle as "affirming the consequent," in which A may be sufficient for B to occur, but not necessary.

17. Leora Broydo, "(Not Such a) Thriller! Critics Give Movie Studios a Thumbs-Down for Twisting Their Words," *Mother Jones*, November/December 1997, http://www.motherjones .com/politics/1997/11/not-such-thriller (accessed July 26, 2017).

18. V. P. Poteat, "Contextual and Moderating Effects of the Peer Group Climate on Use of Homophobic Epithets," *School Psychology Review* 37 (2008): 188–201.

19. Gilbert and Malone, "Correspondence Bias," 21.

20. Malcolm Gladwell, *Blink: The Power of Thinking without Thinking* (New York: Little, Brown, 2005); Timothy D. Wilson, *Strangers to Ourselves: Discovering the Adaptive Unconscious* (Cambridge, MA: President and Fellows of Harvard College, 2002).

21. Myers, *Social Psychology*, 12. In fairness to Myers and the many others who make a similar case, inferring personal values could be accurate some of the time. How often is hard to say and depends on the particulars, but it is less often than most of us think.

22. Poteat, "Contextual and Moderating Effects of the Peer Group Climate"; Francesca M. Franco and Anne Maass, "Intentional Control over Prejudice: When the Choice of the Measure Matters," *European Journal of Social Psychology* 29 (1999): 469–77.

23. J. L. Cowles, "Defeating My Anxiety," *New York Times*, November 10, 2015, http:// opinionator.blogs.nytimes.com/2015/11/10/defeating-my-anxiety/ (accessed July 26, 2017).

24. "Words Can Hurt," Global Down Syndrome Foundation, 2015, http://www .globaldownsyndrome.org/about-down-syndrome/words-can-hurt/ (accessed July 26, 2017).

25. Nick Paumgarten, "Fighting Words: Whatever," *New Yorker*, July 11, 2005, http:// www.newyorker.com/archive/2005/07/11/050711ta_talk_paumgarten (accessed July 26, 2017).

26. Daniel T. Gilbert and Edward E. Jones, "Perceiver-Induced Constraint: Interpretations of Self-Generated Reality," *Journal of Personality and Social Psychology* 50 (1986): 269–80.

CHAPTER 2: POLITICS AND HEARSAY: FAE APPLIED

1. Daniel T. Gilbert and Patrick S. Malone, "The Correspondence Bias," *Psychological Bulletin* 117 (1995): 21–38.

2. Margaret Sullivan, "Editorial Is under Fire for Saying President 'Clearly Misspoke' on Health Care," *Public Editor's Journal* at *New York Times*, November 4, 2013, https:// publiceditor.blogs.nytimes.com/2013/11/04/editorial-is-under-fire-for-saying-president -clearly-misspoke-on-health-care/ (accessed July 26, 2017).

3. Sam Stein, "Mitt Romney Campaign: We Will Not 'Be Dictated by Fact-Checkers,'" *HuffPost*, August 28, 2012, http://www.huffingtonpost.com/2012/08/23/mitt -romney-_n_1836139.html (accessed July 26, 2017).

4. Linda Feldmann, "How 2016 Became the Fact-Check Election," *Christian Science Monitor*, July 1, 2016, https://www.csmonitor.com/USA/Politics/2016/0701/How-2016 -became-the-fact-check-election (accessed July 26, 2017).

5. Julian Zelizer, "Do Facts Matter?" CNN, October 16, 2012, http://www.cnn.com/ 2012/10/15/opinion/zelizer-facts-matter/index.html (accessed July 26, 2017).

6. Feldmann, "How 2016 Became the Fact-Check Election."

7. Jenna Johnson, "Many Trump Supporters Don't Believe His Wildest Promises—And They Don't Care," *Washington Post*, June 7, 2016, https://www.washingtonpost.com/politics/ many-trump-supporters-dont-believe-his-wildest-promises--and-they-dont-care/2016/ 06/06/05005210-28c4-11e6-b989-4e5479715b54_story.html (accessed July 26, 2017).

8. Charles F. Bond Jr. and Bella M. DePaulo, "Accuracy of Deception Judgments," *Personality and Social Psychology Review* 10 (2006): 214–34.

9. Derald W. Sue, *Microaggressions in Everyday Life: Race, Gender, and Sexual Orientation* (Hoboken, NJ: John Wiley & Sons, 2010).

10. Derald W. Sue et al., "Racial Microaggressions in Everyday Life: Implications for Clinical Practice," *American Psychologist* 62 (2007): 276; Sue, *Microaggressions in Everyday Life*.

11. Xuan Thai and Ted Barrett, "Biden's Description of Obama Draws Scrutiny," CNN, February 9, 2007, http://www.cnn.com/2007/POLITICS/01/31/biden.obama/ (accessed July 28, 2017).

12. Sue et al., "Racial Microaggressions in Everyday Life," 276.

13. John McWhorter, "'Microaggression' Is the New Racism on Campus," *Time*, March 21, 2014, http://time.com/32618/microaggression-is-the-new-racism-on-campus/ (accessed July 28, 2017).

14. Scott O. Lilienfeld, "Microaggressions: Strong Claims, Inadequate Evidence," *Perspectives on Psychological Science* 12 (2017): 138–69. Lilienfeld thoroughly described several limitations of microaggression research and noted potential harms from microaggression training programs. Response articles in the same issue of that journal largely concurred.

15. Sue et al., "Racial Microaggressions in Everyday Life," 276.

16. McWhorter, "'Microaggression' Is the New Racism on Campus."

17. Kenneth R. Thomas, Robert E. Wubbolding, and Morris L. Jackson, "Psychologically Correct Race Baiting?" *Academic Questions* 18 (2005): 50.

18. Derald W. Sue et al., "Racial Microaggressions and the Power to Define Reality," *American Psychologist* 63 (2008): 278–79.

19. Kenneth R. Thomas, "Macrononsense in Multiculturalism," *American Psychologist* 63 (2008): 274; Sue et al., "Racial Microaggressions and the Power to Define Reality."

20. Carl Bialik, "The Best Worst Blurbs of 2007," *Gelf Magazine*, January 6, 2008, http://www.gelfmagazine.com/archives/the_best_worst_blurbs_of_2007.php (accessed July 28, 2017).

21. Matt Philbin, "Shameless: NBC Never Tells Viewers It Smeared Zimmerman with Doctored Audio," NewsBusters, June 20, 2013, http://newsbusters.org/blogs/matthew-philbin/2013/06/20/shameless-nbc-never-tells-viewers-it-smeared-zimmerman-doctored-aud (accessed July 28, 2017).

22. "The Splice Channel," *The Daily Show with Jon Stewart*, April 9, 2012, video, 5:15, http://www.cc.com/video-clips/2v4c0b/the-daily-show-with-jon-stewart-the-splice-channel (accessed July 28, 2017).

23. Tobias Greitemeyer, "Article Retracted, but the Message Lives On," *Psychonomic Bulletin and Review* 21 (2014): 557–61.

24. Brian Montopoli, "Mitt Romney Attack Ad Misleadingly Quotes Obama," CBS News, November 23, 2011, http://www.cbsnews.com/news/mitt-romney-attack-ad-misleadingly-quotes-obama/ (accessed July 28, 2017).

25. Lucy Madison and Sarah B. Boxer, "Mitt Romney: 'I Like Being Able to Fire People' for Bad Service," CBS News, January 9, 2012, http://www.cbsnews.com/news/mitt-romney-i-like-being-able-to-fire-people-for-bad-service/ (accessed July 28, 2017).

26. Jim Acosta, "Welcome to the 'Out of Context' Campaign," CNN: Political Ticker, June 12, 2012, http://politicalticker.blogs.cnn.com/2012/06/12/welcome-to-the-out-of-context-campaign/ (accessed July 28, 2017).

27. Matthew S. McGlone, "Contextomy: The Art of Quoting out of Context," *Media, Culture, and Society* 27 (2005): 511–22.

28. John Pieret, "The Quote Mine Project: Or, Lies, Damned Lies, and Quote Mines," The TalkOrigins Archive: Exploring the Creation/Evolution Controversy, October 31, 2006, http://www.talkorigins.org/faqs/quotes/mine/project.html (accessed July 28, 2017).

29. Daniel T. Gilbert, Brett W. Pelham, and Douglas S. Krull, "The Psychology of Good Ideas," *Psychological Inquiry* 14 (2003): 258.

30. Sam Sommers, *Situations Matter: Understanding How Context Transforms Your World* (New York: Riverhead, 2011).

31. Carol S. Dweck, *Mindset: The New Psychology of Success* (New York: Ballantine, 2006), 53, 144. Even if training for particular mind-sets can cause particular behaviors (as demonstrated by some of Dweck's research), that does not mean that we can observe a particular behavior in a colleague or student and conclude there is a particular mind-set behind it (although there might be). Such a conclusion would constitute the converse error. Even if individuals predetermined

to have fixed mind-sets behave differently from those with growth mind-sets, that is technically a correlational outcome, and correlation does not imply causation. If an individual with a fixed mind-set is more likely to become tired or hungry, did the individual "let" it happen, or can regular fatigue and hunger cause a mind-set to become fixed? As I tell my students, it is the curse of the correlation that we can never be sure what causes what in a correlational design. Cause can be effect. Up can be down. But we do know that Dweck's training regarding growth mind-sets has been helpful to many people.

32. Emily Pronin, "The Introspection Illusion," *Advances in Experimental Social Psychology* 41 (2009): 26, 55. Pronin referred in part to a positive correlation between implicit attitudes and nonverbal behaviors, but correlation does not imply causation. And even if correlation did imply causation and implicit attitudes always cause those nonverbal behaviors (that is, even if A implies B), that does not mean that those behaviors automatically reveal attitudes (that is, B does not necessarily imply A).

33. Sue et al., "Racial Microaggressions and the Power to Define Reality," 277, 279.

34. Rafael S. Harris Jr., "Racial Microaggression? How Do You Know?" *American Psychologist* 63 (2008): 275–76.

35. Rafael S. Harris Jr., "Racial Microaggression? How Do You Know?—Revisited," *American Psychologist* 64 (2009): 220; Derald W. Sue, "Racial Microaggressions and Worldviews," *American Psychologist* 64 (2009): 220–21. Mistakes happen. But despite Sue's apology, it was unclear if Sue ever altered his FAE-based reasoning. Sue seemed to continue to draw a connection between Harris's viewpoint and Harris's racial identity. Sue pointed out that people of color who immigrate to the United States (as Harris did) may experience discrimination very differently in their own countries than here and so may deny the existence of microaggressions here. In fact, Harris did not deny the existence of a microaggression in Sue's flight-attendant story but rather raised a question about possible alternative explanations. Harris even tried to contact Sue to gather more information, twice, but Sue either did not reply or replied with a standard letter that did not address Harris's question. I'm not saying that Sue is obligated to answer Harris's question, but the fact that Harris was willing to ask the question (and not assume an answer) reflects Harris's openness to the possibility of Sue's viewpoint. Of course, Sue could be correct and Harris's view could stem from Harris's racial identity. Or maybe Sue was just trying to rationalize his original mistaken position against Harris.

36. Hal R. Arkes and Philip E. Tetlock, "Attributions of Implicit Prejudice, or 'Would Jesse Jackson Fail the Implicit Association Test?'" *Psychological Inquiry* 15 (2004): 257–78; Frederick L. Oswald et al., "Using the IAT to Predict Ethnic and Racial Discrimination: Small Effect Sizes of Unknown Societal Significance," *Journal of Personality and Social Psychology* 108 (2015): 562–71; Daniel R. Stalder, "Thinking We Can See Invisible Racism," PARBs Anonymous (blog), August 18, 2016, https://parbsanonymous.wordpress.com/2016/08/18/thinking-we-can-see-invisible-racism/ (accessed August 18, 2016).

37. Mahzarin R. Banaji and Anthony G. Greenwald, *Blindspot: Hidden Biases of Good People* (New York: Delacorte, 2013), 224.

38. Roy F. Baumeister, *Evil: Inside Human Violence and Cruelty* (New York: W. H. Freeman, 1997), 97.

39. Jonathan Haidt, *The Happiness Hypothesis: Finding Modern Truth in Ancient Wisdom* (New York: Basic Books, 2006), 75.

40. Sommers, *Situations Matter*, 286.

41. Haidt, *Happiness Hypothesis*, 75.

42. David Brooks, "Tools for Thinking," *New York Times*, March 28, 2011, http://www .nytimes.com/2011/03/29/opinion/29brooks.html (accessed October 19, 2017).

43. David C. Funder, "Errors and Mistakes: Evaluating the Accuracy of Social Judgment," *Psychological Bulletin* 101 (1987): 80.

44. Bella M. DePaulo et al., "Lying in Everyday Life," *Journal of Personality and Social Psychology* 70 (1996): 991.

45. Funder, "Errors and Mistakes," 81.

46. Before proceeding, let me briefly acknowledge beyond the issue of the attitude-attribution paradigm that a few researchers have raised questions about whether the FAE even exists as traditionally defined. In a 2001 series of articles in the journal *Psychological Inquiry*, psychologists such as John Sabini and David Funder levied relevant criticism against the FAE concept by delving carefully into the meanings of dispositional versus situational causes. But suffice it to say that the FAE concept survived. Among counterviews, other psychologists pointed out that the critical analysis did not extend to many obvious and central examples of the traditional FAE, including cases of blaming victims for externally caused tragedies.

CHAPTER 3: NONVERBAL DECODING: AN ILLUSION OF INSIGHT

1. Steve Ottman, "New Falcons Take Flight," *Sheboygan Falls News*, January 1, 2014, 4.

2. Jeff Pederson, "As We See It: Perception vs. Reality," *Sheboygan Falls News*, January 16, 2014, https://www.facebook.com/permalink.php?story_fbid=501976516584782&id=29785 9563663146&stream_ref=10 (accessed July 28, 2017).

3. Sheboygan Falls Police Department, "Incident Report F14-00162," Sheboygan Falls, WI, January 13, 2014, http://media.mwcradio.com/mimesis/2014-01/18/Sheboygan%20 Falls%20Police%20Picture%20Investigation_1.pdf (accessed October 28, 2017).

4. WBAY TV-2, "Sheb. Falls Mayor Speaks on Basketball Photo Controversy," Facebook, January 18, 2014, https://www.facebook.com/WBAYTV/posts/10202816064939617 (accessed July 28, 2017).

5. Nicholas Epley, *Mindwise: How We Understand What Others Think, Believe, Feel, and Want* (New York: Alfred A. Knopf, 2014).

6. Pederson, "As We See It."

7. Sheboygan Falls Police Department, "Incident Report F14-00162."

8. Anne M. Paul, "Mind Reading," *Psychology Today*, September 1, 2007, http://www.psychologytoday.com/articles/200708/mind-reading (accessed October 19, 2017).

9. David D. Burns, *The Feeling Good Handbook* (New York: Plume, 1999).

10. Malcolm Gladwell, *Blink: The Power of Thinking without Thinking* (New York: Little, Brown, 2005), 213.

11. Ibid., 12–13; Nalini Ambady and Robert Rosenthal, "Half a Minute: Predicting Teacher Evaluations from Thin Slices of Behavior and Physical Attractiveness," *Journal of Personality and Social Psychology* 64 (1993): 431–41. Another problem with Gladwell's reporting is that the reported results comprised *correlations* between initial snap judgments and end-of-semester ratings, which does not necessarily mean that the ratings were similar in absolute scores. Ambady and Rosenthal acknowledged the potential fallibility in end-of-semester ratings when they suggested that future research should use additional criteria to evaluate teachers' actual effectiveness.

12. Timothy Levine, Kim B. Serota, and Hillary C. Shulman, "The Impact of *Lie to Me* on Viewers' Actual Ability to Detect Deception," *Communication Research* 37 (2010): 847–56.

13. Sharon Weinberger, "Airport Security: Intent to Deceive?" *Nature* 465 (2010): 412–15.

14. John Tierney, "At Airports, a Misplaced Faith in Body Language," *New York Times*, March 23, 2014, http://www.nytimes.com/2014/03/25/science/in-airport-screening-body-language-is-faulted-as-behavior-sleuth.html?hpw&rref=science&_r=0 (accessed July 28, 2017).

15. Jane Fritsch, "The Diallo Verdict: The Overview; 4 Officers in Diallo Shooting Are Acquitted of All Charges," *New York Times*, February 26, 2000, http://www.nytimes.com/2000/02/26/nyregion/diallo-verdict-overview-4-officers-diallo-shooting-are-acquitted-all-charges.html (accessed July 28, 2017).

16. Gladwell, *Blink*, 191.

17. Fritsch, "Diallo Verdict."

18. Camila Domonoske and Bill Chappell, "Minnesota Gov. Calls Traffic Stop Shooting 'Absolutely Appalling at All Levels,'" NPR, July 7, 2016, http://www.npr.org/sections/thetwo-way/2016/07/07/485066807/police-stop-ends-in-black-mans-death-aftermath-is-livestreamed-online-video (accessed July 28, 2017). Of course, the context was more multifaceted than I describe here.

19. Daniel T. Gilbert, Brett W. Pelham, and Douglas S. Krull, "On Cognitive Busyness: When Person Perceivers Meet Persons Perceived," *Journal of Personality and Social Psychology* 54 (1988): 733–40.

20. Amos Tversky and Daniel Kahneman, "Judgment under Uncertainty: Heuristics and Biases," *Science* 185 (1974): 1124–31.

21. Daniel T. Gilbert and Patrick S. Malone, "The Correspondence Bias," *Psychological Bulletin* 117 (1995): 21–38; Fritz Heider, *The Psychology of Interpersonal Relations* (New York: Wiley, 1958).

22. Melvin J. Lerner, *The Belief in a Just World: A Fundamental Delusion* (New York: Plenum, 1980). Of course, sometimes a poor individual may be lazy, as sometimes rich people are, but even then, it is rare that laziness is the *only* reason for poverty, or at least much more rare than most of us think.

23. Daniel R. Stalder, "Competing Roles for the Subfactors of Need for Closure in Committing the Fundamental Attribution Error," *Personality and Individual Differences* 47 (2009): 701–705.

24. Daniel Sullivan, Mark J. Landau, and Zachary K. Rothschild, "An Existential Function of Enemyship: Evidence That People Attribute Influence to Personal and Political Enemies to Compensate for Threats to Control," *Journal of Personality and Social Psychology* 98 (2010): 434–49; Jennifer A. Whitson and Adam D. Galinsky, "Lacking Control Increases Illusory Pattern Perception," *Science* 322 (2008): 115–17.

25. Fritsch, "Diallo Verdict."

26. Alan Feuer, "$3 Million Deal in Police Killing of Diallo in '99," *New York Times*, January 7, 2004, http://www.nytimes.com/2004/01/07/nyregion/3-million-deal-in-police -killing-of-diallo-in-99.html?action=click&module=Search&region=searchResults%230 &version=&url=http%3A%2F%2Fquery.nytimes.com%2Fsearch%2Fsitesearch%2F%23%2 Fdiallo%2Bsettlement%2F (accessed July 28, 2017).

27. Gladwell, *Blink*, 233.

28. B. K. Payne, "Prejudice and Perception: The Role of Automatic and Controlled Processes in Misperceiving a Weapon," *Journal of Personality and Social Psychology* 81 (2001): 181–92.

29. Birt L. Duncan, "Differential Social Perception and Attribution of Intergroup Violence: Testing the Lower Limits of Stereotyping of Blacks," *Journal of Personality and Social Psychology* 34 (1976): 597.

30. John F. Dovidio, Kerry Kawakami, and Samuel L. Gaertner, "Implicit and Explicit Prejudice and Interracial Interaction," *Journal of Personality and Social Psychology* 82 (2002): 62–68.

31. Joseph Cilmi, "Without a Thought!" Amazon.com customer review of *Blink* by Malcolm Gladwell, March 6, 2008, https://www.amazon.com/gp/customer-reviews/ RXELGQDIWU1ZH/ref=cm_cr_srp_d_rvw_ttl?ie=UTF8&ASIN=0316010669 (accessed July 28, 2017).

32. Gladwell, *Blink*, 213–214, 233.

33. Ibid., 196–97.

34. Wikipedia, s.v. "Sheboygan Falls, Wisconsin," last updated November 1, 2017, https:// en.wikipedia.org/wiki/Sheboygan_Falls,_Wisconsin (accessed July 28, 2017).

35. "School Spirit or Gang Signs? 'Zero Tolerance' Comes under Fire," NBC News, March 9, 2014, http://www.nbcnews.com/news/education/school-spirit-or-gang-signs-zero-tolerance -comes-under-fire-n41431 (accessed July 28, 2017).

36. Samantha Grossman, "Deaf Man Stabbed after Sign Language Mistaken for Gang

Signs," *Time*, January 15, 2013, http://newsfeed.time.com/2013/01/15/deaf-man-stabbed -after-sign-language-mistaken-for-gang-signs-2/ (accessed July 28, 2017).

37. Ben Rohrbach, "Illinois Girls Basketball Players Suspended for Racy Hand Gesture," Yahoo! Sports, December 6, 2013, http://sports.yahoo.com/blogs/highschool-prep-rally/ illinois-girls-basketball-players-suspended-racy-hand-gesture-172308236.html (accessed July 28, 2017).

38. If school policies don't care about intentions but only whether specific physical nonverbal signs appear anywhere in a photo, then perhaps these school policies are a form of institutional FAE and need to be reevaluated, because some nonverbal signs have multiple meanings, not all of which are foreseeable when creating policies.

39. Dovidio, Kawakami, and Gaertner, "Implicit and Explicit Prejudice and Interracial Interaction."

40. Tierney, "At Airports, a Misplaced Faith in Body Language."

41. Epley, *Mindwise*.

42. Roger E. Axtell, *Gestures: The DO's and TABOOs of Body Language around the World*, rev. and expanded ed. (New York: John Wiley & Sons, 1997), 130.

43. Ibid., xvii, 49.

44. Dane Archer, "Unspoken Diversity: Cultural Differences in Gestures," *Qualitative Sociology* 20 (1997): 79–105.

45. Axtell, *Gestures*, ix.

46. Archer, "Unspoken Diversity," 103.

47. Axtell, *Gestures*. The Nixon through Japan examples were provided by Axtell.

48. Leila Fadel and Lulu Garcia-Navarro, "How Different Cultures Handle Personal Space," NPR, May 5, 2013, http://www.npr.org/blogs/codeswitch/2013/05/05/181126380/ how-different-cultures-handle-personal-space (accessed July 28, 2017).

49. Roy Wenzl, "KU Researcher Studies Flirting," *Wichita Eagle*, June 4, 2014, http:// www.kansas.com/news/article1145210.html (accessed July 28, 2017).

50. Jessica L. Watkins and Jeffrey A. Hall, "The Association between Nonverbal Sensitivity and Flirting Detection Accuracy," *Communication Research Reports* 31 (2014): 348–56.

51. Paul Ekman and Maureen O'Sullivan, "Who Can Catch a Liar?" *American Psychologist* 46 (1991): 913–20; Paul Ekman, Maureen O'Sullivan, and Mark G. Frank, "A Few Can Catch a Liar," *Psychological Science* 10 (1999): 263–66.

52. Charles F. Bond Jr., "A Few Can Catch a Liar, Sometimes: Comments on Ekman and O'Sullivan (1991), as Well as Ekman, O'Sullivan, and Frank (1999)," *Applied Cognitive Psychology* 22 (2008): 1298–300; Christian A. Meissner and Saul M. Kassin, "'He's Guilty!': Investigator Bias in Judgments of Truth and Deception," *Law and Human Behavior* 26 (2002): 469–80; Carol A. E. Nickerson and Kenneth R. Hammond, "Comment on Ekman and O'Sullivan," *American Psychologist* 48 (1993): 989; Marc-André Reinhard et al., "The Case of Pinocchio: Teachers' Ability to Detect Deception," *Social Psychology of Education* 14 (2011): 299–318. Reinhard et al. showed that more experienced teachers were no more accurate than

less experienced teachers. Bond and Nickerson identified statistical errors or omissions in Ekman and colleagues' research that claimed superior accuracy in certain groups. Ekman and colleagues later disputed or downplayed Bond's and Nickerson's points. But the broader research literature at best shows only a small superiority in nonverbal decoding among "experts."

53. Epley, *Mindwise*.

54. Gladwell, *Blink*.

55. David Myers, *Social Psychology*, 11th ed. (New York: McGraw Hill, 2013).

56. "JSL: Younger Brother," YouTube video, 0:22, posted by "SignTV2009," May 3, 2012, https://www.youtube.com/watch?v=p0_HevkD9Z8 (accessed July 28, 2017); "Taiwan Sign Language VS Japanese Sign Language," YouTube video, 3:30, posted by "jslvideodayo," November 6, 2014, https://www.youtube.com/watch?v=RMbG2d-cNhc (accessed July 28, 2017).

57. Mary E. Kite and Kay Deaux, "Gender Belief Systems: Homosexuality and the Implicit Inversion Theory," *Psychology of Women Quarterly* 11 (1987): 83–96.

58. Gerulf Rieger et al., "Dissecting 'Gaydar': Accuracy and the Role of Masculinity-Femininity," *Archives of Sexual Behavior* 39 (2010): 124–40.

59. Nicholas O. Rule and Nalini Ambady, "Brief Exposures: Male Sexual Orientation Is Accurately Perceived at 50 ms," *Journal of Experimental Social Psychology* 44 (2008): 1100–105.

60. "Ellen on Gaydar," YouTube video, 2:58, posted by "Marianaa18," July 31, 2013, https://www.youtube.com/watch?v=2bCTC0LhF8M (accessed July 28, 2017).

61. "Molly Ringwald Says 'Pretty in Pink' Friend Duckie Was Gay, but Jon Cryer Disputes Allegation," *HuffPost*, May 23, 2012, http://www.huffingtonpost.com/2012/05/23/molly -ringwald-pretty-in-pink-duckie-gay_n_1539778.html (accessed July 28, 2017).

62. Jaroslava Valentova et al., "Judgments of Sexual Orientation and Masculinity-Femininity Based on Thin Slices of Behavior: A Cross-Cultural Comparison," *Archives of Sexual Behavior* 40 (2011): 1150.

63. Rieger et al., "Dissecting 'Gaydar.'"

64. Noah Michelson, "25 Celebrity Coming Out Stories That Shocked the World," *HuffPost*, October 17, 2011, http://www.huffingtonpost.com/2011/10/17/25-celebrity -coming-out-stories_n_1015381.html (accessed July 28, 2017).

65. Nalini Ambady and Mark Hallahan, "Using Nonverbal Representations of Behavior: Perceiving Sexual Orientation," in *The Languages of the Brain*, eds. Albert M. Galaburda, Stephen M. Kosslyn, and Yves Christen (Cambridge, MA: Harvard University Press, 2002), 320–32; David Sylva et al., "Concealment of Sexual Orientation," *Archives of Sexual Behavior* 39 (2010): 141–52.

CHAPTER 4: WHAT'S IN A FACE? PHOTOS CAN LIE

1. Stephen Porter et al., "Is the Face a Window to the Soul? Investigation of the Accuracy of Intuitive Judgments of the Trustworthiness of Human Faces," *Canadian Journal of Behavioral Science* 40 (2008): 176.

2. Mats Larsson, Nancy L. Pedersen, and Håkan Stattin, "Associations between Iris Characteristics and Personality in Adulthood," *Biological Psychology* 75 (2007): 165–75. Of course, when people talk about how expressive someone's eyes are, they might be referring to facial features near or around the eyes. Please read on for a fuller discussion of what can be read from fuller facial expressions.

3. Charles F. Bond Jr. and Bella M. DePaulo, "Accuracy of Deception Judgments," *Personality and Social Psychology Review* 10 (2006): 229, 231.

4. Nicholas O. Rule and Nalini Ambady, "Brief Exposures: Male Sexual Orientation Is Accurately Perceived at 50 ms," *Journal of Experimental Social Psychology* 44 (2008): 1103. Although the photos of gay men's faces were from Facebook, the 52 percent finding resulted from not the gay men themselves posting the photos but rather their friends or acquaintances posting the photos.

5. Jaroslava V. Valentova et al., "Shape Differences between the Faces of Homosexual and Heterosexual Men," *Archives of Sexual Behavior* 43 (2014): 353–61.

6. Nalini Ambady and Mark Hallahan, "Using Nonverbal Representations of Behavior: Perceiving Sexual Orientation," in *The Languages of the Brain*, eds. Albert M. Galaburda, Stephen M. Kosslyn, and Yves Christen (Cambridge, MA: Harvard University Press, 2002), 320–32. The authors described the results as "preliminary."

7. Nalini Ambady, Mark Hallahan, and Brett Conner, "Accuracy of Judgments of Sexual Orientation from Thin Slices of Behavior," *Journal of Personality and Social Psychology* 77 (1999): 544.

8. Wright and his deadpan humor are discussed in detail in this article. Hal Boedeker, "Comedian Steven Wright: Deadpan but Delighted," *Orlando Sentinel*, August 29, 2017, http://www.orlandosentinel.com/entertainment/tv/tv-guy/os-et-comedian-steven-wright -deadpan-but-delighted-20170829-story.html (accessed December 29, 2017).

9. Brian Parkinson, "Do Facial Movements Express Emotions or Communicate Motives?" *Personality and Social Psychology Review* 9 (2005): 278.

10. Lauren Collins, "The Obama Selfie-Face-Gate," *New Yorker*, December 13, 2013, http:// www.newyorker.com/news/news-desk/the-obama-selfie-face-gate (accessed July 24, 2017).

11. Andy Soltis, "Michelle Not Amused by Obama's Memorial Selfie," *New York Post*, December 10, 2013, http://nypost.com/2013/12/10/michelle-annoyed-by-obamas-selfie-at -mandela-memorial/ (accessed July 24, 2017); Linda Stasi, "Stasi: President Obama Cluelessly Joins Danish Prime Minister's Selfie Fun as Wife Makes 'the Face,'" *New York Daily News*, December 15, 2013, http://www.nydailynews.com/new-york/stasi-obama-cluelessly-joins -danish-prime-minister-selfie-fun-article-1.1548216 (accessed July 24, 2017).

12. Eun K. Kim, "First Lady Not Peeved, Says Photographer Who Caught the Obama Selfie," Today, December 11, 2013, http://www.today.com/news/first-lady-not-peeved-says -photographer-who-caught-obama-selfie-2d11723566 (accessed July 24, 2017).

13. Hillel Aviezer et al., "Angry, Disgusted, or Afraid? Studies on the Malleability of Emotion Perception," *Psychological Science* 19 (2008): 724–32.

14. Roxane Gay, "The Media's Michelle Obama Problem: What a Selfie Says about Our Biases," *Salon*, December 10, 2013, http://www.salon.com/2013/12/10/the_medias_michelle _obama_problem_what_a_selfie_says_about_our_biases/ (accessed July 24, 2017).

15. Carol Tavris and Elliot Aronson, *Mistakes Were Made (But Not by Me): Why We Justify Foolish Beliefs, Bad Decisions, and Hurtful Acts* (Orlando, FL: Harcourt, 2007).

16. Paige Lavender, "Obama Takes Selfie with World Leaders at Mandela Memorial, and Michelle Is Having None of It (UPDATED)," *HuffPost*, December 10, 2013, http://www .huffingtonpost.com/2013/12/10/obama-selfie_n_4419349.html (accessed July 24, 2017).

17. Ibid. This comment was made in response to the *HuffPost* article.

18. Roberto Schmidt, Agence France-Presse, *Correspondent/Behind the News* (blog), "The Story Behind 'That Selfie,'" *Tampa Bay Times*, December 11, 2013, http://www.tampabay.com/ opinion/columns/the-story-behind-that-selfie/2156613 (accessed December 14, 2013). These comments were made in response to Roberto Schmidt's *Correspondent* blog post.

19. José-Miguel Fernández-Dols, "Advances in the Study of Facial Expression: An Introduction to the Special Section," *Emotion Review* 5 (2013): 3.

20. Alan J. Fridlund, "The New Ethology of Human Facial Expressions," in *The Psychology of Facial Expression*, eds. James A. Russell and Jose-Miguél Fernández-Dols (New York: Cambridge University Press, 1997), 121, 123.

21. Paul Ekman, "Strong Evidence for Universals in Facial Expressions: A Reply to Russell's Mistaken Critique," *Psychological Bulletin* 115 (1994): 287.

22. James A. Russell, "Facial Expressions of Emotion: What Lies Beyond Minimal Universality?" *Psychological Bulletin* 118 (1995): 388.

23. James A. Russell, "Is There a Universal Recognition of Emotion from Facial Expression? A Review of the Cross-Cultural Studies," *Psychological Bulletin* 115 (1994): 102–41.

24. Ekman, "Strong Evidence for Universals in Facial Expressions."

25. Russell, "Facial Expressions of Emotion."

26. Sara M. Lindberg et al., "New Trends in Gender and Mathematics Performance: A Meta-Analysis," *Psychological Bulletin* 136 (2010): 1123–35.

27. Paul Ekman and Wallace V. Friesen, "Constants across Cultures in the Face and Emotion," *Journal of Personality and Social Psychology* 17 (1971): 124–29.

28. James A. Russell, Jo-Anne Bachorowski, and José-Miguel Fernández-Dols, "Facial and Vocal Expressions of Emotion," *Annual Review of Psychology* 54 (2003): 329–49.

29. José-Miguel Fernández-Dols and Carlos Crivelli, "Emotion and Expression: Naturalistic Studies," *Emotion Review* 5 (2013): 24–29; Mary Kayyal, Sherri Widen, and James A. Russell, "Context Is More Powerful than We Think: Contextual Cues Override Facial Cues Even for Valence," *Emotion* 15 (2015): 287–91; James A. Russell, "A Sceptical Look at Faces as Emotion Signals," in *The Expression of Emotion: Philosophical, Psychological, and Legal Perspectives*, eds. Catharine Abell and Joel Smith (New York: Cambridge University Press, 2016), 157–72. And many others; among a few who still seem to side with Ekman are David

Matsumoto et al., "Cross-Cultural Judgments of Spontaneous Facial Expressions of Emotion," *Journal of Nonverbal Behavior* 33 (2009): 213–38.

30. Tanya L. Chartrand and John A. Bargh, "The Chameleon Effect: The Perception-Behavior Link and Social Interaction," *Journal of Personality and Social Psychology* 76 (1999): 893–910.

31. Phoebe E. Bailey and Julie D. Henry, "Subconscious Facial Expression Mimicry Is Preserved in Older Adulthood," *Psychology and Aging* 24 (2009): 995–1000; Ulf Dimberg, Monkia Thunberg, and Kurt Elmehed, "Unconscious Facial Reaction to Emotional Facial Expressions," *Psychological Science* 11 (2000): 86–89; Katja U. Likowski et al., "Facial Mimicry and the Mirror Neuron System: Simultaneous Acquisition of Facial Electromyography and Functional Magnetic Resonance Imaging," *Frontiers in Human Neuroscience* 6 (2012): 1–10.

32. Patrick Bourgeois and Ursula Hess, "The Impact of Social Context on Mimicry," *Biological Psychology* 77 (2008): 343–52; Evan W. Carr, Piotr Winkielman, and Christopher Oveis, "Transforming the Mirror: Power Fundamentally Changes Facial Responding to Emotional Expressions," *Journal of Experimental Psychology: General* 143 (2014): 997–1003; Ursula Hess and Patrick Bourgeois, "You Smile—I Smile: Emotion Expression in Social Interaction," *Biological Psychology* 84 (2010): 514–20.

33. "Can We All Smile and Be a Villain?" *Toronto Star*, January 23, 2000, 1.

34. Alan J. Fridlund et al., "Social Determinants of Facial Expressions during Affective Imagery: Displaying to the People in Your Head," *Journal of Nonverbal Behavior* 14 (1990): 113–37.

35. Alan J. Fridlund and James A. Russell, "The Functions of Facial Expressions: What's in a Face?" in *The Sage Handbook of Nonverbal Communication*, eds. Valerie Manusov and Miles L. Patterson (Thousand Oaks, CA: Sage, 2006), 299–319.

36. Esther Jakobs, Antony S. R. Manstead, and Agneta H. Fischer, "Social Context Effects on Facial Activity in a Negative Emotional Setting," *Emotion* 1 (2001): 51–69; Parkinson, "Do Facial Movements Express Emotions or Communicate Motives?"; Michelle S. M. Yik and James A. Russell, "Interpretation of Faces: A Cross-Cultural Study of a Prediction from Fridlund's Theory," *Cognition and Emotion* 13 (1999): 93–104.

37. Marwan Sinaceur et al., "Weep and Get More: When and Why Sadness Expression Is Effective in Negotiations," *Journal of Applied Psychology* 100 (2015): 1847–71.

38. Fridlund et al., "Social Determinants of Facial Expressions"; Alan J. Fridlund, "Sociality of Solitary Smiling: Potentiation by an Implicit Audience," *Journal of Personality and Social Psychology* 60 (1991): 229–40.

39. Russell, "Sceptical Look at Faces," 166.

40. Hillary A. Elfenbein, "Nonverbal Dialects and Accents in Facial Expressions of Emotion," *Emotion Review* 5 (2013): 90–96.

41. Adam Carlson, "Man in Viral Beyoncé Photo Explains the Story behind Her Apparent Side Eye: She Was 'Beyond Polite,'" *People*, June 18, 2016, http://people.com/celebrity/beyonce-side-eye-photo-man-explains-the-viral-moment-on-twitter/ (accessed July 25, 2017).

293

42. Daniel Cervone and Tracy L. Caldwell, *Psychology: The Science of Person, Mind, and Brain* (New York: Worth, 2016); Daniel L. Schacter et al., *Psychology*, 4th ed. (New York: Worth, 2017).

43. Sofia Wenzler et al., "Beyond Pleasure and Pain: Facial Expression Ambiguity in Adults and Children during Intense Situations," *Emotion* 16 (2016): 813.

44. "Can We All Smile and Be a Villain?"

45. Kayyal, Widen, and Russell, "Context Is More Powerful than We Think."

CHAPTER 5: SOCIAL ROLES: POPES DON'T BOUNCE

1. Arlin Cuncic, "Shy Actors," Verywell, September 20, 2016, https://www.verywell.com/shy-actors-list-3024270 (accessed October 21, 2017); Arlin Cuncic, "Shy Comedians," Verywell, September 12, 2016, https://www.verywell.com/shy-comedians-3024275 (accessed October 21, 2017); Matthew Jacobs, "Celebrities with Stage Fright Include Adele, Hayden Panettiere, Barbra Streisand, Megan Fox and Many More," *HuffPost*, April 5, 2013, http://www.huffingtonpost.com/2013/04/05/celebrities-with-stage-fright_n_3022146.html (accessed October 21, 2017).

2. David K. Li, "Pope Francis Worked as a Nightclub Bouncer," *New York Post*, December 3, 2013, http://nypost.com/2013/12/03/pope-francis-i-worked-as-a-bouncer/ (accessed October 21, 2017); Michael Solomon, "Holy Rollers: Harley-Davidsons Owned by Pope Francis and Pope Benedict Sell at Auction," *Forbes*, February 11, 2015, https://www.forbes.com/sites/msolomon/2015/02/11/pope-francis-harley-davidson-auction-pope-benedict-xvi/#67287d453dee (accessed October 21, 2017).

3. Louise Wattis and Liz James, "Exploring Order and Disorder: Women's Experiences Balancing Work and Care," *European Journal of Women's Studies* 20 (2013): 264–78.

4. James A. Russell, "A Sceptical Look at Faces as Emotion Signals," in *The Expression of Emotion: Philosophical, Psychological, and Legal Perspectives*, eds. Catharine Abell and Joel Smith (New York: Cambridge University Press, 2016), 169.

5. Alice H. Eagly and Wendy Wood, "The Origins of Sex Differences in Human Behavior: Evolved Dispositions versus Social Roles," *American Psychologist* 54 (1999): 409. This issue is debated, though Alice Eagly has made a strong case over the years.

6. Christian Gollayan, "Bar Explains Why Female Bartenders Are Being Nice to You," *New York Post*, May 30, 2017, http://nypost.com/2017/05/30/bars-message-to-rude-drunk-dudes-goes-viral/ (accessed October 21, 2017).

7. Mark D. Alicke, Jennifer I. Zerbst, and Frank M. LoSchiavo, "Personal Attitudes, Constraint Magnitude, and Correspondence Bias," *Basic and Applied Social Psychology* 18 (1996): 211–28.

8. Eagly and Wood, "Origins of Sex Differences in Human Behavior."

9. My students tell me that "damn" is not technically a swear word. I've checked, and the internet tends to agree.

10. "Do Teachers Swear?" Yahoo! Answers, 2017, https://answers.yahoo.com/question/index?qid=20080109030237AAsNziD (accessed October 21, 2017).

11. Elliot Aronson, *The Social Animal*, 8th ed. (New York: Worth, 1999), 165.

12. A. Pawlowski, "Strict Math Teacher's Secret Identity . . . as a Baby Cuddler," Today, February 27, 2014, http://www.today.com/health/strict-math-teachers-secret-identity-baby-cuddler-2D12172837 (accessed October 21, 2017).

13. Cuncic, "Shy Actors"; Cuncic, "Shy Comedians"; Jacobs, "Celebrities with Stage Fright."

14. Lee Ross and Richard E. Nisbett, *The Person and the Situation: Perspectives of Social Psychology* (London: Pinter & Martin, 2011); Richard E. Nisbett, *Mindware: Tools for Smart Thinking* (New York: Farrar, Straus, and Giroux, 2015).

15. Ryan Howes, "Why People Lie to Their Therapists: You Spend Time, Money, and Energy in Therapy—So Why Not Tell the Truth?" *Psychology Today*, October 26, 2016, https://www.psychologytoday.com/blog/in-therapy/201610/why-people-lie-their-therapists (accessed October 21, 2017); Ryan Howes, "The World's Best Therapy Client: Trying Too Hard in Therapy," *Psychology Today*, April 1, 2011, https://www.psychologytoday.com/blog/in-therapy/201104/the-worlds-best-therapy-client (accessed October 21, 2017); Ryan Howes, "Say Anything: The Joy of Confronting Your Therapist," *Psychology Today*, July 17, 2008, https://www.psychologytoday.com/blog/in-therapy/200807/say-anything (accessed October 21, 2017).

16. And beware the above-average effect in thinking you're a better nonverbal decoder than most other teachers, although you might be.

17. "How to Behave in Class," wikiHow, 2017, http://www.wikihow.com/Behave-In-Class (accessed October 21, 2017).

18. Robert J. Coplan et al., "Is Silence Golden? Elementary School Teachers' Strategies and Beliefs regarding Hypothetical Shy/Quiet and Exuberant/Talkative Children," *Journal of Educational Psychology* 103 (2011): 939–51.

19. "How to Be Smart and Cool at the Same Time," wikiHow, 2017, http://www.wikihow.com/Be-Smart-and-Cool-at-the-Same-Time (accessed October 21, 2017).

20. Rhonda S. Jamison, Travis Wilson, and Allison Ryan, "Too Cool for School? The Relationship between Coolness and Academic Reputation in Early Adolescence," *Social Development* 24 (2015): 384–403; Karolyn Tyson, William Darity Jr., and Domini R. Castellino, "It's Not 'a Black Thing': Understanding the Burden of Acting White and Other Dilemmas of High Achievement," *American Sociological Review* 70 (2005): 582–605.

21. Mary M. Reda, "What's the Problem with Quiet Students? Anyone? Anyone?" *Chronicle of Higher Education*, September 5, 2010, http://www.chronicle.com/article/Whats-the-Problem-With-Quiet/124258/ (accessed October 21, 2017).

22. Shankar Vedantam, "How Stereotypes Can Drive Women to Quit Science," NPR, July

12, 2012, http://www.npr.org/2012/07/12/156664337/stereotype-threat-why-women
-quit-science-jobs (accessed October 21, 2017); Eileen Pollack, "Why Are There Still So Few
Women in Science?" *New York Times*, October 3, 2013, http://www.nytimes.com/2013/10/06/
magazine/why-are-there-still-so-few-women-in-science.html (accessed October 21, 2017).

23. Deborah Hastings, "Engineering Student with No Female Friends Has All Male
Bridesmaids," *Inside Edition*, May 22, 2017, http://www.msn.com/en-us/lifestyle/whats
-hot/engineering-student-with-no-female-friends-has-all-male-bridesmaids/ar-BBBoUfZ?li
=BBnbfcL&ocid=ASUDHP (accessed October 21, 2017).

24. Tyson, Darity, and Castellino, "It's Not 'a Black Thing,'" 582.

25. Claude M. Steele, "Race and the Schooling of Black Americans," *Atlantic Monthly*,
April 1992, https://www.theatlantic.com/magazine/archive/1992/04/race-and-the-schooling
-of-black-americans/306073/ (accessed October 28, 2017).

26. Tyson, Darity and Castellino, "It's Not 'a Black Thing,'" 594–95.

27. Reda, "What's the Problem with Quiet Students?"

28. "Alison Arngrim," tv.com, 2017, http://www.tv.com/people/alison-arngrim/trivia/
(accessed October 21, 2017).

29. John H. Fleming and John M. Darley, "Actors and Observers Revisited:
Correspondence Bias, Counterfactual Surprise, and Discounting in Successive Judgments of
Constrained Behavior," *Social Cognition* 11 (1993): 367–97; Nurit Tal-Or and Yael Papirman,
"The Fundamental Attribution Error in Attributing Fictional Figures' Characteristics to the
Actors," *Media Psychology* 9 (2007): 331–45.

30. Leonard Nimoy, *I Am Not Spock* (Cutchogue, NY: Buccaneer, 1975).

31. John Patterson, "Aubrey Plaza: 'Things Take on a Different Meaning When Death
Comes So Close,'" *Guardian*, August 4, 2016, https://www.theguardian.com/culture/2016/
aug/04/aubrey-plaza-mike-dave-different-meaning-death-so-close (accessed October 21, 2017).

32. Lee D. Ross, Teresa M. Amabile, and Julia L. Steinmetz, "Social Roles, Social Control,
and Biases in Social Perception Processes," *Journal of Personality and Social Psychology* 35 (1977):
486–87.

33. Stephanie Jouffre and Jean-Claude Croizet, "Empowering and Legitimizing the
Fundamental Attribution Error: Power and Legitimization Exacerbate the Translation of Role-
Constrained Behaviors into Ability Differences," *European Journal of Social Psychology* 46
(2016): 621–31.

34. Bertram Gawronski, "On Difficult Questions and Evident Answers: Dispositional
Inference from Role-Constrained Behavior," *Personality and Social Psychology Bulletin* 29
(2003): 1457–75.

35. Ronald Humphrey, "How Work Roles Influence Perception: Structural Cognitive
Processes and Organizational Behavior," *American Sociological Review* 50 (1985): 242–52.
Managers and clerks did not rate themselves but rather fellow managers and fellow clerks,
respectively. Managers and clerks were rated similarly on traits not related to any role.

36. Amanda J. Koch, Susan D. D'Mello, and Paul R. Sackett, "A Meta-Analysis of Gender

Stereotypes and Bias in Experimental Simulations of Employment Decision Making," *Journal of Applied Psychology* 100 (2015): 128–61; Pollack, "Why Are There Still So Few Women in Science?"

37. Janet M. Riggs, "Social Roles We Choose and Don't Choose: Impressions of Employed and Unemployed Parents," *Sex Roles* 39 (1998): 431–43.

38. Gawronski, "On Difficult Questions and Evident Answers," 1460.

39. Sabine Sczesny and Dagmar Stahlberg, "The Influence of Gender-Stereotyped Perfumes on Leadership Attribution," *European Journal of Social Psychology* 32 (2002): 815–28.

40. Katherine H. Karraker, Dena A. Vogel, and Margaret A. Lake, "Parents' Gender-Stereotyped Perceptions of Newborns: The Eye of the Beholder Revisited," *Sex Roles* 33 (1995): 687–701; Laura S. Sidorowicz and G. S. Lunney, "Baby X Revisited," *Sex Roles* 6 (1980): 67–73; Marilyn Stern and Katherine H. Karraker, "Sex Stereotyping of Infants: A Review of Gender Labeling Studies," *Sex Roles* 20 (1989): 501–22.

41. I don't mean to exclude individuals who self-identify as transgender, but researchers know substantially less about transgender roles compared to gender roles.

42. Alice H. Eagly and Wendy Wood, "The Nature-Nurture Debates: 25 Years of Challenges in Understanding the Psychology of Gender," *Perspectives on Psychological Science* 8 (2013): 340, 351.

43. Claire C. Miller, "How to Raise a Feminist Son," *New York Times*, July 1, 2017, https://www.nytimes.com/2017/06/02/upshot/how-to-raise-a-feminist-son.html?ribbon-ad -idx=22&rref=opinion&module=Ribbon&version=origin&region=Header&action=click &contentCollection=Opinion&pgtype=article&_r=0 (accessed October 21, 2017).

CHAPTER 6: DRIVING WITH THE FAE

1. Sam Sommers, *Situations Matter: Understanding How Context Transforms Your World* (New York: Riverhead, 2011), 285–86.

2. Lisa Precht, Andreas Keinath, and Josef F. Krems, "Effects of Driving Anger on Driver Behavior: Results from Naturalistic Driving Data," *Transportation Research Part F* 45 (2017): 75–92.

3. J. L. Deffenbacher, A. N. Stephens, and M. J. M. Sullman, "Driving Anger as a Psychological Construct: Twenty Years of Research Using the Driving Anger Scale," *Transportation Research Part F* 42 (2016): 236–47; Thomas A. Dingus et al., "Driver Crash Risk Factors and Prevalence Evaluation Using Naturalistic Driving Data," *Proceedings of the National Academy of Sciences* 13 (2016): 2636–41; Leon James and Diane Nahl, *Road Rage and Aggressive Driving: Steering Clear of Highway Warfare* (Amherst, NY: Prometheus, 2000); Christine M. Wickens et al., "Driver Anger on the Information Superhighway: A Content Analysis of Online Complaints of Offensive Driver Behaviour," *Accident Analysis and Prevention* 51 (2013): 84–92.

4. Deffenbacher, Stephens, and Sullman, "Driving Anger"; Dwight A. Hennessy, "Social, Personality, and Affective Constructs in Driving," in *Handbook of Traffic Psychology*, ed. Bryan E. Porter (San Diego: Academic Press, 2011), 149–63; Louis Mizell, "Aggressive Driving" (Washington, DC: AAA Foundation for Traffic Safety, 1997); Wickens et al., "Driver Anger on the Information Superhighway."

5. Clayton Neighbors, Nathaniel A. Vietor, and C. Raymond Knee, "A Motivational Model of Driving Anger and Aggression," *Personality and Social Psychology Bulletin* 28 (2002): 324–35.

6. Jennifer S. Lerner and Larissa Z. Tiedens, "Portrait of the Angry Decision Maker: How Appraisal Tendencies Shape Anger's Influence on Cognition," *Journal of Behavioral Decision Making* 19 (2006): 115–37.

7. James and Nahl, *Road Rage and Aggressive Driving*; Jennifer S. Lerner, Julie H. Goldberg, and Philip E. Tetlock, "Sober Second Thought: The Effects of Accountability, Anger, and Authoritarianism on Attributions of Responsibility," *Personality and Social Psychology Bulletin* 24 (1998): 563–74; Brian Parkinson, "Anger on and off the Road," *British Journal of Psychology* 92 (2001): 507–26; Christine M. Wickens et al., "Understanding Driver Anger and Aggression: Attributional Theory in the Driving Environment," *Journal of Experimental Psychology: Applied* 17 (2011): 354–70; Tingru Zhang and Alan H. S. Chan, "The Association between Driving Anger and Driving Outcomes: A Meta-Analysis of Evidence from the Past Twenty Years," *Accident Analysis and Prevention* 90 (2016): 50–62.

8. Mizell, "Aggressive Driving."

9. Frank Schultz, "UW-Whitewater Professors Examine Winter Driving," *Journal Sentinel*, November 30, 2014, http://archive.jsonline.com/news/wisconsin/uw-whitewater -professors-examine-winter-driving-b99399739z1-284275651.html (accesses July 23, 2017).

10. Karin Miller, "This Woman Had a Baby in Her Car on the Way to the Hospital: And That's More Common Than You'd Think," *Self*, May 4, 2016, http://www.self.com/story/this -woman-had-a-baby-in-her-car-on-the-way-to-the-hospital-and-thats-more-common-than-youd -think (accessed July 12, 2017).

11. Marisa Cuellar, "Baby Born in Car on Way to Marshfield Hospital," *Marshfield News-Herald*, September 25, 2014, http://www.marshfieldnewsherald.com/story/news/ local/2014/09/24/baby-born-car-way-marshfield-hospital/16166131/ (accessed July 12, 2017).

12. "Baby Named Camryn After Toyota Camry," Nancy's Baby Names, August 17, 2010, http://www.nancy.cc/2010/08/17/baby-named-camryn-after-toyota-camry/ (accessed July 14, 2017).

13. "Baby Named After Car She Was Born In," What Car?, November 19, 2009, https:// www.whatcar.com/news/baby-named-car-she-born/ (accessed July 14, 2017).

14. Craig A. Anderson and Brad J. Bushman, "Human Aggression," *Annual Review of Psychology* 53 (2002): 27–51.

15. Thomas W. Britt and Michael J. Garrity, "An Integrative Model of Road Rage," *International Review of Social Psychology* 16 (2003): 53–79.

16. James R. Averill, "Studies on Anger and Aggression: Implications for Theories of Emotion," *American Psychologist* 38 (1983): 1145–60.

17. Frank P. McKenna, "Accident Proneness: A Conceptual Analysis," *Accident Analysis and Prevention* 15 (1983): 65–71; Jerry I. Shaw and James A. McMartin, "Perpetrator or Victim? Effects of Who Suffers in an Automobile Accident on Judgemental Strictness," *Social Behavior and Personality* 3 (1975): 5–12.

18. James S. Baxter et al., "Attributional Biases and Driver Behaviour," *Social Behaviour* 5 (1990): 186.

19. Thaddeus A. Herzog, "Automobile Driving as Seen by the Actor, the Active Observer, and the Passive Observer," *Journal of Applied Social Psychology* 24 (1994): 2069.

20. Niki Harré, Theo Brandt, and Carla Houkamau, "An Examination of the Actor-Observer Effect in Young Drivers' Attributions for Their Own and Their Friends' Risky Driving," *Journal of Applied Social Psychology* 34 (2004): 806–24; Dwight A. Hennessy and Robert Jakubowski, "The Impact of Visual Perspective and Anger on the Actor-Observer Bias among Automobile Drivers," *Traffic Injury Prevention* 8 (2007): 115–22; Dwight A. Hennessy, Robert Jakubowski, and Alyson J. Benedetti, "The Influence of the Actor-Observer Bias on Attributions of Other Drivers," in *Contemporary Issues in Road User Behavior and Traffic Safety*, eds. Dwight A. Hennessy and David L. Wiesenthal (Hauppauge, NY: Nova Science Publishers, 2005), 13–20; Alexia Lennon et al., "'You're a Bad Driver but I Just Made a Mistake': Attribution Differences between the 'Victims' and 'Perpetrators' of Scenario-Based Aggressive Driving Incidents," *Transportation Research Part F* 14 (2011): 209–21; Tova Rosenbloom, Adar Ben Eliyahu, and Dan Nemrodov, "Causes of Traffic Accidents as Perceived by Pre-Driving Adolescents," *North American Journal of Psychology* 18 (2016): 533–50.

21. Anderson and Bushman, "Human Aggression"; Christopher R. Engelhardt and Bruce D. Bartholow, "Effects of Situational Cues on Aggressive Behavior," *Social and Personality Psychology Compass* 7 (2013): 762–74; Hennessy, "Social, Personality, and Affective Constructs in Driving"; David Myers, *Social Psychology*, 11th ed. (New York: McGraw Hill, 2013).

22. Anderson and Bushman, "Human Aggression," 38.

23. Redlantrn, "Smells Like Something Died in My Car . . . ," Acurazine forum post, April 9, 2009, https://acurazine.com/forums/3g-tl-problems-fixes-114/smells-like-something-died -my-car-720085/ (accessed August 2, 2017).

24. Hennessy, "Social, Personality, and Affective Constructs in Driving," 156.

25. Mizell, "Aggressive Driving."

26. Ibid.

27. Anderson and Bushman, "Human Aggression"; Hennessy, "Social, Personality, and Affective Constructs in Driving"; David C. Schwebel et al., "Individual Difference Factors in Risky Driving: The Roles of Anger/Hostility, Conscientiousness, and Sensation-Seeking," *Accident Analysis and Prevention* 38 (2006): 801–10.

28. Hennessy, "Social, Personality, and Affective Constructs in Driving," 156.

29. Kenneth A. Dodge, "Translational Science in Action: Hostile Attributional Style

and the Development of Aggressive Behavior Problems," *Development and Psychopathology* 18 (2006): 791–814.

30. Hennessy, "Social, Personality, and Affective Constructs in Driving," 159.

31. Craig A. Anderson et al., "Violent Video Game Effects on Aggression, Empathy, and Prosocial Behavior in Eastern and Western Countries: A Meta-Analytic Review," *Psychological Bulletin* 136 (2010): 151–73; Brad J. Bushman, Mario Gollwitzer, and Carlos Cruz, "There Is Broad Consensus: Media Researchers Agree That Violent Media Increase Aggression in Children, and Pediatricians and Parents Concur," *Psychology of Popular Media Culture* 4 (2015): 200–14. And numerous others.

32. Bryan Gibson et al., "Just 'Harmless Entertainment'? Effects of Surveillance Reality TV on Physical Aggression," *Psychology of Popular Media Culture* 5 (2016): 66–73.

33. Christopher Ferguson is perhaps the most vocal scientific critic of the majority position on media violence, in terms of his articles, books, and popular press interviews. His straw man arguments and ad hominem attacks are also quite evident. But let me acknowledge that identifying an argument as "ad hominem" or an "attack" can have some subjectivity. Let me also acknowledge that heated debates often include such attacks from both sides. Sure enough, I read in one of Ferguson's very recent articles that the majority has made claims against Ferguson's side "remarkably aggressively, with ad hominem comments." But when I chased down the two references Ferguson cited for their ad hominem comments, neither really panned out. In one case, Ferguson said Strasburger and colleagues compared the "scholars" on Ferguson's side to "holocaust deniers," but it turned out that the authors were not labeling scholars that way but rather a subset of nonacademics (perhaps still not a nice thing to do). Christopher J. Ferguson and Eugene Beresin, "Social Science's Curious War with Pop Culture and How It Was Lost: The Media Violence Debate and the Risks It Holds for Social Science," *Preventive Medicine* 99 (2017): 73; Victor C. Strasburger, Ed Donnerstein, and Brad J. Bushman, "Why Is It So Hard to Believe That Media Influence Children and Adolescents?" *Pediatrics* 133 (2014): 572.

34. Arlin J. Benjamin Jr. and Brad J. Bushman, "The Weapons Priming Effect," *Current Opinion in Psychology* 12 (2016): 45–48.

35. Craig A. Anderson, Arlin J. Benjamin, and Bruce D. Bartholow, "Does the Gun Pull the Trigger? Automatic Priming Effects of Weapon Pictures and Weapon Names," *Psychological Science* 9 (1998): 308–14; Engelhardt and Bartholow, "Effects of Situational Cues on Aggressive Behavior."

36. Daniel R. Stalder, "Another School Shooting: Consider the Weapons Effect," PARBs Anonymous (blog), June 8, 2014, https://parbsanonymous.wordpress.com/2014/06/08/another-school-shooting-consider-the-weapons-effect/ (accessed August 2, 2017).

37. Engelhardt and Bartholow, "Effects of Situational Cues on Aggressive Behavior."

38. Ibid.; William Pederson, "Are You Insulting Me? Exposure to Alcohol Primes Increases Aggression Following Ambiguous Provocation," *Personality and Social Psychology Bulletin* 40 (2014): 1037–49.

CHAPTER 7: INTERPERSONAL CONFLICT: OFF THE ROAD

1. Thomas F. Pettigrew, "The Ultimate Attribution Error: Extending Allport's Cognitive Analysis of Prejudice," *Personality and Social Psychology Bulletin* 5 (1979): 461–76.

2. Réjeanne Dupuis and C. W. Struthers, "The Effects of Social Motivational Training Following Perceived and Actual Interpersonal Offenses at Work," *Journal of Applied Social Psychology* 37 (2007): 426–56.

3. Philip Zimbardo, *The Lucifer Effect: Understanding How Good People Turn Evil* (New York: Random House, 2007).

4. Dupuis and Struthers, "The Effects of Social Motivational Training."

5. "Section 6. Training for Conflict Resolution," Community Tool Box, 2017, http://ctb.ku.edu/en/table-of-contents/implement/provide-information-enhance-skills/conflict-resolution/main (accessed August 3, 2017).

6. Birgit Schyns and Tiffany Hansbrough, "The Romance of Leadership Scale and Causal Attributions," *Journal of Applied Social Psychology* 42 (2012): 1870–86; Birgit Schyns and Tiffany Hansbrough, "Why the Brewery Ran Out of Beer: The Attribution of Mistakes in a Leadership Context," *Social Psychology* 39 (2008): 197–203.

7. L. V. Anderson, "Toward a Unified Theory of the Office Kitchen," *Slate*, July 27, 2016, http://www.slate.com/articles/business/the_ladder/2016/07/why_are_office_kitchens_so_filthy_and_disgusting.html (accessed August 3, 2017).

8. David Myers, *Social Psychology*, 11th ed. (New York: McGraw Hill, 2013), 485.

9. Dupuis and Struthers, "The Effects of Social Motivation Training"; C. W. Struthers, Réjeanne Dupuis, and Judy Eaton, "Promoting Forgiveness among Co-Workers Following a Workplace Transgression: The Effects of Social Motivation Training," *Canadian Journal of Behavioural Science* 37 (2005): 299–308.

10. Valerie S. Folkes, "Consumer Reactions to Product Failure: An Attributional Approach," *Journal of Consumer Research* 10 (1984): 398–409; Valerie S. Folkes, Susan Koletsky, and John L. Graham, "A Field Study of Causal Inferences and Consumer Reaction: The View from the Airport," *Journal of Consumer Research* 13 (1987): 534–39.

11. Elizabeth Cowley, "Views from Consumers Next in Line: The Fundamental Attribution Error in a Service Setting," *Journal of the Academy of Marketing Science* 33 (2005): 139–52.

12. Brad Tuttle, "We Hate You Too: Pet Peeves from Consumers—and from Retail Workers," *Time*, August 24, 2010, http://business.time.com/2010/08/24/we-hate-you-too-pet-peeves-from-consumers-and-from-retail-workers/ (accessed August 3, 2017).

13. Brian Alexander, "Low Blood Sugar Tied to 'Hangry' Fights with Spouse," *Today*, April 14, 2014, http://www.today.com/health/low-blood-sugar-tied-to-hangry-fights-spouse-2D79526249 (accessed August 3, 2017).

14. Bernard Weiner, "Searching for Order in Social Motivation," *Psychological Inquiry* 7 (1996): 199–216.

15. In fairness to these authors, their studies were rarely a simple two-variable correlational study but rather more complicated forms of correlational analysis, including partial correlations that control for some third variables. None of these designs technically justify a cause-effect conclusion, but they can come close. Also, these authors sometimes cited other studies that were true experiments.

16. Clive Seligman et al., "Manipulating Attributions for Profit: A Field Test of the Effects of Attributions on Behavior," *Social Cognition* 3 (1985): 313–21.

17. Weiner, "Searching for Order."

18. Kenneth A. Dodge, "Social Cognition and Children's Aggressive Behavior," *Child Development* 51 (1980): 162–70.

19. Jason E. Plaks, Sheri R. Levy, and Carol S. Dweck, "Lay Theories of Personality: Cornerstones of Meaning in Social Cognition," *Social and Personality Psychology Compass* 3 (2009): 1069–81; David S. Yeager et al., "Implicit Theories of Personality and Attributions of Hostile Intent: A Meta-Analysis, an Experiment, and a Longitudinal Intervention," *Child Development* 84 (2013): 1651–67.

20. Myers, *Social Psychology*, 138.

21. Karl Ask and Pär A. Granhag, "Hot Cognition in Investigative Judgments: The Differential Influence of Anger and Sadness," *Law and Human Behavior* 31 (2007): 537–51; Karl Ask and Afroditi Pina, "On Being Angry and Punitive: How Anger Alters Perception of Criminal Intent," *Social Psychological and Personality Science* 2 (2011), 494–99; Dacher Keltner, Phoebe C. Ellsworth, and Kari Edwards, "Beyond Simple Pessimism: Effects of Sadness and Anger on Social Perception," *Journal of Personality and Social Psychology* 64 (1993): 740–52.

CHAPTER 8: VICTIM BLAMING

1. David Myers, *Social Psychology*, 11th ed. (New York: McGraw Hill, 2013), 131.

2. Juliana Breines, "Why Do We Blame Victims? When Others' Misfortune Feels Like a Threat," *Psychology Today*, November 24, 2013, https://www.psychologytoday.com/blog/in-love-and-war/201311/why-do-we-blame-victims (accessed August 8, 2017).

3. Brandon Smith, "Orlando Victims Died Because They Were Unarmed—Not Because They Were Gay," Alt-Market.com, June 15, 2016, http://alt-market.com/articles/2921-orlando-victims-died-because-they-were-unarmed-not-because-they-were-gay (accessed August 8, 2017).

4. M. J. Davis and T. N. French, "Blaming Victims and Survivors: An Analysis of Post-Katrina Print News Coverage," *Southern Communication Journal* 73 (2008): 243–57; Thomas Gilovich and Lee Ross, *The Wisest One in the Room: How You Can Benefit from Social Psychology's Most Powerful Insights* (New York: Free Press, 2015).

5. Peter Jamison, "These 8th-Graders from New Jersey Refused to Be Photographed with Paul Ryan," *Washington Post*, May 28, 2017, https://www.washingtonpost.com/politics/these-8th-graders-from-new-jersey-refused-to-be-photographed-with-paul-ryan/2017/05/28/

ca46b116-43b9-11e7-bcde-624ad94170ab_story.html?utm_term=.b0c1a38bb752 (accessed August 8, 2017); Kelly Wallace, "Gorilla Tragedy: Why Are We So Quick to Blame the Parents?," CNN, June 1, 2016, http://www.cnn.com/2016/06/01/health/gorilla-tragedy -parenting-blame/ (accessed August 8, 2017).

6. Kees van den Bos and Marjolein Maas, "On the Psychology of the Belief in a Just World: Exploring Experiential and Rationalistic Paths to Victim Blaming," *Personality and Social Psychology Bulletin* 35 (2009): 1567–78; Carolyn L. Hafer and Laurent Bègue, "Experimental Research on Just-World Theory: Problems, Developments, and Future Challenges," *Psychological Bulletin* 131 (2005): 128–67.

7. Thomas Gilovich and Richard Eibach, "The Fundamental Attribution Error Where It Really Counts," *Psychological Inquiry* 12 (2001): 23–26.

8. Warren J. Blumenfeld, "Why Do Christians Always Blame LGBT People for Natural Disasters?" *LGBTQ Nation*, October 12, 2016, https://www.lgbtqnation.com/2016/10/ christians-always-blame-lgbt-people-natural-disasters/ (accessed July 23, 2017).

9. Kent D. Harber, Peter Podolski, and Christian H. Williams, "Emotional Disclosure and Victim Blaming," *Emotion* 15 (2015): 603.

10. Kathleen A. Fox and Carrie L. Cook, "Is Knowledge Power? The Effects of a Victimology Course on Victim Blaming," *Journal of Interpersonal Violence* 26 (2011): 3407–27; Harber, Podolski, and Williams, "Emotional Disclosure and Victim Blaming"; Annemarie Loseman and Kees van den Bos, "A Self-Regulation Hypothesis of Coping with an Unjust World: Ego-Depletion and Self-Affirmation as Underlying Aspects of Blaming of Innocent Victims," *Social Justice Research* 25 (2012): 1–13.

11. Bernard Weiner, "Searching for Order in Social Motivation," *Psychological Inquiry* 7 (1996): 199–216; Hanna Zagefka et al., "Donating to Disaster Victims: Responses to Natural and Humanly Caused Events," *European Journal of Social Psychology* 41 (2011): 353–63.

12. Harber, Podolski, and Williams, "Emotional Disclosure and Victim Blaming."

13. Ellen Berscheid, David Boye, and Elaine Walster, "Retaliation as a Means of Restoring Equity," *Journal of Personality and Social Psychology* 10 (1968): 370–76; David C. Glass, "Changes in Liking as a Means of Reducing Cognitive Discrepancies between Self-Esteem and Aggression," *Journal of Personality* 32 (1964): 520–49.

14. Harber, Podolski, and Williams, "Emotional Disclosure and Victim Blaming"; Melvin J. Lerner, *The Belief in a Just World: A Fundamental Delusion* (New York: Plenum, 1980).

15. Hafer and Bègue, "Experimental Research on Just-World Theory," 145; Melvin J. Lerner, "The Justice Motive: Where Social Psychologists Found It, How They Lost It, and Why They May Not Find It Again," *Personality and Social Psychology Review* 7 (2003): 388–99.

16. Hafer and Bègue, "Experimental Research on Just-World Theory."

17. Jennifer A. Whitson and Adam D. Galinsky, "Lacking Control Increases Illusory Pattern Perception," *Science* 322 (2008): 115–17.

18. Shelley E. Taylor, *Positive Illusions: Creative Self-Deception and the Healthy Mind* (New York: Basic Books, 1989).

19. Lerner, *Belief in a Just World*, 9.

20. Hafer and Bègue, "Experimental Research on Just-World Theory."

21. Whitson and Galinsky, "Lacking Control Increases Illusory Pattern Perception," 116.

22. Daniel R. Stalder, "Competing Roles for the Subfactors of Need for Closure in Committing the Fundamental Attribution Error," *Personality and Individual Differences* 47 (2009): 701–705.

23. Yamiche Alcindor, "Ben Carson Calls Poverty a 'State of Mind,' Igniting a Backlash," *New York Times*, May 25, 2017, https://www.nytimes.com/2017/05/25/us/politics/ben-carson-poverty-hud-state-of-mind.html (accessed August 8, 2017).

24. Emily Badger, "Does 'Wrong Mind-Set' Cause Poverty or Vice Versa?" *New York Times*, May 30, 2017, https://www.nytimes.com/2017/05/30/upshot/ben-carsons-thinking-and-how-poverty-affects-your-state-of-mind.html (accessed August 8, 2017).

25. "Obama's Own Story Defines His American Dream," NPR, May 30, 2012, http://www.npr.org/2012/05/30/153994202/obamas-own-story-defines-his-american-dream (accessed August 8, 2017).

26. Please forgive me if phrases like these are part of how you support your loved ones and you are aghast at the notion that you could be victim blaming even a little. I am only raising the possibility. And as I said, phrases like these can be helpful. You know your loved ones better than I do!

27. Carolyn Gregoire, "This Is Scientific Proof That Happiness Is a Choice," *HuffPost*, December 13, 2013, http://www.huffingtonpost.com/2013/12/09/scientific-proof-that-you_n_4384433.html (accessed August 8, 2017).

28. "Quotes about Victim Blaming," Goodreads, 2017, http://www.goodreads.com/quotes/tag/victim-blaming (accessed August 8, 2017).

29. Barbara S. Held, "The Tyranny of the Positive Attitude in America: Observation and Speculation," *Journal of Clinical Psychology* 58 (2002): 965–92.

30. Louis Mizell, "Aggressive Driving" (Washington, DC: AAA Foundation for Traffic Safety, 1997), 17.

31. Alexandra Brodsky, "Blame Rape's Enablers, Not the Victims," *New York Times*, October 23, 2013, http://www.nytimes.com/roomfordebate/2013/10/23/young-women-drinking-and-rape/blame-rapes-enablers-not-the-victims (accessed August 8, 2017).

32. Kayleigh Roberts, "The Psychology of Victim-Blaming," *Atlantic*, October 5, 2016, https://www.theatlantic.com/science/archive/2016/10/the-psychology-of-victim-blaming/502661/ (accessed August 8, 2017).

33. Mei-whei Chen, Thomas Froehle, and Keith Morran, "Deconstructing Dispositional Bias in Clinical Inference: Two Interventions," *Journal of Counseling and Development* 76 (1997): 74–81; Yael Idisis, Sarah Ben-David, and Efrat Ben-Nachum, "Attribution of Blame to Rape Victims among Therapists and Non-Therapists," *Behavioral Sciences and the Law* 25 (2007): 103–20.

34. Karen Kleiman, "Lying in Therapy: Is It Self-Preservation or Intentional

Manipulation?" *Psychology Today*, February 1, 2013, https://www.psychologytoday.com/blog/isnt-what-i-expected/201302/lying-in-therapy (accessed August 8, 2017); Gordon Shippey, "My Client, the Liar," Counselling Resource, January 4, 2011, http://counsellingresource.com/features/2011/01/04/my-client-the-liar/ (accessed August 8, 2017).

35. Joseph Burgo, "Lying to Our Clients," After Psychotherapy, April 12, 2013, http://www.afterpsychotherapy.com/lying-to-our-clients/ (accessed August 8, 2017).

36. Harber, Podolski, and Williams, "Emotional Disclosure and Victim Blaming."

37. John Barton, "The Great CBT Debate," John Barton Therapy (blog), November 18, 2014, http://www.johnbartontherapy.com/blog/the-great-cbt-debate (accessed August 8, 2017); William J. Lyddon and Robin Weill, "Cognitive Psychotherapy and Postmodernism: Emerging Themes and Challenges," *Journal of Cognitive Psychotherapy: An International Quarterly* 11 (1997): 75–90.

38. David D. Burns, *The Feeling Good Handbook* (New York: Plume, 1999), 77–78, 314; Daniel R. Stalder, "It's Not the End of the World: Comforting but Illogical," PARBs Anonymous (blog), February 21, 2016, https://parbsanonymous.wordpress.com/2016/02/21/its-not-the-end-of-the-world-comforting-but-illogical/ (accessed August 9, 2017).

39. Karl Ask and Pär A. Granhag, "Hot Cognition in Investigative Judgments: The Differential Influence of Anger and Sadness," *Law and Human Behavior* 31 (2007): 537–51; Michael T. Moore and David M. Fresco, "Depressive Realism: A Meta-Analytic Review," *Clinical Psychology Review* 32 (2012): 496–509; John H. Yost and Gifford Weary, "Depression and the Correspondent Inference Bias: Evidence for More Effortful Cognitive Processing," *Personality and Social Psychology Bulletin* 22 (1996): 192–200.

40. Taylor, *Positive Illusions*; Shelley E. Taylor et al., "Are Self-Enhancing Cognitions Associated with Healthy or Unhealthy Biological Profiles?" *Journal of Personality and Social Psychology* 85 (2003): 605–15.

41. Timothy P. Baardseth et al., "Cognitive-Behavioral Therapy versus Other Therapies: Redux," *Clinical Psychology Review* 33 (2013): 395–405; Gro Janne H. Wergeland et al., "An Effectiveness Study of Individual vs. Group Cognitive Behavioral Therapy for Anxiety Disorders in Youth," *Behaviour Research and Therapy* 57 (2014): 1–12; Henny A. Westra and David J. A. Dozois, "Preparing Clients for Cognitive Behavioral Therapy: A Randomized Pilot Study of Motivational Interviewing for Anxiety," *Cognitive Therapy and Research* 30 (2006): 481–98.

CHAPTER 9: THE INDIVIDUAL MATTERS TOO

1. David Myers, *Social Psychology*, 11th ed. (New York: McGraw Hill, 2013).

2. Ibid.

3. Rachel Manning, Mark Levine, and Alan Collins, "The Kitty Genovese Murder and the Social Psychology of Helping: The Parable of the 38 Witnesses," *American Psychologist* 62 (2007): 555–62.

4. John M. Darley and Bibb Latané, "Bystander Intervention in Emergencies: Diffusion of Responsibility," *Journal of Personality and Social Psychology* 8 (1968): 377–83.

5. Joachim I. Krueger, "A Componential Model of Situation Effects, Person Effects, and Situation-by-Person Interaction Effects on Social Behavior," *Journal of Research in Personality* 43 (2009): 127–36.

6. Ibid.; Scott O. Lilienfeld, "Further Sources of Our Field's Embattled Public Reputation," *American Psychologist* 67 (2012): 808–809.

7. "SITUATIONS MATTER by Sam Sommers," YouTube video, 2:46, posted by "RiverheadBooks," March 15, 2011, https://www.youtube.com/watch?v=90YC_yReluc (accessed August 18, 2017).

8. Sam Sommers, *Situations Matter: Understanding How Context Transforms Your World* (New York: Riverhead, 2011), 201. Sommers's ultimate message in his book did leave some room for the individual, though sometimes he didn't get to it until the ends of chapters. I will discuss more of Sommers's romance message later in this chapter.

9. "When Situations Not Personality Dictate Our Behaviour," PsyBlog, December 15, 2009, http://www.spring.org.uk/2009/12/when-situations-not-personality-dictate-our -behaviour.php (accessed August 18, 2017); Allen R. McConnell, "Paterno Surprise Reflects Ignoring the Power of the Situation," *Psychology Today*, November 10, 2011, https://www .psychologytoday.com/blog/the-social-self/201111/paterno-surprise-reflects-ignoring-the -power-the-situation (accessed August 18, 2017).

10. Leonard S. Newman and Daria A. Bakina, "Do People Resist Social-Psychological Perspectives on Wrongdoing? Reactions to Dispositional, Situational, and Interactionist Explanations," *Social Influence* 4 (2009): 256–73; Leonard S. Newman, Daria A. Bakina, and Ying Tang, "The Role of Preferred Beliefs in Skepticism about Psychology," *American Psychologist* 67 (2012): 805–806; Lilienfeld, "Further Sources of Our Field's Embattled Public Reputation"; Daniel R. Stalder, "A Role for Social Psychology Instruction in Reducing Bias and Conflict," *Psychology Learning and Teaching* 11 (2012): 245–55.

11. Craig Haney and Philip G. Zimbardo, "Persistent Dispositionalism in Interactionist Clothing: Fundamental Attribution Error in Explaining Prison Abuse," *Personality and Social Psychology Bulletin* 35 (2009): 807; Philip G. Zimbardo, *The Lucifer Effect: Understanding How Good People Turn Evil* (New York: Random House, 2007).

12. Daniel R. Stalder, "Revisiting the Issue of Safety in Numbers: The Likelihood of Receiving Help from a Group," *Social Influence* 3 (2008): 24–33.

13. Manning, Levine, and Collins, "Kitty Genovese Murder."

14. Darley and Latané, "Bystander Intervention in Emergencies"; Bibb Latané and Steve Nida, "Ten Years of Research on Group Size and Helping," *Psychological Bulletin* 89 (1981): 308–24. Darley and Latané did not report exact probabilities, but Latané and Nida did report them for the Darley and Latané study.

15. Latané and Nida, "Ten Years of Research on Group Size and Helping."

16. Stalder, "Revisiting the Issue of Safety in Numbers."

17. Robert C. MacCallum et al., "On the Practice of Dichotomization of Quantitative Variables," *Psychological Methods* 7 (2002): 19–40.

18. Arthur L. Beaman et al., "Increasing Helping Rates through Information Dissemination: Teaching Pays," *Personality and Social Psychology Bulletin* 4 (1978): 406–11.

19. Sommers, *Situations Matter*, 64–65. Other authors besides Sommers have pointed to computer-mediated communication as a likely place to find evidence of the bystander effect.

20. Daniel R. Stalder, "Updating the Bystander-Effect Literature: The Return of Safety in Numbers" (presentation, Annual Convention of the Midwestern Psychological Association, Chicago, IL, May 5–7, 2011).

21. Cara Buckley, "Man Is Rescued by Stranger on Subway Tracks," *New York Times*, January 3, 2007, http://www.nytimes.com/2007/01/03/nyregion/03life.html (accessed August 19, 2017).

22. Scott O. Lilienfeld et al., *50 Great Myths of Popular Psychology: Shattering Widespread Misconceptions about Human Behavior* (Chichester, UK: Wiley-Blackwell, 2010).

23. Manning, Levine, and Collins, "The Kitty Genovese Murder."

24. Craig Haney, Curtis Banks, and Philip Zimbardo, "Interpersonal Dynamics in a Simulated Prison," *International Journal of Criminology and Penology* 1 (1973): 69–97.

25. Joachim I. Krueger, "Lucifer's Last Laugh: The Devil Is in the Details," *American Journal of Psychology* 121 (2008): 338; Stephen Reicher and S. A. Haslam, "Rethinking the Psychology of Tyranny: The BBC Prison Study," *British Journal of Social Psychology* 45 (2006): 4.

26. Thomas Carnahan and Sam McFarland, "Revisiting the Stanford Prison Experiment: Could Participant Self-Selection Have Led to the Cruelty?" *Personality and Social Psychology Bulletin* 33 (2007): 603–14.

27. Ibid., 612.

28. Haney and Zimbardo, "Persistent Dispositionalism in Interactionist Clothing."

29. Jared M. Bartels, Marilyn M. Milovich, and Sabrina Moussier, "Coverage of the Stanford Prison Experiment in Introductory Psychology Courses: A Survey of Introductory Psychology Instructors," *Teaching of Psychology* 43 (2016): 136–41.

30. Myers, *Social Psychology*; Sommers, *Situations Matter*.

31. Donald G. Dutton and Arthur P. Aron, "Some Evidence for Heightened Sexual Attraction under Conditions of High Anxiety," *Journal of Personality and Social Psychology* 30 (1974): 510–17.

32. Tom Bartlett, "Does Familiarity Breed Contempt or Fondness," *Chronicle of Higher Education*, December 9, 2013, http://www.chronicle.com/blogs/percolator/does-familiarity-breed-contempt-or-fondness/33767 (accessed August 19, 2017).

33. Richard L. Moreland and Scott R. Beach, "Exposure Effects in the Classroom: The Development of Affinity among Students," *Journal of Experimental Social Psychology* 28 (1992): 255–76. This study was not a classically designed experiment in that participants were not randomly assigned to different exposure conditions with the same actress, but the researchers did control how often the multiple actresses visited the classroom. And the actresses were prerated as similar in attractiveness.

34. Sommers, *Situations Matter*, 209.

35. Shelley E. Taylor, *Positive Illusions: Creative Self-Deception and the Healthy Mind* (New York: Basic Books, 1989), 135.

36. Stephen J. Blumberg and David H. Silvera, "Attributional Complexity and Cognitive Development: A Look at the Motivational and Cognitive Requirements for Attribution," *Social Cognition* 16 (1998): 253–66; Lou E. Hicks, "Is There a Disposition to Avoid the Fundamental Attribution Error?" *Journal of Research in Personality* 19 (1985): 436–56; Daniel R. Stalder, "Does Logic Moderate the Fundamental Attribution Error?" *Psychological Reports* 86 (2000): 879–82.

37. Paul R. D'Agostino and Rebecca Fincher-Kiefer, "Need for Cognition and the Correspondence Bias," *Social Cognition* 10 (1992): 151–63.

38. Whitney L. Heppner et al., "Mindfulness as a Means of Reducing Aggressive Behavior: Dispositional and Situational Evidence," *Aggressive Behavior* 34 (2008): 486–96.

39. Nurit Tal-Or and Yael Papirman, "The Fundamental Attribution Error in Attributing Fictional Figures' Characteristics to the Actors," *Media Psychology* 9 (2007): 331–45.

40. Dale T. Miller, Stephen A. Norman, and Edward Wright, "Distortion in Person Perception as a Consequence of the Need for Effective Control," *Journal of Personality and Social Psychology* 36 (1978): 598–607; Daniel R. Stalder, "Competing Roles for the Subfactors of Need for Closure in Committing the Fundamental Attribution Error," *Personality and Individual Differences* 47 (2009): 701–705.

41. Garth J. O. Fletcher et al., "Attributional Complexity: An Individual Difference Measure," *Journal of Personality and Social Psychology* 51 (1986): 875–84.

42. Garth J. O. Fletcher, Glenn D. Reeder, and Vivian Bull, "Bias and Accuracy in Attitude Attribution: The Role of Attributional Complexity," *Journal of Experimental Social Psychology* 26 (1990): 275–88.

43. Daniel R. Stalder, "Are Attributionally Complex Individuals More Prone to Attributional Bias?" (presentation, Annual Convention of the Midwestern Psychological Association, Chicago, IL, May 1–3, 2014). For readers who are curious, Cohen's *d* averaged .18 for the AC-FAE relation in my meta-analysis. Also, the same meta-analysis found that high-AC people were consistently less prone to intergroup prejudice, though more prone to self-serving biases. High-AC people are an interesting group.

44. Chi-yue Chiu, Ying-yi Hong, and Carol S. Dweck, "Lay Dispositionism and Implicit Theories of Personality," *Journal of Personality and Social Psychology* 73 (1997): 19–30; Carolyn L. Hafer and Laurent Bègue, "Experimental Research on Just-World Theory: Problems, Developments, and Future Challenges," *Psychological Bulletin* 131 (2005): 128–67; Yexin J. Li et al., "Fundamental(ist) Attribution Error: Protestants Are Dispositionally Focused," *Journal of Personality and Social Psychology* 102 (2012): 281–90; Charles G. Lord et al., "Leakage Beliefs and the Correspondence Bias," *Personality and Social Psychology Bulletin* 23 (1997): 824–36; Linda J. Skitka et al., "Dispositions, Scripts, or Motivated Correction? Understanding Ideological Differences in Explanations for Social Problems," *Journal of Personality and Social*

Psychology 83 (2002): 470–87.

45. Daniel T. Gilbert and Patrick S. Malone, "The Correspondence Bias," *Psychological Bulletin* 117 (1995): 21–38; Kimberly J. Duff and Leonard S. Newman, "Individual Differences in the Spontaneous Construal of Behavior: Idiocentrism and the Automatization of the Trait Inference Process," *Social Cognition* 15 (1997): 217–41; Takahiko Masuda and Shinobu Kitayama, "Perceiver-Induced Constraint and Attitude Attribution in Japan and the US: A Case for the Cultural Dependence of the Correspondence Bias," *Journal of Experimental Social Psychology* 40 (2004): 409–16.

46. Fredda Blanchard-Fields and Michelle Horhota, "Age Differences in the Correspondence Bias: When a Plausible Explanation Matters," *Journal of Gerontology: Psychological Sciences* 60B (2005): 259–67.

47. Igor Grossmann and Michael E. W. Varnum, "Social Class, Culture, and Cognition," *Social Psychological and Personality Science* 2 (2011): 81–89; Michael W. Kraus, Paul K. Piff, and Dacher Keltner, "Social Class, Sense of Control, and Social Explanation," *Journal of Personality and Social Psychology* 97 (2009): 992–1004.

48. Jack Block and David C. Funder, "Social Roles and Social Perception: Individual Differences in Attribution and Error," *Journal of Personality and Social Psychology* 51 (1986): 1200–207; Liz Goldenberg and Joseph P. Forgas, "Can Happy Mood Reduce the Just World Bias? Affective Influences on Blaming the Victim," *Journal of Experimental Social Psychology* 48 (2012): 239–43; Joseph P. Forgas, "On Being Happy and Mistaken: Mood Effects on the Fundamental Attribution Error," *Journal of Personality and Social Psychology* 75 (1998): 318–31; Daniel R. Stalder and Jessica A. Cook, "On Being Happy and Mistaken on a Good Day: Revisiting Forgas's (1998) Mood-Bias Result," *Journal of Social Psychology* 154 (2014): 371–74.

CHAPTER 10: PROS AND CONS OF BEING BIASED: TO BE OR NOT TO BE

1. Faith H. Brynie, *Brain Sense: The Science of the Senses and How We Process the World around Us* (New York: AMACOM, 2009); Thomas Gilovich and Lee Ross, *The Wisest One in the Room: How You Can Benefit from Social Psychology's Most Powerful Insights* (New York: Free Press, 2015).

2. Daniel R. Stalder, "The Bias Myth: Bias Is All Bad," PARBs Anonymous (blog), June 3, 2015, https://parbsanonymous.wordpress.com/2015/06/03/the-bias-myth-bias-is-all-bad/ (accessed September 2, 2017); R. W. Sternglanz and Bella M. DePaulo, "Reading Nonverbal Cues to Emotions: The Advantages and Liabilities of Relationship Closeness," *Journal of Nonverbal Behavior* 28 (2004): 245–66.

3. Anjelica Oswald, "Even Rockstar Author J. K. Rowling Has Received Letters of Rejection," *Business Insider*, July 29, 2016, http://www.businessinsider.com/jk-rowlings

-rejection-letters-2016-7 (accessed September 2, 2017). Of course, many persevering authors' manuscripts are never published.

4. David S. Greenawalt and Adele M. Hayes, "Is Past Depression or Current Dysphoria Associated with Social Perception?" *Journal of Social and Clinical Psychology* 31 (2012): 329–55; Michael T. Moore and David M. Fresco, "Depressive Realism: A Meta-Analytic Review," *Clinical Psychology Review* 32 (2012): 496–509.

5. Shelley E. Taylor, *Positive Illusions: Creative Self-Deception and the Healthy Mind* (New York: Basic Books, 1989); Shelley E. Taylor et al., "Psychological Resources, Positive Illusions, and Health," *American Psychologist* 55 (2000): 99–109; Shelley E. Taylor et al., "Are Self-Enhancing Cognitions Associated with Healthy or Unhealthy Biological Profiles?" *Journal of Personality and Social Psychology* 85 (2003): 605–15. A primary critique was written by C. R. Colvin and Jack Block, "Do Positive Illusions Foster Mental Health? An Examination of the Taylor and Brown Formulation," *Psychological Bulletin* 116 (1994): 3–20.

6. Shelley E. Taylor et al., "Portrait of the Self-Enhancer: Well Adjusted and Well Liked or Maladjusted and Friendless?" *Journal of Personality and Social Psychology* 84 (2003): 174.

7. Ibid.

8. Daniel T. Gilbert and Patrick S. Malone, "The Correspondence Bias," *Psychological Bulletin* 117 (1995): 34.

9. Mei-whei Chen, Thomas Froehle, and Keith Morran, "Deconstructing Dispositional Bias in Clinical Inference: Two Interventions," *Journal of Counseling and Development* 76 (1997): 74–81.

10. David Myers, *Social Psychology*, 11th ed. (New York: McGraw Hill, 2013), 291.

11. Lissa Rankin, "The Nocebo Effect: Negative Thoughts Can Harm Your Health," *Psychology Today*, August 6, 2013, https://www.psychologytoday.com/blog/owning-pink/201308/the-nocebo-effect-negative-thoughts-can-harm-your-health (accessed September 2, 2017); Sternglanz and DePaulo, "Reading Nonverbal Cues to Emotions."

12. Gilbert and Malone, "Correspondence Bias," 35.

13. Daniel R. Stalder, "Using Social Psychology Instruction to Reduce Bias, Defensiveness, and Conflict" (presentation, Annual Teaching Institute of the Association for Psychological Science and Society for the Teaching of Psychology, Chicago, IL, May 22–25, 2008).

14. Earl Hunt, "Situational Constraints on Normative Reasoning," *Behavioral and Brain Sciences* 23 (2000): 680.

15. James Friedrich, "On Seeing Oneself as Less Self-Serving than Others: The Ultimate Self-Serving Bias?" *Teaching of Psychology* 23 (1996): 107–109; Emily Pronin, Daniel Y. Lin, and Lee Ross, "The Bias Blind Spot: Perceptions of Bias in Self versus Others," *Personality and Social Psychology Bulletin* 28 (2002): 369–81; Daniel R. Stalder, "A Role for Social Psychology Instruction in Reducing Bias and Conflict," *Psychology Learning and Teaching* 11 (2012): 245–55.

16. Gilovich and Ross, *Wisest One in the Room.*

17. Kathleen A. Fox and Carrie L. Cook, "Is Knowledge Power? The Effects of a

Victimology Course on Victim Blaming," *Journal of Interpersonal Violence* 26 (2011): 3407–27; Scott O. Lilienfeld, Rachel Ammirati, and Kristin Landfield, "Giving Debiasing Away: Can Psychological Research on Correcting Cognitive Errors Promote Human Welfare?" *Perspectives on Psychological Science* 4 (2009): 393; Heidi R. Riggio and Amber L. Garcia, "The Power of Situations: Jonestown and the Fundamental Attribution Error," *Teaching of Psychology* 36 (2009): 108–12; Stalder, "Role for Social Psychology Instruction."

18. Leonard S. Newman and Daria A. Bakina, "Do People Resist Social-Psychological Perspectives on Wrongdoing? Reactions to Dispositional, Situational, and Interactionist Explanations," *Social Influence* 4 (2009): 256–73; Ying Tang, Leonard S. Newman, and Lihui Huang, "How People React to Social-Psychological Accounts of Wrongdoing: The Moderating Effects of Culture," *Journal of Cross-Cultural Psychology* 45 (2014): 752–63.

19. Vincent Y. Yzerbyt et al., "The Dispositional Inference Strikes Back: Situational Focus and Dispositional Suppression in Causal Attribution," *Journal of Personality and Social Psychology* 81 (2001): 365–76.

20. Stalder, "Role for Social Psychology Instruction."

21. Gilovich and Ross, *Wisest One in the Room*, 70.

22. "Author Malcolm Gladwell on His Best-Selling Books," interview by Anderson Cooper, 60 Minutes Overtime, November 24, 2013, video, http://www.cbsnews.com/news/author-malcolm-gladwell-on-his-best-selling-books/ (accessed July 25, 2017).

23. Jerry M. Burger, "Changes in Attributions over Time: The Ephemeral Fundamental Attribution Error," *Social Cognition* 9 (1991): 182–93.

24. Didier Truchot, Gwladys Maure, and Sonia Patte, "Do Attributions Change over Time When the Actor's Behavior Is Hedonically Relevant to the Perceiver," *Journal of Social Psychology* 143 (2003): 202–208.

25. Gilbert and Malone, "Correspondence Bias."

26. Daniel T. Gilbert et al., "Blurry Words and Fuzzy Deeds: The Attribution of Obscure Behavior," *Journal of Personality and Social Psychology* 62 (1992): 18–25.

27. Jennifer S. Lerner and Philip E. Tetlock, "Accounting for the Effects of Accountability," *Psychological Bulletin* 125 (1999): 255–75; Philip E. Tetlock, "Accountability: A Social Check on the Fundamental Attribution Error," *Social Psychology Quarterly* 48 (1985): 227–36.

28. Sean Illing, "Why We Pretend to Know Things, Explained by Cognitive Scientist," *Vox*, April 16, 2017, http://www.vox.com/conversations/2017/3/2/14750464/truth-facts-psychology-donald-trump-knowledge-science (accessed September 2, 2017).

29. Mark Schaller et al., "Training in Statistical Reasoning Inhibits the Formation of Erroneous Group Stereotypes," *Personality and Social Psychology Bulletin* 22 (1996): 829–44.

30. Joseph P. Forgas, "On Being Happy and Mistaken: Mood Effects on the Fundamental Attribution Error," *Journal of Personality and Social Psychology* 75 (1998): 318–31; Daniel R. Stalder and Jessica A. Cook, "On Being Happy and Mistaken on a Good Day: Revisiting Forgas's (1998) Mood-Bias Result," *Journal of Social Psychology* 154 (2014): 371–74; John H. Yost and Gifford Weary, "Depression and the Correspondent Inference Bias: Evidence for More

Effortful Cognitive Processing," *Personality and Social Psychology Bulletin* 22 (1996): 192–200.

31. Liz Goldenberg and Joseph P. Forgas, "Can Happy Mood Reduce the Just World Bias? Affective Influences on Blaming the Victim," *Journal of Experimental Social Psychology* 48 (2012): 239–43.

32. Annemarie Loseman and Kees van den Bos, "A Self-Regulation Hypothesis of Coping with an Unjust World: Ego-Depletion and Self-Affirmation as Underlying Aspects of Blaming of Innocent Victims," *Social Justice Research* 25 (2012): 1–13.

33. Kent D. Harber, Peter Podolski, and Christian H. Williams, "Emotional Disclosure and Victim Blaming," *Emotion* 15 (2015): 604.

34. Chen, Froehle, and Morran, "Deconstructing Dispositional Bias in Clinical Inference."

35. David Aderman, Sharon S. Brehm, and Lawrence B. Katz, "Empathic Observation of an Innocent Victim: The Just World Revisited," *Journal of Personality and Social Psychology* 29 (1974): 342–47.

36. Theresa K. Vescio, Gretchen B. Sechrist, and Matthew P. Paolucci, "Perspective Taking and Prejudice Reduction: The Mediational Role of Empathy Arousal and Situational Attributions," *European Journal of Social Psychology* 33 (2003): 455–72.

37. Mariëlle Stel, Kees van den Bos, and Michèlle Bal, "On Mimicry and the Psychology of the Belief in a Just World: Imitating the Behaviors of Others Reduces the Blaming of Innocent Victims," *Social Justice Research* 25 (2012): 14–24.

38. Seiji Takaku, "The Effects of Apology and Perspective Taking on Interpersonal Forgiveness: Introducing a Dissonance-Attribution Model of Interpersonal Forgiveness," *Journal of Social Psychology* 141 (2001): 494–508; Seiji Takaku, "Reducing Road Rage: An Application of the Dissonance-Attribution Model of Interpersonal Forgiveness," *Journal of Applied Social Psychology* 36 (2006): 2362–78.

39. Jon Kabat-Zinn, *Wherever You Go There You Are: Mindfulness Meditation in Everyday Life* (New York: Hyperion, 1994).

40. Jennifer Block-Lerner et al., "The Case for Mindfulness-Based Approaches in the Cultivation of Empathy: Does Nonjudgmental, Present-Moment Awareness Increase Capacity for Perspective-Taking and Empathic Concern?" *Journal of Marital and Family Therapy* 33 (2007): 501–16.

41. Tim Hopthrow et al., "Mindfulness Reduces the Correspondence Bias," *Quarterly Journal of Experimental Psychology* 70 (2017): 351–60.

42. J. D. Creswell, "Mindfulness Interventions," *Annual Review of Psychology* 68 (2017): 491–516.

43. "Raisin Meditation," Greater Good in Action, 2017, http://ggia.berkeley.edu/practice/raisin_meditation (accessed September 2, 2017). Also try entering "raisin meditation" on YouTube.

44. Pema Chödrön, *Comfortable with Uncertainty: 108 Teachings on Cultivating Fearlessness and Compassion* (Boston: Shambhala, 2002); Jamie Holmes, *Nonsense: The Power of Not Knowing* (New York: Crown, 2015).

45. Daniel R. Stalder, "How to Reduce Biases: Accept Uncertainty," PARBs Anonymous (blog), March 23, 2015, https://parbsanonymous.wordpress.com/2015/03/23/how-to-reduce -biases-accept-uncertainty/ (accessed September 2, 2017).

46. Jason E. Plaks, Sheri R. Levy, and Carol S. Dweck, "Lay Theories of Personality: Cornerstones of Meaning in Social Cognition," *Social and Personality Psychology Compass* 3 (2009): 1069–81.

47. Adrienne Shaw et al., "Serious Efforts at Bias Reduction: The Effects of Digital Games and Avatar Customization on Three Cognitive Biases," *Journal of Media Psychology*, May 20, 2016, https://doi.org/10.1027/1864-1105/a000174 (accessed September 2, 2017).

48. Chi-yue Chiu, Ying-yi Hong, and Carol S. Dweck, "Lay Dispositionism and Implicit Theories of Personality," *Journal of Personality and Social Psychology* 73 (1997): 19–30.

49. "Resources for Teaching Growth Mindset," Edutopia, January 5, 2016, https://www .edutopia.org/article/growth--resources (accessed September 2, 2017).

50. Jesse Chandler and Norbert Schwarz, "How Extending Your Middle Finger Affects Your Perception of Others: Learned Movements Influence Concept Accessibility," *Journal of Experimental Social Psychology* 45 (2009): 123–28; Myers, *Social Psychology*; Simone Schnall and James D. Laird, "Keep Smiling: Enduring Effects of Facial Expressions and Postures on Emotional Experience and Memory," *Cognition and Emotion* 17 (2003): 787.

51. Manizeh Khan and Meredyth Daneman, "How Readers Spontaneously Interpret Man-Suffix Words: Evidence from Eye Movements," *Journal of Psycholinguistic Research* 40 (2011): 351–66.

52. Elizabeth F. Loftus and John C. Palmer, "Reconstruction of Automobile Destruction: An Example of the Interaction between Language and Memory," *Journal of Verbal Learning and Verbal Behavior* 13 (1974): 585–89.

53. Klaus Fiedler and Tobias Krüger, "Language and Attribution: Implicit Causal and Dispositional Information Contained in Words," in *The Oxford Handbook of Language and Social Psychology*, ed. Thomas M. Holtgraves (New York: Oxford University Press, 2014), 250–64.

54. Gün R. Semin and Christianne J. De Poot, "The Question-Answer Paradigm: You Might Regret Not Noticing How a Question Is Worded," *Journal of Personality and Social Psychology* 73 (1997): 472–80.

EPILOGUE: RATIONAL WELL-BEING

1. Barnaby D. Dunn, "Helping Depressed Clients Reconnect to Positive Emotion Experience: Current Insights and Future Directions," *Clinical Psychology and Psychotherapy* 19 (2012): 326–40; Catherine J. Harmer, Guy M. Goodwin, and Philip J. Cowen, "Why Do Antidepressants Take So Long to Work? A Cognitive Neuropsychological Model of

Antidepressant Drug Action," *British Journal of Psychiatry* 195 (2009): 102–108.

2. Alexander Pope, as quoted in Jonathan Swift, *Swift's Miscellanies* (1727). The quote from Socrates might be apocryphal.

3. Jordi Quoidbach, Moïra Mikolajczak, and James J. Gross, "Positive Interventions: An Emotion Regulation Perspective," *Psychological Bulletin* 141 (2015): 655–93.

INDEX

995   Psy